INTERNATIONAL CONSTRUCTION CONTRACTS MANAGEMENT WITH PARTICULAR REFERENCE TO FIDIC CONTRACTS

International Construction Contracts Management with Particular Referenced to FIDIC Contracts

ISBN: 9781731533203

Published by:

Dr. W. A. Khan
Uxbridge, London
First Edition – 2018
ISBN: 9781731533203

Table of Contents

FOREWORD

International Construction Contract Management with particular reference to FIDIC contracts' is a comprehensive easy to understand and practical reference book for construction professionals working on construction projects internationally. Written by Dr Wazir Khan, International Contracts and claims Management consultant with over 40 years' experience of construction project management in the UK and internationall including many Mega Projects and programmes. This book has been designed specifically to help in overcoming the day-to-day contractual problems encountered in the constructional projects.

It is acknowledged fact that construction industry professionals produce terms of contracts all the time; e.g. whenever they write a specification clause or put a dimension on a drawing. Unfortunately, a lot of graduates leave university without realising this importance, or the significance of contracts in general, where misunderstandings and mistakes can be extremely expensive and cause considerable delay. The text in this Book is a practical and reader-friendly approach for students and new professionals in the fields Civil Engineering and the Built Environment, starting at the very beginning of construction projects and making important connections between all stages of constructional projects execution.

Since, management of projects is frequently problematic because they are rarely comprised of straightforward buildings or procured under standard forms of contract, therefore it is vital to find a practical solution to solve project problems. The author has attempted to clarify terms and points of law and offered guidance that can be applied in most situations, helping the reader resolve problems quickly and without outside assistance or resorting to expensive litigation proceedings.

The Book consists of 19 Chapters. Chapter 1 consists of Introduction. Chapter 2 consists of Common Methods Of Procurement And Types Of Construction Contracts and include: Introduction; Lump Sum Contract; Unit Price Contract; Cost Plus Fixed Percentage Contract; Cost Plus Fixed Fee Contract; Cost Plus Variable Percentage Contract; Target Estimate Contract; Guaranteed Maximum Cost Contract; Partnering: Emerging Method Of Procurement; and To Be Collaborative Contract (BCC). Chapter 3 Consists Of Major Forms Of Contracts Used In International Construction and include: Institution Of Civil Engineers (ICE); The New Engineering Contract (NEC); The Joint Contracts Tribunal (JCT); PPC 2000; The NEC Partnering Option X12; and The FIDIC Suite Of Contracts covering: General, The New Red, Yellow And Silver Books, FIDIC Red Book Construction Contract, FIDIC Yellow Book - Plant And Design Build Contract, FIDIC Silver Book - Epc Turnkey Contract 1st Edition 1999, FIDIC Green Book Short Form Of Contract, Orange Book Conditions Of Contract For Design-Build And Turnkey, Red Book (Mdb Edition), Design, Build And Operate Form (Fidic "Gold Book"), and NEC Contract Vs FIDIC Contract.

Chapter 4 Consists Of Selection Of Consultants In Construction Process and include: General Aspects; Selection Procedure; Terms Of Reference (TOR); Pre-Qualification; Prepare The Short List; Call For Request For Proposals (RFP); Assessment Of Proposals; Value Analysis/Cost Effectiveness; and Forms Of Agreement . Chapter 5 Consists Of Review Of Design And Technical Documents. Chapter 6 Consists Of Value Management/Value Engineering In Construction Process and include: Value Management (Vm) Process;

Stakeholder Management – Role Of Stakeholders And Facilitators; Principal Objectives Of Value Management; Principal Benefits Of Value Management; Risks Associated With Value Management; and Value Management In The Design Process. Chapter 7 Consists Of Pre-Construction Contract Management and include: Pre-Qualifications And Selection Of Tenderers; Call For Tenders; Tendering Process covering: Introduction, The Content Of Tendering Process, Competitive Bidding, and Types Of Competitive Bidding; Receiving And Evaluating Tender Documents covering: Receiving Tender Documents, and Evaluation And Comparison Of Tender; and Award Of Contract.

Chapter 8 Consists Of Construction Management Agreement Under Fidic Contracts. Chapter 9 Concists Of Selection Of Fidic Form Of Contract And Include: Introduction; And Selection Of Appropriate Form Of Contract. Chapter 10 Consists The Obligations Of The Employer Under The Construction Contracts and include: Right Of Access To The Site; Permits, Licences Or Approval; Employer's Personnel; Employer's Claims; and Nominated Subcontractors covering: Introduction, Definition Of "Nominated Subcontractor", Objection To Nomination, Payments To Nominated Subcontractors, and Evidence Of Payments. Chapter 11 Consists Of Supervision, Management And Control) With Particular Reference To Fidic Contracts and include: Employer's Personnel; and The Engineer covering: Engineer's Duties And Authority, Delegation By The Engineer, Instructions Of The Engineer, Replacement Of The Engineer, and Employer's Representative.

Chapter 12 Consists Of Commencement Of Construction Work Under Fidic Contracts. Chapter 13 Consists Of Programme Of Construction Works Under

Fidic Contracts And Include: Programme Under Fidic Contracts; Programme And Follow-Up And Updating Schedule. Chapter 14 Consists Of General Aspects Of Contracts Management And Administration Of Construction Phase. Chapter 15 Consists Of Supervision, Management And Control Of Construction In General. Chapter 16 Consists Of Supervision, Management And Control Of Construction With Particular Reference To Fidic Contacts and include: Cooperation, Coordination Meeting And Progress Reports; Delays And Suspension Of Works covering: Extension Of Time, Delay Caused By Authorities, and Progress Reports; Contracts Variations And Adjustments covering: General, Right To Vary, Value Engineering, Variation Procedure, Adjustments For Changes In Legislation, and Adjustments For Changes In Cost; and Measurement And Evaluation covering: General , Works To Be Measured, Method Of Measurement, and Evaluation; and Contract Price And Payments covering: The Contract Price, Advance Payment, Interim Payment, Schedule Of Payments, Payment, Delayed Payment, Payment Of Retention Money, Final Payment, Payment In Applicable Currencies, Provisional Sums, Daywork, and Release From Performance.

Chapter 17 consists of ISO 9000 – Quality Management In Construction and include: Introduction; Transition Of Iso 9001: 2008 To ISO 9001:2015; and The Cost Of Quality; QC And QA Under FIDIC Contracts covering: Quality In Construction Process, and Contractor's Specific Obligations To Control Quality Of Works. Chapter 18 Consists Of Risk Management & Responsibility In Constructional Projects and includes: Risk Management; and Transfer Of Risk. Chapter 19 consists of Summary and Conclusion. The Book is supported by Bibliography.

If the reader wishes to gain a further comprehensive knowledge and deep understanding of the subject matters, he or she is directed to consult scholastic work listed under 'Bibliography' and the author feels great pleasure in acknowledging his gratitude to all the authors and publishers of this scholastic work which has been consulted and may have been quoted in the text of this book.

The author earnestly hopes that the matters raised in this book will help professional involved in construction process and other professional to participate in total project management of construction process

Finally, the readers and the users of this book are cordially invited to point out errors/ mistakes and forward their comments/suggestions, which may bring about improvement to the next edition of this publication.

Dr Wazir Ali Khan
Retired Chartered Engineer and Chartered Surveyor
Advocate of Peace and Social Reforms Activist
Research Scientist, Author and Publisher
Uxbridge, Greater London, United Kingdom
Email: drwakhan@aol.com
Published Books link:
http://www.amazon.co.uk/s/ref=nb_sb_noss?url=search-alias%3Ddigital-text&field-keywords=Wazir+Khan
Dr W A Khan_Publisher Global Bookshelf Link:
HTTPS://WWW.SFSMGROUP.COM/PUBLISHERS-BOOKSHELF

Chapter 1

INTRODUCTION

The construction industry in the UK encompasses all the sectors of building, civil engineering and process plant and includes the projects of different type, size and complexity and demands extensive professional services and skills of different trades. The scope of construction industry is well described by Morledge, Smith, and Kashiwagi (2006, p.1) in these words:

"The building industry produces a diverse range of outputs, ranging from products verging on mass production in the construction of houses, through bespoke service facilities such as schools and hospitals, elements of production in the form of industrial premises to house the manufacturing operations of organisations both large and small, to minor repair and maintenance work. Civil engineering on the other hand provides for many of our transportation needs in the form of roads, tunnels and bridges, railways, docks and airports, and other energy needs in the form of pipelines and power-lines, and the essentials of civilised life in the form of water and sewage treatment facilities, distribution and disposal systems".

Construction industry is essentially a service industry as what is sold to the client is not a product but a capacity to produce (Winch, 2002). Unlike manufacturing industry and retail sectors, construction industry is an agglomeration of projects than a discrete or a fixed constellation of firms (Groak, 1994).

Construction industry is an important contributor to the national economy and without adequate construction capacity aspirations for economic growth cannot be accomplished, thereby implying that economic activity and self-identity are two primary drivers for construction activity, which are inextricably linked together. Researchers have found that the capital assets of any country predominantly consist of its built environment assets and in the UK built environment assets, such as: housing, infrastructure and other buildings represents 76% (£3800 billion) of a total assets base worth around £5000 billion at 2005 prices (Morledge, Smith, and Kashiwagi, 2006).

However, since there is, by and large, an extended time period between the initiation of project procurement process and its eventual completion and handover to the client, this time period may encompass significant changes in economic activity, which in turn may provoke changes to the initial rationale of the construction process. Also unlike the manufacturing industry and retail sectors the supply process of construction industry is more of an inconsistent network than a well coordinated and carefully managed supply chain.

These inherent problems of construction industry bring conceptual difficulties for clients coming to the industry with value propositions associated with delivery of projects, thereby needing considerable assistance from the professionals in formulating a suitable framework of the project implementation process i.e. project strategy for the client who is in fact is purchasing undefined, unspecified project where both price and delivery are vague at the outset.

Such a framework include: carrying out a detailed assessment of the: client's characteristics, client's overall needs and goals by identifying specific primary and secondary objectives of the project, and the risks inherent in the proposal, and then determining the environment in which the project will be delivered and finally selecting the most appropriate method of project procurement (Masterman, 2002).

Selecting a suitable method of project procurement is fundamental to the success of a project. In the past, by and large, traditional method of project procurement based on price-led traditional practices were used, the main method consisted of procuring designer to design the job and then selecting a constructor on the basis of low bid and the construction management function was carried out by client's in-house project team or through a project manager separately procured by the client.

However, traditional methods are being replaced over the past three decades by less conventional approaches based on the principles of building trust between all parties by incorporating more co-operative means of project implementation. However, increased trust and collaboration tend to be resisted where a cultural rooted in conformance with the contract and price exists and gained only limited increased support from experienced construction clients where they can see that progressive measurable value-based improvement has been accomplished by adopted such practices.

Due to this limited support, collaborative arrangements, such as partnering have therefore tended to gain relatively less acceptance by the overall UK construction industry. This gave rise to the needs for strategic procurement initiatives to satisfy the construction clients with the quality and predictability of construction work together with developing increasingly knowledgeable and influential corporate and public sector clients.

The construction business in the United Kingdom is worth over £65 billion a year, of which direct expenditure by government departments and their agencies accounted for almost £7.5 billion in 2000, which ever-since has increased manifold due to substantial increase in Government spending on creating increased and improved facilities such as: transport, school and hospitals. In view of this higher level of spending on capital projects increased the urgency of the need for improvements in public sector procurement and management of new construction, refurbishment, repairs and maintenance, etc.

A series of major studies during the 1990s highlighted the inefficiencies of tradition methods of procurement and management of major projects, primarily due to the problems created by awarding contract solely on the basis of lowest bid. As long back as 1860, John Ruskin perceived this problem and he advised in the following words (Egan, 2002):

"It is unwise to pay too much, but it is worse to pay too little. When you pay too much, you lose a little money – that is all. When you pay too little, you sometimes lose everything, because the thing you bought was incapable of doing the thing it was bought to do. The common law of business balance prohibits paying a little and getting a lot – It can't be done with the lowest bidder, it is well to add something for the risk you run. And if you do that, you will have enough to pay for something better".

British industry for centuries ignored this advice and continued to adopt a lowest bid principle of selection of procurement without realising that this does not provide value for money in either the final cost of construction or through life and operational costs. Also, over this period, by and large, professional relationships between the government departments and the construction industry were often typically characterised by distrust and conflict, which in turn contributed to poor performance of control of costs.

Among the series of major studies during the 1990s, the most significant ones include: 'Constructing the Team' by the forum led by Sir Michael Latham (1994); 'The Levene Efficiency Scrutiny into Construction Procurement' by the UK Government (1995); 'The Procurement Guide – RICS; 'Rethinking Construction' by the forum led by Sir John Egan (1998); 'Efficiency in Civil Government Procurement' – the Gershon Report (1999); 'Modernising Construction – the National Audit Office of the UK Government (2001); and 'Accelerating Change' by the strategic forum led by Sir John Egan (2002).

In the 'Constructing the Team report Sir Michael Latham highlighted that the construction industry's traditional methods of procurement and contract management and its adversarial culture caused ineffectiveness and inefficiency and concluded that by addressing these issues could have 30% potential savings over 5 years period and made a number of recommendations to improve the procurement process as well as management of construction project.

These recommendations included: better communication with the construction industry to reduce conflict; increased training of civil servants on procurement and risks management; adoption of a more commercial approach; and negotiation of deals justified on value for money ground. In the same year, the Royal Institute of Chartered Surveyors published 'The Procurement Guide' (RICE, 1996) in which much valuable advise to the professionals to adopt a more strategic and comprehensive approach to construction procurement was provided.

However, the progress in achieving improvements following the Latham report was perceived to be slow and as a result in 1998, this issue was given significant emphasis in Egan's report on 'Rethinking Construction' in which Sir John challenged the construction industry to commit itself to change so that by working together a modern industry could be created, ready to face the future (Egan, 1998).

This report saw a need for a change of style, culture and process and towards this end the report identified five 'drivers', which needed to be in place to secure improvement in construction industry. These drives are: (i) committed leadership, (ii) focus of the customer, (iii) integration of process and team around the project, (iv) a quality driven agenda, and (v) commitment to people.

The report also identified four key processes which required to be significantly enhanced. The processes are: (i) partnering the supply chain, (ii) components and parts, (iii) focus on end products, and (iv) construction process (elimination of waste). The report also has set seven quantified targets to achieve the desired level of improvements. These targets are: (i) reduce capital costs by 10%, (ii) reduce construction time by 10%, (iii) reduce defects by 20%, (iv) reduce by 20%, (v) improve cost and time predictability by 10%, (vi) increase productivity by 10%, and (vii)increase profitability by 10%. This report has since been adopted as major initiative by the UK Government in its procurement policy.

Also considerable efforts have been devoted to examining the ways to transfer technology, in which both procurement process and project supply chains are managed in other heavy industries e.g. ship building, oil exploration and car/aeroplane manufacturing, to construction (Cox and Townsend, 1998), but no significant success is achieved due to the reasons that these techniques required significant modification and adaptation to meet the special needs of construction industry.

In January 2001, the National Audit Office published its report 'Modernising Construction' about how the construction procurement and delivery of construction projects in the UK can be modernised with benefits for all involved in the construction industry. 'Modernising Construction' report highlighted best practice being adopted by government departments and industry, which if applied more widely could achieve sustainable improvements in construction performance, which in turn will achieve better value for money for taxpayers. The report made recommendation to four key groups in the industry including the need for the UK government departments to develop more sophisticated performance measures and also to actively measure improvements in construction performance.

In view of the progress being made the 'Rethinking Construction' initiative was given continuing financial support by the UK Government and a Strategic Forum for Construction under the Chairmanship of Sir John Egan was set up. This forum produced a report on 'Accelerating Change' (Egan, 2002) in which key measures to accelerate change were proposed, which included Vision; Strategic Targets, Future Actions by the

Forum; Future actions agreed by others; and Forum recommendations. Sir John Egan, Chairman – strategic Forum for Construction made the detailed statement by summarising the report on 'Acceleration Change, which is reproduced, with permission of the 'Strategic Forum for Construction', herein below:

"In my foreword ....'Accelerating Change': Although the above mentioned difficulties of construction have been adequately addressed by some sectors of the construction industry and construction process is improved by implementing various initiatives but, nevertheless the perceived performance of the construction industry appears to be historically poor. In this context the classical example of the extreme poor performance of the Holyrood Project for the Scottish Parliament is noteworthy, which was completed in October 2004, three years late and at final costs of £431 Million - over ten time the initial estimate of 40 Million -(NCE 7, 2004). This leads us to believe that further efforts and initiatives are needed to further improve the construction process.

Because of relevance to our study, Part 3 i.e. "Procuring and Managing Construction" of the report on "Modernising Construction" demand detailed review is warranted to discuss and identify the possible efficiency gains as well as inefficiencies. This part of the report examines how better value for money can be achieved by adopting good practice in (i) selecting contractors, (ii) designing, (iii) planning, (iv) project management, (v) measuring construction performance, and (vi) remunerating contractors. The analysis in the report is based on an examination of case studies of typical projects intended to reflect good construction practice as part of the movement for innovation programme, advice of experts appointed on the panel, and discussion with the contractors. Each area is further examined herein below:

Selecting contractors: The report has identified the weakness and inefficiencies in the selection of designer and contractor through traditional competitive tendering practice, which has led to a number of problems, throughout the construction process, e.g. in selecting design consulting very little emphasis is place on the quality of the design proposal, thereby forcing design team to spend less time on the design to keep within the contract price, and giving less time attention for constructability review and value management by the consultants. This practice not only created problem during construction phase by increasing health and safety risks but also caused unnecessary design changes with associated cost increases.

The Government Construction Client Panel's Benchmarking study in 1999 showed that three-quarters of the 66 projects studied exceeded the contract price by up to 50 per cent and two-third had exceeded their original date by 63% (Benchmarking the Government Client Stage 2 Study 1999). This practice provided an incentive for the consultant to win the job on minimum price criteria, on the understanding and assumption that there would inevitably be design changes, delays, new requirements of the clients, environmental or physical constraints, unforeseeable before, that would no doubt increase costs, which will allow them to make substantial claims and increased profit margins. Accordingly traditional competitive tendering basis was found extremely inefficient and providing less value for money.

It is encouraging that the Government's treasury and the OGC has departed from the traditional practice and emphasised the need to achieve value for money in all forms of procurement including construction, while having due regard to propriety and regularity. Also a number of central government and other public sector bodies as well as private sector clients have departed from the traditional practice and have significantly changed the way in which they select and procure construction services i.e. by taking a longer term view of the likely quality of the finished building rather than just concentrate on contract price alone. Since, estimating the likely costs of building over its whole life can be difficult therefore to overcome this difficulty Defence Estates in Building Down Barriers pilot project has developed a framework for making decisions on through life costs and requires all parties in the supply chain, including material and component suppliers and specialist contractors, to have reliable data on the operational costs of their products including running and maintenance costs.

Key features of this approach include: (a) strategic alliances between the prime contractor and its sub-contractors; (b) continuous improvement targets to reduce costs and enhance quality; (c) the use of a systematic analysis of the weaknesses and strengths in existing design and construction process; and (d) focus on the through-life cost and functional performance of the building.

Following Building Down Barriers, Defence Estates has extended the use of prime contracting across all its procurement expenditure, Defence Estates is fundamentally has changed the way it procures construction for both capital and maintenance, with a policy of using Prime Contracting as the preferred procurement route where Private Finance Initiatives (PFIs) are inappropriate.

Prime Contracting involves the integration of design, construction and maintenance under the control of a fully accountable Prime Contractor who is responsible for: (i) the selection of sub contractors; (ii) the management of procurement from the rest of the supply chain; (iii) the design of the facility; (iv) the co-ordination and overall systems, engineering and testing; (v) planning, programming and cost control; and (vi) total delivery of the facilities ensuring that they are fit for, the specified purpose and in line with through life cost predictions and delivered by the target completion date.

This report must be viewed as a way forward for the UK construction industry to move into modernising construction and effectively participate in providing more value for money for all including tax payers, government departments, consultants, contractors and private clients. The report has included some example of good practice adopted by various government agencies in selecting contractors. For example, the Highway Agencies emphasised in balancing quality and price, which is having distinct benefits, such as: greater consideration to quality of final construction; more incentive for contractors to put forward innovative design, etc.

Defence Estates has given more emphasis in integrating design and construction, which is having distinct benefits, such as: (a) considering the through life costs of the building; to sect competent contractors having a proven ability to manage both design and construction and manage their supply chain; (b) and producing design of a building based on specifications framed in terms of outputs; etc. The Environmental Agency emphasised in reducing the number of contractors and developing longer term relationships, which having distinct benefits, such as: having ability to gain greater assurance as to the likely quality and performance; etc.

Designing buildings: The report has stated that "badly designed buildings can fail to meet the needs of end users, may cause operational problems, have high maintenance or running costs and can be inefficient and costly to build as well as dangerous. It is at the design stage that most can be done to optimise the value of a building to its end users. Private sector experience shows that involvement of a facilities manager at this stage has many benefits, as they can contribute their experience of operating in and maintaining the building. Capital costs are an important factor in the overall costs of buildings but investment in good quality design and construction can result in a more efficient operating environment and lower running costs".

Furthermore, information technologies has the potential to improve quality of building design, e.g. integrating design process with construction so that design, risk allocation and project management all draw on one database. The report has given examples of good design practice adopted by various authorities. Essex County Council adopted the approach of integrating the design team with consideration of sustainability and whole-life costs, which is having distinct benefits, such as: innovative design that made good use of available space by adopting a compact triangular shape at lower construction costs and adoptable to other projects i.e. replicated to other schools.

The Highway Agency on M60-3 contracted emphasised the design practice by involving the contractor at an early stage, which is having distinct benefits, such as: in the design planning the construction secured cost reductions and environmental benefits, etc. Defence Estate Building Down Barriers emphasised a focus of the design on the needs of end user, which is having distinct benefits, such as: users satisfaction on operational point of view, etc. Kingston Hospital trust emphasised the pre-fabrication and standardisation in design, which is having distinct benefits, such as: Terrapin, the main contractor handed over the building in 20 weeks compared with original estimated completion time by all potential contractors of over 35 weeks; etc.

Planning: The report states that "construction projects in the public sector can have a long lead time - the examples in our case studies range from 4 months to 30 months, from the time when the need for a new building is agreed to when construction work starts." This long lead time should be utilised for planning construction process, as once initial formalities are over, there can be construction pressure for building to start with insufficient time available for planning the construction process. Good planning involves: (a) risk assessment, allocation and management; (b) linking the design of the building to its construction; and (c) value management. In the report, the case study of Dudley Southern Bypass provides an example of how investing time upfront in planning the construction demonstrates benefits of planning. The project was completed within target cost and the agreed budget and 5 months ahead of schedule.

Project Management: The report states that "a well-thought-through design and a comprehensive plan are essential for efficient and effective construction but equally important is good project management." Good project management is the key to the success of the project and its responsibilities must be clearly defined and understood and it must be supported by clearly defined delegated authority to make project decisions and its structure should be uncomplicated and reflect good practice.

Some researchers have shown that poor project management has contributed to construction projects being delivered late or over budget. Ministry of Defence: Building Down Barriers has set a good project management example which has secured distinct benefits when prime contractor and project management has contributed to the success of the construction by reducing time by 20%, reducing wastage to 0% and increasing labour productivity by 11% to 16%.

Measuring construction performance: The report states that "Sir John Egan in his review "Rethinking Construction" drew attention to the lack of firm quantitative information with which to evaluate the success or otherwise of construction projects." The key elements and processes which the Egan Report - Rethinking Construction (1998) recommended need to be in place to secure significant improvement in construction performance. For example, Egan report recommended that five key drivers to achieve better construction, namely: (i) committed leadership; (ii) Focus on the customer; (iii) integration of process & team around the project; (iv) a quality driven agenda; and (v) commitment to people Must need to be in place to achieve better construction.

The report has also recommended that the four key projected process, namely: (i) Partnering the Supply Chain; (ii) Components and Parts; (iii) Focus on End Products; and (iv) Construction Process are needed to achieve change. The report also identified seven annual achievable targets for improving the performance of construction that should be pursued. These are: (1) Reduce capital costs by 10%. (2) Reduce construction time by 10%. (3) Reduce defects by 20%. (4) Reduce accidents by 20%. (5) Increase predictability of projected cost and time by 10%. (6) Increase productivity by 10%. And Increase turnover and profits by 10%.

It must be understood that these key performance indicators are not a substitute for companies' own performance measurement systems and benchmarking but they do however, enable companies to gauge their performance in relation to their competitors. These indicators have been particularly useful for companies having unsophisticated performance systems. Measuring construction performance has distinct benefits, e.g. Defence Estates consider measurement to be key to improve construction performance and manage contracts by way of external benchmarking, etc. Another example: Mansell plc, a major construction firm have a number of indicators to assess their business performance.

Remunerating suppliers: There is a golden principle in construction contracts that work must be done at a sufficient contract price and not necessary at minimum price criteria of competitor tendering. If price is too low contractors are likely to seek every opportunity to increase costs through claims often leading to lengthy litigation. Although, it is obvious that all suppliers need to make a reasonable profit margin to continue to exist, but nevertheless if a contract price which allows firms to earn excessive profits will not represent value for money. Some balance is needed so that contractors have reasonable financial incentives to deliver good quality buildings on time and to budget while departments need to be able to demonstrate that their contract strategy includes a form of remuneration that ensures that taxpayers' money is being well spent.

The report states that: (a) it is necessary to provide incentives which promote a co-operative team approach; (b) essential to ensuring effective partnering arrangements; qnd (c) to designing out risk and to tackling any unforeseen difficulties that arise. It is likely that this will involve an equitable allocation of "the pains and gains of such arrangements."

The reports sets out a table of 'methods of remuneration to incentivise contractors, which are having a range of benefits as well as some potential disadvantages which need careful management, e.g. Fixed Price (Design and Build) method has distinct benefits as the client has certainty as to final price of the building, but it has potential disadvantages as the client still carries the risk of delay to handover of the building on time in spite of the facts that transferring all risks to the contractors may not be cost effective.

Target price method has distinct benefits for client as well as the contractor i.e. client having greater certainty over price and for the contractor having incentive to make cost saving for the benefit of both the client and the contractor, but potential disadvantages should be well managed by ensuring value for money through efficiency sharing and cost savings, etc. There are other two methods, namely: payment on the basis of outcomes; and Target price with agreed profit and overheads (prime contractor). These too have distinct benefits and inherent potential disadvantages.

Finally, studies have identified the potential for major savings up to 30% in the cost of construction, specifically by industry and its clients adopting a more collaborative approach founded on a competitive process with appropriate risk sharing in which value for money is obtained for all parties through a clear understanding of various factors, such as: (i) the project's requirements; (ii) transparency as to costs and profits; and (iii) clear understanding to mutual rights and obligations, and appropriate incentives. The studies have also identified that more attention to design and early involvement of the whole construction team could also improve the operational efficiency of completed buildings resulting in potentially greater savings over the whole life of the building.

This report highlights good practice being adopted by departments and industry which if applied more widely could achieve sustainable improve-ments in construction performance achieving better value for money for all the parties having interest in the projects. This report is therefore a forward looking and, through changing their approach to the procurement and management of construction, the larger spending departments and agencies estimate that they will achieve efficiency gains of over £600 million annually and improve the quality of the construction. For industry the application of best practice has the potential to lead to improved profitability compared with the current industry average of one per cent of turnover.

The studies have also concluded that there needs to be a greater concentration on achieving a better construction, which meets the needs of the end user at lower through life costs. This demands that the entire supply chain including clients, professional advisers, contractors, sub-contractors and suppliers of materials must be integrated to manage risk and apply engineering techniques and value management methodology to improve constructability and drive waste out of the process, thereby reducing it through life and operational costs, leading to greater certainty of project time and budgeted costs, fewer accidents and more sustainable construction.

Now moving from the United Kingdom's construction process to the construction process in Europe there are many factors that contribute to barriers to free competition in the construction market, such as: (a) education and training of construction professionals; (b) construction organization; and (c) barriers to free trade in the construction market.

Unlike the olden days, now construction professionals are highly educated and trained people and they are equipped with adequate skills to enable them to execute the construction with full regards to the quality and safety of the buildings and structure most economically. In today's project environment the success of any project is measured by three performance indicators or constraints, i.e. (1) Time, (2) Costs and (3) Quality. This is why it is a normal practice in big projects for Design and Construction Management teams to become part of the quality circuit where they economically, safely and efficiently engineer the serviceability and reliability attributes called for. The education of these professionals may be different in each of the EU countries.

In the olden days none of these professional existed as, by and large, buildings were constructed by craftsmen, who had the manual skills to build , and master craftsmen, who would perform the design function and direct construction. However, from 17th century onwards the professionals have developed themselves to meet the demand of the construction larger buildings and associated infra-structure, such as:

roads, canals, railways, water supply and other systems.

By and large, construction professionals include: architects, engineers, and quantity surveyors in the UK. In the EU countries other than the UK, quantity surveyors do not exist. In the major EU countries, the education for architects varies between 4 to 6 years of degree, whilst for engineers and quantity surveyors between 3 to 4 years followed by post graduate professional training between 2 to 3 years to achieve professional status. In some countries of EU, the standard of the professional's training is set by the respective government regulations

The main purpose of construction organisation is to organise resources in such manner that it produces efficiency and cost effectiveness in design and construction so that the client gets best value for money he is spending. The major players in the construction sector include: architects, engineers, quantity surveyors, general/management contractors, sub-contractors, and specialists and their mutual working relationships are formalised by means of contract between the parties. For example, a client wanting some construction work will have to enter into contract with the designer and the contractor, which often requires formal contract documents i.e. drawings and specifications, etc. and the conditions of contract. However, construction contracts for the state sector will be different and more controlled than private sector construction contracts.

Many clients who require construction do not have sufficient knowledge and know-how and in-house capabilities to manage the designers and the contractors. Such client often employ either construction manager (a firm) or project manager (a firm) to administer contracts on behalf of the client.. In some countries of EU, this aspect is recognised in the 'Standard Conditions of contract' where a particular person is identified to administer the contract on behalf of the client.

There are a number of laws including planning law that exist all over Europe to control construction and one of these would be the right to carry out construction something in the first place. However, consent of the state is mandatory before building can proceed. However, as far as the competition, the EU has produced building directives which have been incorporated in national laws. Also, to control health and safety, the EU has introduced further directives, which have also been incorporated in the laws of member countries.

In construction industry I Europe, it seems to have many different firms contracted together with contracts, which is considered a major barrier, but to overcome this it may be possible for one firm to employ all the people required for the construction of a facility and then to effect only one contract between the client and the firm.

Research has shown that not only in the UK and Europe but also world-wide, many mistakes, in the construction industry have been made through carelessness, overconfidence, lack of adequate knowledge and experience, or the pressure of time, etc. which turned out costly in both human and financial terms. Each time when such catastrophes occurred, the importance of quality was felt. In quantitative terms some have estimated the cost of poor quality to be at least 7.5% of the total project costs. Although the Quality is dependent upon the Client Quality Agenda

Priorities based upon his budget and facility management needs, but the fact remains that Quality needs to be considered as a common place necessity rather than a paid for luxury, as it results in mitigation of recurring deficiencies, improvement in design, satisfaction of end users (customer: Client: Owner, etc.) and reduction in cost growth.

Under the current competitive business environment, business enterprises, particularly major companies operating in EU countries are becoming more and more quality conscience having objectives to produce high level products and services to meet their customers'/clients' requirements. In this context, it must be remembered that quality is not something that occur automatically and it is not enough to establish whether the result of work performed meets the requirements. But it demands avoidance of faults during the various work stages through corporate efforts in directing and controlling various processes, e.g., planning, design & development, purchasing, production, inspection, testing, etc. Therefore, the aim should be directed towards achieving a high degree of quality in all of the operational areas of the respective company. The company top management should issue a quality policy. Based on the quality policy, a comprehensive quality system needs to be developed and introduced in all organizational units in the form of a QA Program.

The purpose of QA Program, particularly on any major construction project should be to make optimum use of both QA documents and organization as management tools and take all those planned and systematic actions necessary to provide adequate confidence that all the elements of work will satisfy given requirements for quality. It is important to remember in this context that for effectiveness, Quality Assurance usually requires a continuing evaluation of factors that affect the adequacy of the design or specification or both for intended application as well as verification and audits of construction, installation and inspection operations.

The European Council has adopted a detailed and comprehensive text towards a strategic partnership with Africa, which shall have a great impact on construction industry in a very large single European market. If the resolution contained therein will be adopted then, no doubt, the construction industry will have a bright future as a very large single European construction market.

Now moving from Europe to Global Construction industry as a result of a research for independent expert consultants for the World Fair Exhibitions in 1913, a number of consulting engineers met to discuss the possibility of forming a global Federation with an objective to apply the founding principles of Quality, Integrity, and Sustainability to Global construction industry.

The meeting with 59 participants was a success in that it led to the formal constitution on 22 July 1913 of FIDIC, Fédération Internationale des Ingénieurs Conseils, or later, the International Federation of Consulting Engineers. There were; official delegates from Austria, Belgium, Canada, Denmark, France, Germany, Hungary, Netherlands, Russia, Switzerland, the United Kingdom and the USA. Three countries, Belgium, France and Switzerland decided to found the Federation.

The other countries maintained provisional links during the initial years. However, due to the World Wars and other major political disturbances, FIDIC development was slow until the late 1940's. The number of member countries changed constantly, and all came from Europe. In 1959, they were joined by Australia, Canada, South Africa, and the USA. This made FIDIC a truly international Federation. The Federation developed gradually over the years into a truly global organisation with Member Associations representing countries from all regions of the world.

Today, more than ever, the role of FIDIC has become essential for the consulting engineering industry. FIDIC not only represents the countries where Member Association are located, it has become the voice of the consulting engineering industry in a globalised world. For instance, FIDIC partnership with the World Bank and other Multinational Development Banks working in the different geographical regions ensure the application of international standards designed by engineers for engineers to finance and deliver the world infrastructure.

Other FIDIC partnerships with the United Nations and international humanitarian organisations allow the industry to join forces with other sectors to achieve common goals! Dedicated professionals from consulting engineering firms and associations contribute day-to-day with their work to develop and promote FIDIC over the world: the FIDIC President, the FIDIC Executive Committee, members of FIDIC committees; members of task forces and working groups; FIDIC Directors and Secretaries, FIDIC Past Presidents; FIDIC Adjudicators; FIDIC Accredited Trainers; and Young Professionals. FIDIC is, today, the result of a century of volunteer and committed leadership! Its core principles remain unaltered after 100 years: Quality, Integrity and Sustainabiliy.

Over the last century, consulting engineers have made a truly significant impact on society worldwide. Innovative advances in transport, energy, water supply, buildings, and vital infrastructure have all led to improved health and economic development, and hence a much better quality of life. The past one hundred years of engineering excellence contribution have shown what can be achieved. The foundations for a sustainable future have been provided, with the consulting engineer now established as an essential partner for an improved society. Effective engineering is clearly fundamental for humankind, but the strategic planning skills of engineers need to be universally recognised and used for the benefit of everyone

FIDIC's promise is to be recognised as a trusted adviser to decision makers involved in the planning and construction of a sustainable infrastructure for future generations! FIDIC will collaborate with other like minded organisations to achieve this objective. FIDIC have developed various form of contracts which are being used in international construction in the global economy, particulary in Middle East Mega construction industry.

FIDIC forms of contracts have been in use in the Middle East since the 1970s. Although the FIDIC conditions of contract have been drafted on the basis of English common law principles, bur nevertheless the public and private sectors in Gulf countries who source their law from a mixture of civil law such as the UAE, , Kuwait and Oman, and Shari'ah Law in the Kingdom of Saudi Arabia have based their conditions of contract on the FIDIC forms. Historically, the public sector in those countries have led the way for FIDIC to be adopted or used in response to the national tendering laws and the corresponding various government ministries' requirements. However, Public sector employers in the Middle East, similar to those internationally, tend to prefer lump sum fixed price contracts.

Particular to UAE: Construction contracts in the UAE are predominantly based upon the FIDIC forms of contract. Due to the growing number of major repeat clients and large scale developers in the region has given rise to the development of bespoke forms of contract, tailored to each individual client's needs. Such contracts, by and large, are using the FIDIC 4 'Red Book' Form as a basis, modified to a greater or lesser degree depending upon the risk profile of each client. This also applies to works procured by Dubai Municipality. Abu Dhabi Municipality, however, bases its contract on a modified FIDIC 3 form, taken from the 3rd edition of the FIDIC Conditions of Contract for Works of Civil Engineering Construction.

Contracts based on the 1999 'red book' are now starting to be used in the UAE, but in general the market remains firmly rooted in the FIDIC 4 form. Civil works contracts within the UAE are mostly procured on a remeasurable basis, whereas building works will generally be based on a fixed-price lump sum. However, there are some exceptions. More and more clients are procuring projects using a fast track approach and will therefore incorporate a remeasurable element, reflecting those parts of the design which are incomplete at tender stage. Although design-build contracts are used on some major projects, but this procurement route is not yet common.

Particular to Qatar: In Qatar the most common forms for building works are those issued by the Public Works departments through the Ministry of Municipal Affairs and Agriculture (MMAA) and the Qatar Petroleum Company (QP). These are lump sum contracts, generally using bills of quantities or specifications and drawings. These contracts are slanted towards the client, but are usually administered in a reasonable manner.

The market has seen an increase in the number of FIDIC based contracts being implemented for both private and key public sector clients. In addition, in some very long duration contracts, the government is beginning to introduce a price adjustment mechanism to allow compensation for fluctuations in market prices. Before any contract is awarded, there are commonly a number of sessions of negotiation, during which the price and other contractual terms can be modified to respond to a reduction in contract price.

Particular to Kingdom of Saudi Arabia: Within the public sector construction contracts are based on the Standard Conditions for Public Works, which are amended to suit particular projects. These conditions are generally based on those given in the 4th edition of the FIDIC Conditions of Contract for Works of Civil Engineering Construction, the FIDIC 4 'Red Book', but with greater control given to the employer for the administration of the contract. All public work contracts are let on remeasured basis and subject to the Saudi Government Tendering and Procurement Regulations, as issued by Royal Decree M/58 dated 4.7.1427 AH. Disputes are referred to the Grievance Board and will not be dealt with under arbitration, unless a Special Council of Ministers Resolution is issued.

Construction contracts, however, in the private sector are generally based on FIDIC forms of contract and are amended to suit the particular conditions for each project. Employers prefer lump sum versus remeasured contracts and normally exercise great control in the administration of the construction process by imposing various restrictions on the engineer's (consultant) authorities under the contract. All contracts are subject to Saudi laws where Islamic Sharia is the prime source of legislation. Litigation and arbitration are both available for resolution of disputes in the private sector.

Particular to Kuwait: The Ministry of Public Works in Kuwait has historically issued its own set of contractual conditions based on FIDIC conditions. However, where such conditions have been heavily modified to reflect a lump sum fixed price requirement primarily driven by local public tender laws.

Particular to Bahrain: Government work in the Bahrain is now being undertaken using a bespoke suite of contract forms that were issued in 2009. Private developers predominantly use the current FIDIC Conditions of Contract for Construction, the

1999 edition of the 'Red Book', which is well understood in the local market but often heavily modified for specific use. Most of the work completed in Bahrain is under a traditional lump sum form of contract, where the design is completed upfront and a price agreed with a contractor before work begins on site. However, many of the new developments are looking at faster procurement routes to adapt to market difficulties that are prevalent within the Middle East. Progress is slow as Bahrain has a limited number of contractors with the capacity and capability to undertake large scale projects.

Design and build and two-stage procurement are in use across the state but are not considered to be the industry norm. As more international private developers have started working in Bahrain with time constraints as their main driver, the market has adjusted to accommodate this demand. Design and build contracts, however, are rarely used. This is largely due to the Committee for Organising Engineering Professional Practice (COEPP) restrictions on contractors undertaking in-house design that necessitates the novation of the client's architect or a sub consultant appointment.

Particular to Lebanon: Construction contracts in Lebanon are generally based upon the FIDIC forms of contract. Some large scale developers in Lebanon, as well as the Lebanese government, have promoted the development and use of bespoke forms of contract, tailored to each client. Such contracts generally use the FIDIC 4 'Red Book' form as a basis, amended to a greater or lesser degree depending upon the risk profile of each client. In the public sector, all works are procured on a remeasurement basis. The private sector, however, uses either fixed-price lump-sum or remeasured contracts. It is worth noting that there is no standard method of measurement of building works for Lebanon and the RICS Principles of Measurement (International) for Works of Construction (POMI) is widely used. Design and build contracts are not yet popular in Lebanon. Both arbitration and litigation methods are available for dispute resolutions in the private and public sectors.

Particular to Oman: Public works in Oman are undertaken using a bespoke government contract *known as the Standard Documents for Building and Civil Engineering Works*, 4th edition, 1999. The document is based on early FIDIC contracts with the 4th edition containing only minor changes from the previous 3rd edition, 1981. The most important change is that the contract is now printed in Arabic. The Ministry of Legal

Affairs is in the process of preparing a new edition but its launch date is yet to be published. The Standard Document facilitates both a remeasurement and lump-sum contract dependent on a choice of clauses, and is based upon a fully completed design, specification and bill of quantities. The RICS Principles of Measurement (International) are the most widely used method of measurement.

Infrastructure projects have their own method of measurement, as detailed within the Ministry of Transport and Communications document, Highway Design Standards. Oman Tender Board laws require all government projects to utilise the Standard Documents on every project, without amendment. In addition, the Tender Board facilitates all government tenders, centrally, through the tender board process. Only Royal Office and Royal Court of Affairs projects are exempt from this process although they do go through a similar internal tender process.

Standard Documents are commonly used by private sector clients in the local market, particularly for small-to-medium sized contracts. Private clients tend to prefer the 3rd edition as this is written in English, but varies only in a minor way from the Arabic 4th edition — preferred by the government ministries. International and private sector clients with large project contracts, US$150 million-plus, commonly use an amended version of the FIDIC "Red Book." Whilst some of the larger integrated tourism developments have used a design build form of contract, design and build as a procurement route is not routinely used.

Accordingly, throughout Middle East either FICD Forms of Contract have been used bespoke and/or modified contracts based on FIDIC contracts used.

International Construction Contracts Management with Particular Referenced to FIDIC Contracts

In this Book we will discuss in detail the International Construction contracts management in general and FIDIC contracts in particular

Chapter 2

COMMON METHODS OF PROCUREMENT AND TYPES OF CONSTRUCTION CONTRACTS

2.1 INTRODUCTION

While construction contracts serve as a means of pricing construction on competitive basis, they also structure the allocation of risk to the various parties involved. The owner has the sole power to decide what type of contract should be used for a specific building/facility to be constructed and to set forth the terms in a contractual agreement. It is important to understand the risks of the contractors associated with different types of construction contracts.

2.2 LUMP SUM CONTRACT

In a lump sum contract, the owner has essentially assigned all the risk to the contractor, who in turn can be expected to ask for a higher mark-up in order to take care of unforeseen contingencies. Beside the fixed lump sum price, other commitments are often made by the contractor in the form of submittals such as a specific schedule, the management reporting system or a quality control program. If the actual cost of the project is underestimated, the underestimated cost will reduce the contractor's profit by that amount. An overestimate has an opposite effect, but may reduce the chance of being a low bidder for the project.

2.3 UNIT PRICE CONTRACT

In a unit price contract, the risk of inaccurate estimation of uncertain quantities for some key tasks has been removed from the contractor. However, some contractors may submit an "unbalanced bid" when it discovers large discrepancies between its estimates and the owner's estimates of these quantities. Depending on the confidence of the contractor on its own estimates and its propensity on risk, a contractor can slightly raise the unit prices on the underestimated tasks while lowering the unit prices on other tasks. If the contractor is correct in its assessment, it can increase its profit substantially since the payment is made on the actual quantities of tasks; and if the reverse is true, it can lose on this basis. Furthermore, the owner may disqualify a contractor if the bid appears to be heavily unbalanced. To the extent that an underestimate or overestimate is caused by changes in the quantities of work, neither error will effect the contractor's profit beyond the mark-up in the unit prices.

2.4 COST PLUS FIXED PERCENTAGE CONTRACT

For certain types of construction involving new technology or extremely pressing needs, the owner is sometimes forced to assume all risks of cost overruns. The contractor will receive the actual direct job cost plus a fixed percentage, and have little incentive to reduce job cost. Furthermore, if there are pressing needs to complete the project, overtime payments to workers are common and will further increase the job cost. Unless there are compelling reasons, such as the urgency in the construction of military installations, the owner should not use this type of contract.

2.5 COST PLUS FIXED FEE CONTRACT

Under this type of contract, the contractor will receive the actual direct job cost plus a fixed fee, and will have some incentive to complete the job quickly since its fee is fixed regardless of the duration of the project. However, the owner still assumes the risks of direct job cost overrun while the contractor may risk the erosion of its profits if the project is dragged on beyond the expected time.

2.6 COST PLUS VARIABLE PERCENTAGE CONTRACT

For this type of contract, the contractor agrees to a penalty if the actual cost exceeds the estimated job cost, or a reward if the actual cost is below the estimated job cost. In return for taking the risk on its own estimate, the contractor is allowed a variable percentage of the direct job-cost for its fee. Furthermore, the project duration is usually specified and the contractor must abide by the deadline for completion. This type of contract allocates considerable risk for cost overruns to the owner, but also provides incentives to contractors to reduce costs as much as possible.

2.7 TARGET ESTIMATE CONTRACT

This is another type of contract which specifies a penalty or reward to a contractor, depending on whether the actual cost is greater than or less than the contractor's estimated direct job cost. Usually, the percentages of savings or overrun to be shared by the owner and the contractor are predetermined and the project duration is specified in the contract. Bonuses or penalties may be stipulated for different project completion dates.

2.8 GUARANTEED MAXIMUM COST CONTRACT

When the project scope is well defined, an owner may choose to ask the contractor to take all the risks, both in terms of actual project cost and project time. Any work change orders from the owner must be extremely minor if at all, since performance specifications are provided to the owner at the outset of construction. The owner and the contractor agree to a project cost guaranteed by the contractor as maximum. There may be or may not be additional provisions to share any savings if any in the contract. This type of contract is particularly suitable for turnkey operation.

2.9 PARTNERING: EMERGING METHOD OF PROCUREMENT

The origins of partnering, as a construction management concept, are relatively recent in the UK and date from the mid-1980s. Extensive examples of partnering can, however, be found in the USA, Australia and New Zealand. According to the National Economic Development Office (NEDC) report *Partnering: contracting without conflict,* published in June 1991, true partnerships in the formal sense only became established in the mid-1980s with the first being between Shell and partners in 1984.

The increased growth of interest in partnering in the construction industry can be traced to the Latham report *Constructing the Team* published in 1994 which said; 'Partnering includes the concepts of teamwork between supplier and client, and of total continuous improvement. It requires openness between the parties, ready acceptance of new ideas, trust and perceived mutual benefit .... We are confident that partnering can bring significant benefits by improving quality and timeliness of completion whilst reducing costs'.

In 1995 the Reading Construction Forum (RCF)

published *Trusting the Team - the Best Practice Guide to Partnering in Construction* by Professor John Bennett and Dr Sarah Jayes of Reading University. This document drew the key distinction between project partnering (as applied to one-off schemes or teams) and strategic partnering (as applied to a series of projects, and often also referred to as 'alliancing' or 'strategic alliancing').

In 1996 the Construction Industry Board (CIB) report 'Partnering in the Team' defined partnering as follows: "Partnering is a structured management approach to facilitate team working across contractual boundaries. Its fundamental components are formalised mutual objectives, agreed problem resolution methods, and an active search for continuous measurable improvements".

In 1998 the RCF's follow-up report 'The Seven Pillars of Partnering' suggested the evolution of a third generation of partnering, in which 'modernised construction firms will use co-operation throughout their supply chains to build up efficient "virtual organisations" that respond to and shape rapidly changing markets'.

Also in1998 Sir John Egan's 'Rethinking Construction' identified five drivers for change, and four process improvements, one of which was partnering the supply chain. Shortly after the publication of the report the construction industry and Government established the Movement for Innovation (M4I) in response to the reports call for a movement for change.

In 1999 the Achieving Excellence programme sought to promote the change agenda in public sector procurement by reference to a series of targets for improved performance and the Construction Industry Council published the first edition of its document 'A Guide to Project Team Partnering'. This contained suggested heads of terms for a partnering contract. In March 2000 the Local Government Task Force was set up to encourage and assist local authorities to adopt the principles of Rethinking Construction.

In 2001 the Construction Clients' Charter was launched by the Confederation of Construction Clients. The Charter sets out a commitment in the four key areas of client leadership, integrated team working, a quality agenda and people. One of the Charter's key tenets of client leadership is to "adopt a partnering approach wherever possible" and promote a "team-based, non-adversarial approach amongst clients, advisers and the supply chain". In 2002 the Strategic Forum, which succeeded the CIB in July 2001, published 'Accelerating Change', a manifesto for the next phase of change in the industry. This set the target that by the end of 2004, 20% by value of construction projects let in the UK would be delivered by 'integrated teams'.

The project partnering team must include the client together with consultants, constructor/construction manager, key specialists, and key suppliers. The team members form a 'virtual company', acting co-operatively and making decisions in a blame-free environment of trust. This will raise the collective performance and aid more effective working, with the focus firmly on agreed common goals. Underpinning the successful project partnering team will be openness, clearly articulated mutual objectives, a problem resolving structure, a commitment to continuous improvement - measured against Key Performance Indicators (KPIs) - and a mechanism to manage the risks and fairly share the rewards.

There are two different categories of partnering

and within these categories there are a number of different types. The two categories are: (a) project partnering; and (b) strategic partnering.

Project partnering is often referred to as 'single project partnering' or sometimes as 'first-level partnering'. Project partnering occurs when two or more firms come together in a partnering arrangement for a single project. In the USA 90% of all partnering is project partnering. Strategic partnering is sometimes referred to as 'multi-project partnering' and occasionally as 'second-level partnering'. It takes place when two or more firms use partnering on long-term basis to undertake more than one construction project.

Strategic partnership is a business relationship, based on risk sharing as against risk transfer principle, for the benefit of all parties as it is built on mutual trust, openness and respect. It evolves to bring all parties together to form common goals, to integrate design and construction by involving contractors at an earlier stage, to share the risk and rewards of projects and to set up mechanisms to resolve disputes.

Because partnering has a lot to do about establishing long-term relationships it is evident that more gains and benefits are likely to be achieved from the longer-term strategic partnering than shorter term project partnering. However, project partnering is sometimes seen as a 'trial' for longer term strategic partnering. In the effort to modernising construction during the last decade, strategic partnering is emerged as a suitable procurement option.

The researchers have found that strategic partnering can provide many inherent benefits, such as but not limited to: (i) it provides better projects by engaging the supply chain in project management teams; (ii) it saves substantial management time as it allows the management team to be open and put issues on the table; (iii) it provides better and dispute-free relationships, e.g. no litigations or claims; (iv) it provides high levels of client and user satisfaction; (v) it provides better time performance i.e. project completion is ahead of schedule; and (vi) it provides better value, with an average of 25% cost savings on the trades engaged on a strategic basis.

In Rethinking Construction, Sir John Egan expressed the view that "Effective partnering does not rest on contracts. Contracts can add significantly to the cost of a project and often add no value to the client. If the relationship between a constructor and employer is soundly based and the parties recognise their mutual dependence then formal contract documents should gradually become obsolete". Historically, standard form construction contracts tend to provide for what happens when something goes wrong. The philosophy behind the new standard forms of partnering contract is geared more towards ensuring project success.

Those undertaking partnering arrangements in the UK also need to be aware of European Law as it affects trading within the European Union. The 1995 report, *Trusting the Team: Best Practice Guide to Partnering in Construction* gives detailed information upon contractual and legal issues as they affect the UK and the following statement from the report clearly identifies some of the problems associated with EU legislation:

'Partnering will always be unlawful in EU law if its effect is to discriminate against undertakings on national grounds, or breach the fundamental freedoms of the European Union – namely the freedom of movement of goods, services, workers and capital. Even if a partnering arrangement does not affect trade between member states, it may still be void, punishable by fine or liable in damages under English law if the agreement imposes restrictions on the price and supply of goods'.

It needs to be recognised that the standard forms of partnering contract which have recently been published and which are identified below are still in an embryonic state of development. As definitions of collaborative working evolve and are agreed, so too should the contractual arrangements that support such processes as a greater understanding of their constraints and limitations are gained.

2.10 TO BE COLLABORATIVE CONTRACT (BCC)

This type was developed originally under the auspices of 'The Reading Construction Forum' and is currently being trialled on a number of projects. BCC comprises a Purchase Order and a set of standard conditions. This standard form is intended for use as a design and construct contract. Unlike the public sector standard forms discussed below, this form does not expressly deal with operational performance of the asset once construction completion is achieved.

Interestingly, this form takes a middle line between PPC2000 and the charter option. In common with the NEC Option X12 and the JCT Partnering Charter, BCC recognises the use of non-contractually binding statements of aspiration. Therefore, under BCC the parties are expected to enter into a "project protocol" which not only sets out what the parties hope to achieve from their collaboration but also sets out the means by which such aspiration may be achieved. That protocol is not intended, however, to be contractually binding.

An important feature of the BCC is the inclusion within the contract of a risk register. Such registers are commonly used on large projects and PFI/PPP schemes as well as in the standard form Prime Contract. The Project Team is required to be consulted on issues that cannot be resolved between constructing parties, so as to make objective recommendations as to their resolution. The parties are required to give serious consideration to such recommendations. Although risk allocation remains unchanged throughout the life of the contract, (unless both parties agree otherwise), the risk register (including cost and time consequences) should be regularly updated.

Chapter 3

MAJOR FORMS OF CONTRACTS USED IN INTERNATIONAL CONSTRUCTION

3.1 INSTITUTION OF CIVIL ENGINEERS (ICE)

ICE is an independent engineering body having principal membership in the United Kingdom, but it has memberships in China, Hong Kong, Russia, India and roughly 140 other countries of the World. The ICE documents are traditionally for Engineering Constructional Projects. **Pre 1987 versions of FIDIC** were very much based on ICE forms but there is far less similarity now. Traditionally they were Engineer based contracts where the Employer appointed the Engineer. Available Documents

1. ICE Conditions of Contract Measurement Version 7th Edition: July 2004
2. ICE Conditions of Contract Design and Construct 2nd Edition: July 2004
3. ICE Conditions of Contract Minor Works 3rd Edition: July 2004
4. ICE Conditions of Contract Term Version: July 2004
5. ICE Conditions of Contract Ground Investigation 2nd Edition: July 2004
6. Agreement for Consultancy Work in respect of Domestic or Small Works: amendments Dec 1999

These are briefly discussed herein below:

1. ICE Conditions of Contract, 7th Edition: July 2004: This Contract is based on the traditional pattern of engineer designed contractor built works with valuation by admeasurements. The traditional role of the engineer in advising the client, designing the works, supervising construction, certifying payment and adjudicating in cases of dispute is fully maintained.

2. ICE Conditions of Contract Design and Construct 2nd Edition - July 2004: This contract radically departs from the normal ICE Conditions of Contract concept with the contractor responsible for all aspects of design and construction, including any design originally provided by or on behalf of the employer. The Form of Tender provides for payment on a lump sum basis but other forms of payment may be used.

3. ICE Conditions of Contract Minor Works 3rd Edition - July 2004: This is intended for use in contracts where: (a) the potential risks involved for both the employer and the contractor are adjudged to be small; (b) the works are of a simple and straightforward nature; (c) the design of the works, save for any design work for which the contractor is made responsible is complete in all essentials before tenders are invited; (d) the contractor has no responsibility for the design of the permanent works other than possibly design of a specialist nature; (e) nominated sub-contractors are not employed; and (f) the contract value does not exceed £500,000 and the period for completion of the contract does not exceed 6 months except where the method of payment is on either a daywork or a cost plus fee basis.

4. ICE Conditions of Contract Term Version - July 2004: The concept of a term contract is to carry out routine maintenance and remedial work within a set geographical area. A contractor is appointed to carry out such work for an agreed period of time (the term) carrying out such packages of work as may be required by the employer under conditions set out in the Term Version. The contract should be suitable for planned and reactive maintenance or refurbishment work as well as for new work and emergency works where a contractor may be on call. Each package of work to be carried out is identified in a works order which defines the works required and their location sets any programming needs and also states any special requirements or payment terms. Payments will normally be valued by measurement using rates set down in the term contract but specially agreed prices or a cost plus arrangement may also be used.

5. ICE Conditions of Contract Ground Investigation, 2nd Edition - July 2004: The conditions are very closely based on the ICE General Conditions of Contract 5th Edition. The contract conditions specify that the work will be under the full direction and control of the engineer, and on site, under the supervision of the engineer's representative or other person appointed by the engineer. The company or firm undertaking the physical work is referred to as the contractor. With limited exceptions, the role of the contractor is to perform the physical works and testing included within the contract documents, the control, direction and interpretation of such work generally being in the hands of the engineer or his representatives. In following the ICE General Conditions of Contract 5th Edition, the contract price is indeterminate at tender stage and is only finally derived on final measurement of the work undertaken.

6. Agreement for Consultancy Work in respect of Domestic or Small Works - amendments Dec 1999: ICE has produced this contract for domestic or small works in the form of a checklist for discussion with the client. It is divided into five sections, four of which reflect the type of services most often provided and the fifth deals with payment.

3.2 THE NEW ENGINEERING CONTRACT (NEC)

The NEC Form of Contract was developed by ICE in the early 1990s with the aim of introducing a new form of non-adversarial form of contract strategy which would contribute towards the more effective and smoother management of projects. It is now in its Third Edition and was the preferred form of contract for works relating to the 2012 Olympics facilities in London. It is radically different from other English style forms of Building and Civil Engineering Contracts, in that it has a core contract form, written in simple terms and substantial bolt ones to enable use in a variety of circumstances. The choice of options will have to be a subject for advice in each case.

The NEC Form of contract is a legal framework of project management procedures designed to handle all aspects of the management of engineering and construction projects. It is in use across the spectrum of engineering and construction projects by a wide range of clients, consultants and contractors. Its use encompasses projects both large and small, civil engineering and building, national and international.

The NEC Form of contract comprises a suite of contract documents and range of support services consisting of training, consultancy, software and a users group.

Since the original launch of the main engineering and construction contract and subcontract, the NEC has been extended to include a professional services contract, an adjudicator's contract; a short contract; and a term services contract, are under development.

The NEC Form of contract is being used for:

- Engineering and construction work containing any or all of the traditional disciplines such as civil, electrical, mechanical and building work.
- Projects where the Contractor has full design responsibility, partial design responsibility or no design responsibility.
- All the normal current options such as competitive tender, target contracts, cost reimbursable contracts and management contracts.
- Contracts in the UK and around the world.

Structure of The NEC 2 Form of contract: The main NEC 2 contract, the Engineering and Construction Contract - omnibus edition, and its associated sub-contract, are based on the employer selecting a contract form from six options as follows:

Option A: Priced contract with activity schedule

Option B: Priced contract with bill of quantities

Option C: Target contract with activity schedule

Option D: Target contract with bill of quantities

Option E: Cost reimbursable contract

Option F: Management contract

The chosen contractual strategy is then further refined by selecting from up to 15 secondary options depending on the main option selected. These are as follows:

Option G: Performance bond

Option H: Parent company guarantee

Option J: Advance payment to the Contractor

Option K: Multiple currencies

Option L: Sectional completion

Option M: Limitation of the Contractor's liability for his design to reasonable skill and care

Option N: Price adjustment for inflation

Option P: Retention

Option Q: Bonus for early completion

Option R: Delay damages

Option S: Low Performance Damages

Option T: Changes in the law

Option U: The Construction (Design and Management) Regulations 1994

Option V: Trust Fund

Option Z: Additional conditions of contract

The Engineering and Construction Short Contract follows the same principles as the main contract but with a reduced number of clauses and no secondary options. It can be used on projects which: (a) do not require sophisticated management techniques; (b) comprise straightforward work; and (c) impose only low risks on both the employer and the contractor.

The Professional Services Contract also follows the broad principles of other NEC Form of Contract documents but has been modified to cover the procurement of professional services. It is designed to be used in one of four main options:

Option A: Priced contract with activity schedule

Option B: Time based contract

Option C: Target contract

Option D: Term contract

These may be supplemented by up to 14 secondary option clauses.

Each contract document is supported by guidance notes and printed flow charts which set out the logic behind all contract decisions. In addition to the contract documents themselves, there are a range of support products and services covering training, consultancy, software, an active users group and a web site.

3.3 THE JOINT CONTRACTS TRIBUNAL (JCT)

Since 1931, the JCT, based in London, England, has been producing standard forms of contract, guidance notes and other standard documents used in the construction industry. The JCT range of contracts are fundamentally building rather than civil engineering contracts but are used for projects where both building and civil engineering works are involved. They cover, primarily, contracting and design and build and management contracts. Some forms deal with less complicated or expensive forms of contract.

The major types of form are traditionally English building contracts having been divided into with and Without Quantities forms to cover both methods of measurement. These are listed below:

The JCT helpfully publish a document entitled - Practice Note - Deciding on the appropriate JCT Contract, which provides guidance on what they would consider to be the appropriate JCT Contract for different situations - e.g. design and build, traditional contracting, cost plus or management. The note also contains a detailed list of JCT style contracts available. The current note sets out the position as at February 2007.

In a radical departure from previous JCT forms, the JCT launched on 1 March 2007, a new set of contract documents entitled JCT - Constructing Excellence.

Available Documents Include:

1. Major Project Form
2. PCC 2005 Standard Form of Prime Cost Contract
3. WCD 2005 Standard Form of Building Contract With Contractor's Design
4. 2005 Standard Form of Building Contract
5. MC 2005 Standard Form of Management Contract
6. IC 2005 Intermediate Form of Building Contract

7. MW 2005 Agreement for Minor Building Works
8. MTC 2005 Standard Form of Measured Term Contract

In addition JCT publish subcontracts, trade contracts and forms of warranty to be used with the particular contract in question.

Also in addition forms of framework agreement and facilities management agreements are available.

Details of some of the major forms of contract available are discussed herein below:

1. Major Project Form (MPF): The Major Project Form has been developed to meet the needs of clients who regularly procure the construction of major buildings. It reflects those amendments frequently made to JCT- developed standard form building contracts by developers and other large commercial organizations. This form is suitable for experienced users who require limited procedural provisions in the contract form and have their own in-house procedures, for experienced knowledgeable contractors who can put in place a proper system of risk management, and for significant projects in terms of size and complexity. MPF is the first JCT form specifically to provide for third party rights. It caters to various levels of design input on the part of the client and the contractor and incorporates a design submission procedure. The MPF also provides for projects carried out in phases, and therefore does not require a supplement, and it also requires the parties to establish their own insurance requirements, in contrast to other JCT forms.

Other key provisions are those dealing with: (a) acceleration of project; (b) bonus for early completion; (c) cost savings and value improvements; the Client's pre-appointed consultants; and mediation.

2. PCC 2005 Standard Form of Prime Cost Contract: This form is appropriate for use where the employer wants the earliest possible start. There may be insufficient time to prepare detailed tender documents; or circumstances such as an inability to accurately define the work may make the use of the detailed tender documents inappropriate, necessitating the appointment of a contractor simply on the basis of an estimate of the total cost.

3. WCD 2005 Standard Form of Building Contract With Contractor's Design: This form is appropriate for use where the employer wishes the contractor not only to carry out and complete works, but also to have a design responsibility for the works.

4. 2005 Standard Form of Building Contract: Appropriate for use on building contracts where the Employer appoints an Architect or Supervising Officer to be the interface between he and the Contractor.

5. MC 2005 Standard Form of Management Contract: This form is appropriate for use with large scale projects where an early start and the earliest possible completion are required. In such situations it is not always possible to prepare full design information before work commences, and much of the detail design may be of a sophisticated or innovative nature requiring proprietary systems or components designed by specialists.

6. IC2005 Intermediate Forms of Building Contract: Suggested for prospects of between £250,000 and £5,000,000 or where more detailed condition than the Minor Works form (No. 7) are required.

7. MW 2005 Agreement for Minor Building Works: This form is appropriate for new works, alterations and extensions to all types of building, such as: (a) where the proposed works are to be carried out for an agreed lump sum; (b) where the work involved is simple in character; and (c) where an architect or contract administrator has been appointed to advise on and to administer its terms. It is, however, not suitable for use where detailed control procedures are needed.

8. MTC 2005 Standard Form of Measured Term Contract: This form is appropriate for use by employers who have a regular flow of maintenance and minor works, including improvements, to be carried out by a single contractor over a specified period of time and all under a single contract. The JCT Constructing Excellence Contract shares certain basic principles with the BE Collaborative Contract (3.4) below and has some common authors. Its principles are stated to be collaboration and partnership within a rigorous legal framework, but a framework that has many options (like the NEC forms) to cover particular situations.

The JCT Practice Note 4: Non-Binding Partnering Charter for Single Project: The JCT adopts a relatively simple approach. It is a guidance/practice note plus a two page Partnering Charter, which is non-binding in its nature and available for multi-party use. Like the NEC Option X12, it is designed to operate alongside the use of an existing JCT Standard Form of Contract and aims to promote good teamwork within that context. The Charter contains only two brief statements; the first being how the parties are to conduct the dealings between themselves, and the second being the 4 objectives to be achieved by the team under the headings of (1) Delivery, (2) People, (3) Team working, and (4) Commercial. As to how the signatories to the Charter are to act, this includes statements of aspiration (acting in a way to avoid disputes by adopting a "no-blame culture") as well as more explicit terms such as to act "in a co-operative way" and "fairly towards each other". However, such terms are nonetheless not intended to create legally enforceable terms as between the signatories to the Charter.

As to the four stated objectives in the Charter, these are to be measured against performance indicators to be established. An agreement to agree is, in English Law, void for uncertainty unless the parameters of the agreement are set out with sufficient precision so as to enable the court to say what the terms of the agreement should be. Such concerns do not, of course, concern a non-contractual Charter. Thus, the signatories are left to agree as loosely or precisely as they wish; ultimately no party can enforce its "rights" under the Charter because it has no such rights.

3.4 PPC 2000

PPC 2000 is the first multi-party standard form partnering contract to be published by a professional body. Launched in September 2000 (amended in June 2003) by the Association of Consulting Architects (ACA), PPC 2000 introduces a contractually binding partnering agreement that seeks to integrate the entire project team using a single multi-party approach. It is also intended to cover the entire duration of the design and construction process, from inception including the feasibility and design phases through to completion of the works. The "partnering team members" will include the client, the construction contractor, all consultants and key selected specialists or suppliers.

The associated contract SPC 2000 is designed to enable the partnering team members to the PPC 2000 to enter into back-to-back arrangements with their subcontractors referred to as "Specialists". The structure of SPC 2000 reflects that of PPC 2000. PPC 2000 has enjoyed wide use since publication, particularly in the housing sector where Housing Associations have been driven by Housing Corporation requirements to embrace the Egan philosophy in their procurement of projects.

3.5 THE NEC PARTNERING OPTION X12

The New Engineering Contract core conditions were first published in 1993. They reflect an approach and contain a number of features that are consistent with a partnering approach to procurement. In this sense, advocates of the NEC form claim that it is the earliest of standard form partnering contracts.

The NEC expressly introduces the concept of partnering by the act of the parties including Option X12 into the contract. Within the NEC framework, the partnering Option X12 is selected for use with an "Own Contract", namely another contractually binding contract between the parties. The NEC Option X12 does not expressly create legally enforceable obligations or contractual relations between Partners, other than those between parties to the "Own Contract". It is intended more as guide to collaborative project management, with references to "Partnering Information" including any requirements on the use of common information systems, as well as participations in workshops, arrangements for joint design development, value engineering, value management, risk management and the like.

3.6 THE FIDIC SUITE OF CONTRACTS

3.6.1 General

Please note that the FIDIC 1999 contracts are not a revision of previous forms; hence "First Edition" within their titles as sponsored by perhaps a desire to create the dominant forms of contract relative to all forms of construction project coupled with the changing face of construction a complete overhaul took place. The most fundamental change to the new contracts being the abandonment of the work based contract; it being replaced by contracts that recognised which party was to be responsible for the design of the Works (or the vast majority of the Works) and where risk would be allocated.

The FIDIC publishes internationally recognised forms of contract for infrastructure works. These are in broad term called Rainbow Suite encompassing seven Books: (1) Conditions of Contract for Construction For Building and Engineering Works designed by the Employer - Red Book. (2) Conditions of Contract for Plant and Design Build For Electrical and Mechanical Plant and for Building and Engineering Work Designed by the Contractor - Yellow Book. (3) Conditions of Contract for EPC/Turnkey Projects - Silver Book. (4) Conditions of Contract for Design, Build and Operate Projects - Gold Book. (5) Conditions of Contract for Construction MDB Harmonised Edition For Building and Engineering Works designed by the Employer - Pink Book. (6) Short Form of Contract - Green Book. (7)The FIDIC Contract Guide - Blue Book

See picture below:

Red Book, Yellow Book, and Silver Book are commonly used on International construction projects. These Forms share the Project Risks between the Employer and the Contractor as shown in the diagram below:

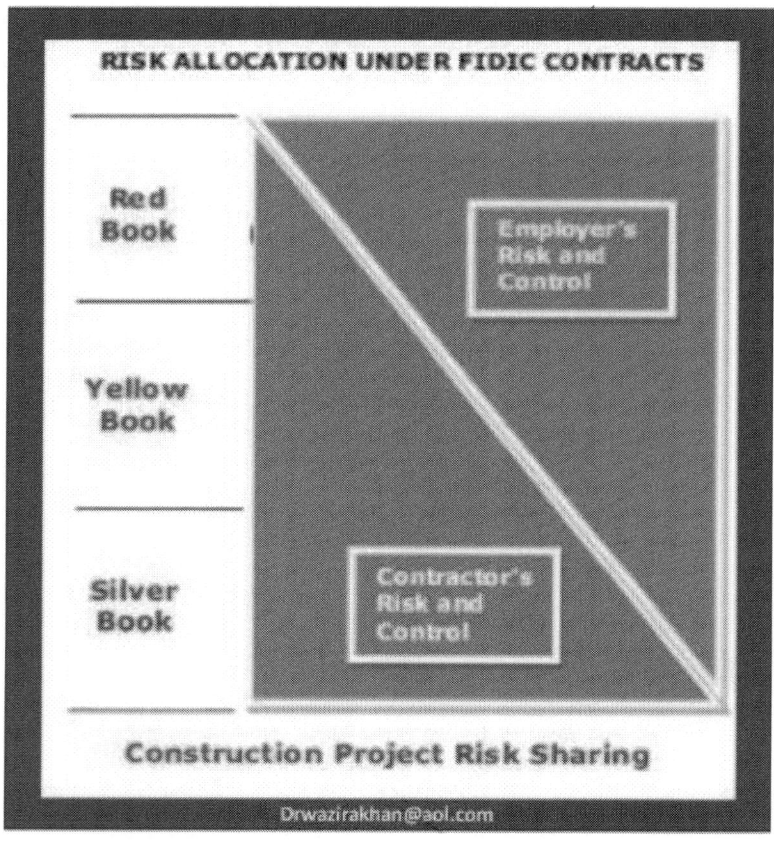

3.6.2 The New Red, Yellow and Silver Books

A fundamental change adopted by FIDIC when drafting these contracts was to move away from a work style to a contract that reflected where the responsibility for design would be allocated. FIDIC not only sought to issue a new suite of contracts but also sought to make the contracts user friendly and create a best practice manual for contract administration.

To aid all users the task group drafting the contracts were instructed to standardise the three new major forms. The results being that, unless differences were essential, definitions, layout, clause numbering, and clause wording were identical. Accordingly the Red, Yellow and Silver Books contain only twenty clauses; the last edition of the old Red Book contained seventy two clauses whilst the old Yellow Book fifty one clauses.

The general layout of the Contracts is as follows:

- General Conditions; including an Appendix entitled General Conditions of Dispute Adjudication Agreement which includes the Procedural Rule for a DAB.
- A section giving guidance for the preparation of any Particular Conditions; this section also includes examples of guarantees, securities and bonds that are commonplace on international projects.
- A section entitled Forms; here FIDIC provide examples of:
    - Letter of Tender with supporting Appendix to Tender;
    - Contract Agreement;
    - DAB Agreements (either a one-person DAB or three person DAB).

FIDIC have continued to be helpful to those using its contracts. With respect to the position of 'The Engineer', from the impartial, quasi arbitral role of previous editions, FIDIC have amended the role of the Engineer in the Red and Yellow Books (the Silver Book has an Employer's Representative). The Engineer is clearly stated to act for the Employer. He is no longer required to be impartial but whenever required to make a determination in respect of value, cost or time related matter he has to make his determination fairly, and in accordance with the Contract, having taken into consideration all relevant circumstances.

3.6.3 FIDIC Red Book Construction Contract

The FIDIC Red Book Construction Contract comprise the "General Conditions", which form part of the "Conditions of Contract for Construction" First Edition 1999 published by the Fédération Internationale des Ingénieurs-Conseils (FIDIC), and the following "Particular Conditions", which include amendments and additions to such General Conditions.

The salient features of this Contract can be summarised as:

- FIDIC Red Book Construction Contract which is recommended for building or engineering works designed by the Employer or by his representative, the Engineer. Accordingly, it is suitable for all types of project where the main responsibility for design lies with the Employer (or its Engineer) although provision is made for the Contractor to design elements of the Works
- Under the usual arrangements for this type of contract, the Contractor constructs the works in accordance with a design provided by the Employer. However, the works may include some elements of Contractor-designed civil, mechanical, electrical and/or construction works.
- The forms are recommended for general use where tenders are invited on an international basis.

- Modifications may be required in some jurisdictions, particularly if the Conditions are to be used on domestic contracts. FIDIC considers the official and authentic texts to be the versions in the English language.
- The administration of the Contract and approval of work is carried out by the Engineer as is certification of payments and determination of extensions of time.
- Payment to the Contractor is based upon work done and rates as per a Bill of Quantities (a Standard Method thus reflecting the likely on site nature of the Works (a reflection that the Red Book will most likely be used for building and civil engineering projects).
- Risk sharing is balanced between Parties such as the Employer taking the risks of "adverse physical conditions" and the "operation of the forces of nature" that are considered to be unforeseeable.
- Claims by both Parties have to follow procedures, albeit the conditions imposed upon the Contractor are harsher with the inclusion of a "fatal" notice provision.
- The Contractor has some financial protection in that it can request evidence from the Employer that it has the finances to pay the estimated Contract Price.
- Materials can be paid for both on and off site if strict criteria are followed, including the listing of materials for which payment maybe sought within the Contractor's tender.

In the preparation of this FIDIC Red Book Construction Contract for Construction, it was recognised that, while there are many sub-clauses which will be generally applicable, there are some sub-clauses which must necessarily vary to take account of the circumstances relevant to the particular contract. The sub-clauses which were considered to be applicable to many (but not all) contracts have been included in the General Conditions, which will facilitate their incorporation into each contract.

The General Conditions and the Particular Conditions will together comprise the Conditions of Contract governing the rights and obligations of the parties. It will be necessary to prepare the Particular Conditions for each individual contract, and to take account of those sub-clauses in the General Conditions which mention the Particular Conditions.

3.6.4 FIDIC Yellow Book - Plant and Design Build Contract

FIDIC Yellow Book - Plant and Design Build Contract 1st Edition 1999 FIDIC Conditions of Contract for Plant and Design Build, which is recommended for the provision of electrical and/or mechanical plant, and to the design and execution of building or engineering works. Under the usual arrangements to this type of contract, the Contractor designs and provides, in accordance with the Employer's requirements, plant and/or other works; which may include any combination of civil, mechanical, electrical and/or construction works. In structure this is very similar to the Red Book.

The salient features of this Contract can be summarised as:

- It is suitable for all projects where the main responsibility for design lies with the Contractor based upon the Employer's Requirements although provision is made for the Employer (or his Engineer) to design elements of the Works.

- The administration of the Contract and approval of work is carried out by the Engineer as is certification of payments and determination of extensions of time
- Payment to the Contractor is based upon a Lump Sum price and normally against a schedule of milestones to be achieved by the Contractor. This reflects that the Yellow Book will most likely be used for process plants and the like where a high degree of offsite manufacture of plant and equipment is foreseen and payment terms can be drafted to recognise this situation subject to the listing of such plant and equipment within the Contractor's tender as within the Red Book
- Testing procedures leading to completion are likely to be more complicated than within the Red Book, again reflecting the likely nature of the project
- The Yellow Book shares with the Red Book the provisions noted above relative to:
    - Risk sharing;
    - Claims by both Parties; and
    - Financial protection for the Contractor.

Note: The Red and Yellow Books are said to provide contracts with a balanced view of risk sharing meaning: (i) the Employer pays the Contractor only when specific risks occur; (ii) the Contractor does not have to include within its tender for risks that are difficult to value. This means that the Employer has a great degree of uncertainty in respect of the final price and the final time for completion

3.6.5 FIDIC Silver Book - EPC Turnkey Contract 1st Edition 1999

Under the usual arrangements for this type of contract, the entity carries out all the Engineering, Procurement and Construction: providing a fully-equipped facility, ready for operation (at the "turn of the key"). This type of contract is usually negotiated between the parties.

The Conditions of Contract to EPC/Turnkey Projects FIDIC silver book, which are recommended where one entity takes total responsibility to the design and execution of an engineering project.

The Silver Book reflects a market desire for certainty of cost and time. The Contractor is asked to allow within its tender for a wide range of risks relative to cost and time; such risks will most likely include all ground conditions (i.e. the Contractor may have little knowledge of the country where contract is executed) and the completion of the Works will be based upon a strict but often brief performance related specification. The Employer will still bear some risks such as those related to war, terrorism and Force Majeure but the unbalanced risk profile of this Contract will undoubtedly be a higher price; a factor that Employer's must accept.

The Salient features of the Silver Book can be summarised as:

- Design liability rests solely with the Contractor, the Employer will provide its requirements but these are often in the form of a brief performance specification.

- The Contractor carries out all engineering, procurement and construction often including performance tests after completion; a "turn-key" project allowing operation of the facility upon completion.
- There is not an Engineer within the Contract; the Employer may appoint an Employer's Representative.
- It is lump sum Contract with payment terms most likely similar to those envisaged under the Yellow Book.

Employer whilst selecting a Silver Book Contract should recognise the significant costs for a Contractor to produce a tender. Accordingly it advisable that Employer's recognising this selects only a small number of Contractors to tender. Since Employers have chosen a turnkey style of contract and therefore should allow the Contractor complete freedom to carry out the Works in its chosen manner in order to reach any performance criteria laid down by the Employer. If the Employer unwilling to grasp such factors, or the tender time is too short to allow the Contractor to compile an adequate tender, or considerable amounts of work are underground, or difficult to inspect then the Contractor must ask the Employer to use Yellow Book Contract, thereby accepting some additional risks and receiving a lower tender price.

3.6.6 FIDIC Green Book Short Form of Contract

The final contract to be issued in 1999 was the Green Book or Short Form of Contract. This Contract recognised a need for a much simpler and shorter contract to suit projects with a relatively low Contract Price and short time duration. However, depending on the type of work and the circumstances, the Conditions may be suitable for contracts of considerably greater value. This Book is considered most likely to be suitable for fairly simple or repetitive work or work of short duration without the need for specialist sub-contracts. This form may also be suitable for a contract which include, or wholly comprise, contractor-designed civil engineering, building, mechanical and/or electrical works.

The Contract itself is very flexible, any reader will however recognise the Contract as being from the same family albeit it has only fifteen clauses and a total of ten pages. The clauses are short and easily understood; whilst design can be carried out by either party an Engineer is not foreseen, however the Employer may appoint a Representative. Payment can be made on either a lump sum or remeasured basis.

As with the major forms the Green Book Contract includes guidance notes (noted as not forming part of the Contract) as well as an Agreement together with its Appendix and Rules for Adjudication, whilst the noticeable absentee being the Particular Conditions section. In this respect FIDIC consider that the Green Book can work without such conditions but, a cautionary note is provided should an Employer deem it necessary to amend the drafted Contract.

3.6.7 Orange Book Conditions of Contract for Design-Build and Turnkey

The Contents of this Contract Book include: (i) General Conditions; (ii) Guidance for the Preparation of the Particular Conditions; and (iii) Forms of Tender and Agreement.

When the Orange book was published the Red and Yellow Books were still aimed at procurement of civil engineering and plant installation respectively. At the time it added a clear design and build and turnkey option into the available suite of contracts.

Since the publication in 1999 of the latest Red and Yellow Books there is now less focus on the type of project and more focus on the implementation of different procurement strategies

3.6.8 Red Book (MDB edition)

The FIDIC MDB edition of the Red Book simplifies the use of the FIDIC contract for the MDBs, their borrowers and others involved with project procurement, such as consulting engineers, contractors and contract lawyers.

The following MDBs that have all participated in the preparation of this edition of the Red Book:

i. African Development Bank;
ii. Asian Development Bank;
iii. Black Sea Trade and Development Bank;
iv. Caribbean Development Bank;
v. European Bank for Reconstruction and Development;
vi. Inter-American Development Bank;
vii. International Bank for Reconstruction and Development (The World Bank);
viii. Islamic Bank for Development Bank; and (ix) Nordic Development Fund.

3.6.9 Design, Build and Operate form (FIDIC "Gold Book")

The Gold Book form of contract is probably the most radical of the new colours; it represents a contract period of over 20 years! It is a design, build and operate (DBO) contract that the industry has needed for some time to reflect the ever growing trend that contractors no longer construct something then go away but also maintain and operate the facility for many years to come. It has been described as a Yellow Book with an operate and maintenance contract bolted on; the First Edition of the Conditions of Contract for Design, Build and Operate Projects was issued in 2008.

In the Foreword to the Gold Book, FIDIC envisaged that it would be used by separate construction and operating companies acting as the "Contractor" under a joint venture/consortium agreement. However, imposing obligations on the JV/Consortium as a whole causes particular problems in a DBO project. For example in Sub-Clause 4.1 of the Gold Book, a duty is imposed on the Contractor to ensure that the Works are "fit for the purposes for which the Works are intended as defined in the Contract" and states that the "Contractor shall be responsible for ensuring that the Works remain fit for such purposes during the Operation Service Period".

The Gold Book without doubt fills one of the last gaps in FIDIC"s toolbox of contracts. Its use is growing especially as government departments such as water authorities warm to the idea of having foreign contractors bring their knowledge of providing water treatment and supply at a profit but also having to be responsible for remedying defects whilst remaining in the country. Accordingly FIDIC has not only responded to employers who crave to outsource but also the changing face of contractors who are now operators too.

Any potential disputes between contractors carrying out a design and build contract to questionable standards leading to poor performance, defects and disputes whilst leaving the employer to struggle through a 20 year life time of a plant have, potentially, been negated. In The Gold Book that is, provided and the whole scheme is fully thought through and both parties, as with all contracts, are willing and able to act responsibly towards each other such that a balance is struck between the constructions and operating elements of the contract.

The salient features of Gold Book include:

- Design, build plus operation and maintenance for 20 years by the contractor on a green field site.
- Design and build phase risk allocation similar to the Yellow Book with exacting completion criteria but also a cut off date should the contractor be 182 days late leading to termination if desired.
- Payment on a lump sum basis but a defined asset replacement fund and schedule that notes the timing and cost of the replacement of certain assets. Costs of replacing plant and equipment outside of the schedule will be the responsibility of the contractor, as is a cost over that stated on the schedule. Any surplus in the fund at the end of the twenty years is divided equally.
- The employer is entitled to deduct 5% from payments during the "operation service period" (OPS) in case the contractor does not fulfil its maintenance obligations. The fund is to be released, if not spent, within the final payment to the contractor. The contractor being responsible for its own defects arising from design and construction in this period.

- An independent audit body is jointly appointed for the duration of the OPS to monitor the performance of the contractor and employer. Whilst having no power, the parties are intended to give "due regard" to matters raised by the audit body.
- A joint inspection is required at least two years before the end of the OPS; any works identified must be carried out by the contractor who will also face completion tests similar to those at the end of the design and build phase. Defaulting contractors risk losing the 5% maintenance retention fund.
- A standing DAB is established from a set date for the design and build phase and a new one every 5 years during the OPS.

In the Gold Book Contract, the key to success appears to be with the contractor who must design and build a quality plant with low operating and maintenance costs; fit for purpose and built to last, but this has to be tested in the years to come. However, like any relationship time gives rise to change and only time will tell if FIDIC have considered all factors such as changes in the deliverables required by the employer, but to its credit, FIDIC has recently issued its guide to this form.

3.7 NEC CONTRACT VS FIDIC CONTRACT

Both NEC and FIDIC contracts are standard forms of contract that are part of standard families for procuring works or consultancy services (FIDIC) and goods, works or services (NEC).

Both contracts provide for a person to act on behalf of the employer should the employer not have appropriate people in-house in terms of capacity or capability; the project manager acts on behalf the employer in NEC, the engineer in FIDIC.

FIDIC focuses on liabilities and risk in the manner of traditional contracts whereas NEC requires and enables a more proactive and collaborative approach to managing the contract.

With respect to Cost, NEC and FIDIC (Red Book) both provide for the price payable to the contractor to be based on bills of quantities, and both allow for stage payments.

NEC3 and FIDIC Conditions of Contract for EPC/Turnkey Projects (FIDIC Silver Book) are both popular standard forms of engineering and construction contract, used on a variety of projects both in the UK and internationally. However, they have fundamentally different approaches to the way projects should be managed and conducted.

In this, the first of a two-part series assessing NEC3 against the more conventional FIDIC Silver Book in terms of its suitability for substantial international construction and engineering projects, the contrasting approaches and philosophies of the two forms in relation to structure, portability, risk and administration are observed. In his 1994 report entitled Constructing the Team, Michael Latham commented that *"The client who wishes to accept little or no risk should take different routes for procuring advice from the client who places importance on detailed, hands-on control."* This comment characterises the difference in approach between a more traditional form of contract (such as FIDIC Silver Book) and the new NEC3 form, which embraces a more collaborative approach.

FIDIC Silver Book is specifically designed as a turnkey contract, where an employer hands full responsibility over to the contractor for all design, engineering and construction. This approach expects the employer to "wait for the keys" and to have little day-to-day management of the project as work progresses. NEC3 envisages the project as a collaborative process, with an emphasis on contract administration. The parties are obliged to "act in a spirit of mutual trust and co-operation", an obligation which is central to the philosophy and concept of NEC3.

As every project will be different, and every employer will have a different appetite for risk, therefore, regardless whether an NEC3 or FIDIC Silver Book standard form contract is used for a large-scale project, there will inevitably be considerable scope for tailoring and amendment to suit the project and the parties.

NEC3, in structure, language and terminology, is different from more traditional forms such as FIDIC. It shies away from the traditional language of construction contracts, such as "extensions of time" or "variations," and even avoids the use of mandatory wording such as "shall" – instead, verbs are used in the present tense. This takes some getting used to, but is deliberately done to reflect the underlying collaborative philosophy of the NEC3 approach. NEC3 is drafted to operate in a "common sense" manner. The language is intended to operate flexibly; as design responsibility and pricing structure are not "nailed down" in the draft it should, theoretically, be adaptable for any project which may make it more portable internationally.

Structurally, NEC3 is made up of core conditions, six main options (reflecting the price/procurement strategy, analysed further in the second of this two-part series) and various secondary options ("W," "X" and "Y" clauses). The parties can tailor their contract to fit a project by selecting which of the optional clauses they would like to incorporate. Optional clauses include: dispute resolution procedures; provision for bonds or parent company guarantees; and limitations on liability and advance payment. The parties can also include further "Z clauses" if they want to amend any of the NEC clauses or include additional provisions. The structure reflects NEC3's primary purpose as a management tool. It is often said that a "good" contract will never be taken out of a cupboard unless and until something goes wrong; this is wholly untrue of NEC3, which is intended to utilise involved project management and where the intent is that the contract remains an active tool throughout the life of a project.

Many of the provisions intrinsic within FIDIC appear as secondary options in NEC3 (such as performance security and liquidated damages), and others are missing altogether. If adopting a less traditional approach, an employer will need to have a good understanding of how NEC3 works so as to ensure that nothing important is missed; assuming that the "usual" clauses are present within NEC3 would be a mistake. FIDIC Silver is more traditional in nature. It sets out a series of "General Conditions" and the parties will tailor this to their project through the use of "Particular Conditions." The contract is part of the FIDIC "rainbow" of contracts, a well-established family of standard forms designed for use in a variety of projects and approaches, including design and build, employer-design, dredging, and smaller projects. The forms all follow a similar format; international contractors are likely to be familiar with this as it is used as the basis for a variety of projects around the world.

There is also a well-established body of case law interpreting traditional contracts such as FIDIC Silver Book and its forerunners. Its principles are therefore well-understood. There is significantly less case law looking at NEC3 or its predecessors.

Familiarity, however, does not automatically mean that the form is superior or more user-friendly; "different" is not the same as "bad." NEC3 does require an employer willing to embrace its approach, as well as a project manager who is experienced in following it; but those who are experienced at using it will often be found singing its praises.

A standard form of engineering and construction contract, for use in international projects, needs to be portable and easily adaptable for a variety of jurisdictions. FIDIC is designed for international use and is the most common international standard form, available in a number of languages. NEC3 has widespread use in the UK, aided by the backing that it has received from the UK Office of Government Commerce for public sector projects – recent high-profile examples include construction of Terminal 5 at Heathrow Airport and the 2012 Olympic Stadium. However, it is intended to be fully portable and is now being seen in a number of international projects and markets.

NEC3's approach could, albeit as a gross generalisation, be summarised as being that employers should pay for risks as and when they occur, rather than paying a high er price to pass these risks to the contractor up front. The consequence of this is that the employer bears more risk than it would under more traditional forms but it will likely to achieve lower contract price.. FIDIC Silver Book has a different philosophy: as a turnkey contract, it aims to pass, as far as possible, full responsibility to the contractor and the situations which entitle the contractor to claim more time and/or money are more limited. This approach is often preferred, and may even be dictated, by financiers. Many employers and contractors will also prefer this more conventional approach as it provides greater certainty about where the risk portfolio is distributed.

On the face of it, many employers would opt for the risk position under FIDIC Silver as providing a clear dividing line between the parties' respective positions. That said, others may prefer a more collaborative approach that seeks to manage risks rather than simply allocate responsibility. The theme of risk management underpins NEC3's approach to risk, and the employer is expected to take a proactive approach. Through the use of optional clauses, the employer can also incentivise the contractor – the target cost options, for example, include shared savings mechanisms, and there are also optional clauses to incorporate key performance indicators and early completion bonuses. None of these concepts are found in FIDIC Silver Book.

NEC3's collaborative approach to risk is further represented by the "risk register" and "early warning" concepts that allow more "hands on" time and delay management. The risk register is intended to be a project management tool to manage those risks which arise over the course of a project. Risks should be notified by the contractor or project manager as an "early warning matter" and will then be added to the risk register. The parties are encouraged to have risk reduction meetings to review registered risks and decide on solutions. NEC3's collaborative approach is also represented in its unusual approach to delay and/or cost entitlement.

Rather than the usual retrospective approach represented in FIDIC and other traditional contracts, under NEC3 an award is forward-looking, based upon a quotation-style approach: when an event occurs which is the employer's risk, the contractor is required to notify the anticipated effects of this event and, once agreed or determined, these anticipated effects (in terms of time and/or cost) are developd irrespective of the actual effects. The FIDIC Silver Book approach is much more traditional, with the contractor expected to manage risks as the project develops and deliver a complete solution on time. For employers and contractors who are used to the more traditional balance of risk in an EPC contract, the FIDIC Silver Book approach is likely to be more attractive.

NEC3 places obligations on the employer, the contractor, the project manager and the supervisor and clearly anticipates, and in fact heavily relies on parties other than the employer and the contractor to ensure that the contract is administered correctly. The role of the project manager is central to NEC3. FIDIC Silver places obligations on the employer and the contractor only insofar as the day-to-day administration of the contact is concerned.

Although selected by, and acting on behalf of, the employer, the project manager is required to act fairly and impartially and heavy reliance is placed on the project manager in terms of making various decisions and issuing various key notices, including notifying compensation events. The party selected to act as project manager will therefore undoubtedly need to be very involved in the project on a daily basis and will also need to have a very detailed knowledge of the NEC3 form and how it works. FIDIC Silver Book is drafted on the basis that the employer will generally leave the contractor to progress with the works, in accordance with the contract.

FIDIC Silver does not envisage that the contract will be "administered" by any third party and works generally on the basis that the employer accepts that the contractor will progress the works, address any issues as and when these arise and hand over a fully functional product at the end of the works. That said, there is nothing to prevent the employer from engaging a technical advisor or engineer to monitor compliance with the contract. For example the rights for the employer to approve the contractor's documents and inspect the work or plant are clearly intended to allow the input of a technical advisor; it is simply that there is nothing in FIDIC Silver Book to restrain the employer's discretion. In practice, an employer using FIDIC Silver Book with its technical advisor is likely to have a high degree of involvement in the project.

We can conclude by stating that when assessing these contracts, it is not so much a case of better or worse, but a difference in approach, and the question of which contract will work best for a specific project and the parties involved. NEC3 relies on good management and is designed to flesh out problems as the project progresses. Although FIDIC Silver Book is designed as a true turnkey contract, with the intention that the contractor will, for the most part, take responsibility for ongoing problems, but in the majority of international high-value projects conducted under FIDIC Silver Book, the employer is seen to be actively involved throughout and often takes a collaborative approach. FIDIC, for example, has a concept of the dispute adjudication board, which can be used by the parties to manage problems as they arise and avoid more formal dispute resolution procedures.

In international constructional project, inevitability, there are pros and cons to both approaches but because of choice, a heavy emphasis on management comes with cost implications and may not suit every project owner, but it could have the advantage of fixing problems earlier. But how well the contracts work depends to a large extent on how they are used in practice.

Chapter 4

SELECTION OF CONSULTANTS IN CONSTRUCTION PROCESS

4.1 GENERAL ASPECTS

The most important standards by which to judge a consultant's suitability to carry out a particular project include: professional competence; managerial ability; availability of resources; impartiality; fairness of fee structure; professional integrity; and quality assurance system. These are briefly discussed herein below:

Professional Competence: The competent professional consultant will be able to offer the client a team that will have the education, training, practical experience and judgement to carry out the project. The client can evaluate the professional competence of the team by examining; (i) the detailed resumes of key staff members and their relevant experience on similar assignments; (ii) the list of similar projects carried out by the firm and present staff; (ii) the approach to and methodology for the proposed assignment. In addition, the client should validate the performance of the consultant on similar previous assignments with owners and examine the performance history of the consultant in similar foreign countries.

Managerial Ability: To successfully achieve project objectives, a consultant must have managerial skills to match the size and type of the project. The consultant will need to marshal skilled manpower and adequate resources, maintain schedules and ensure that the work is planned in the most efficient manner. The consultant will need to be able to deal competently with contractors, suppliers, loan agencies, government agencies and the public during the course of the project. At the same time, the client must be informed of the development of the project to be able to make decisions quickly and accurately. The client can assess the managerial ability of the consultant team by examining: (i) past projects performance record; (ii) the documentation and project control procedures which guide the performance of the consultant's services; (iii) the success record of the proposed project manager on previous projects; (iv) the project management and quality control approach proposed for the new assignment; (v) the progress reporting and client communication techniques proposed for the assignment; and (vi) the success rate on previous projects of the consultant in transferring technology.

Availability of Resources: When selecting a consultant it is important to establish whether the firm has sufficient financial and manpower resources to carry out the project to the necessary detail and standards commensurate with the time and fee schedule. This will indicate the extent to which the firm's current resources are committed. The client should verify that the consultant has sufficient staff available at the relevant experience levels and that there are sufficient financial resources to carry out the work. The client can validate the adequacy of the consultant's resources by reviewing: (i) the number of qualified professional and managerial personnel committed to the project team; (ii) the deployment of the project staff and how the team will be organised with lines of responsibility; (iii) the credit worthiness of the firm; (iv) the ready access to supporting resources; and (v) the proximity of the firm's offices to the proposed work.

Impartiality: When the Employer/Client employs a consultant who is a member of one of FIDIC's member associations, such as: ACEI, the client has the assurance that the consultant subscribes to FIDIC's Code of Ethics, is competent, and provides impartial professional advice. The consultant is remunerated solely by the fees paid by the clients. The consultant has no commercial ties which can prejudice his/her impartial judgement. If the consultant is a member of a consortium, he/she may be remunerated from the proceeds of the consortium. In this case, the consultant must consider the consortium partners to be clients. The consultant is therefore able to approach all assignments objectively and by exercising sound professional judgement and prudent economic principles, can provide solutions to serve the clients best interests. The client may wish the consultant to furnish an affidavit confirming that no potential conflict of interest in the performance of the proposed assignment exists.

Fairness of Fee Structure: Consultants need to be adequately compensated to ensure that they are able to provide high-quality services with proper attention to details, alternative considerations, innovation and cost effective solutions. Consultants must maintain highly competent staff through continuous education and training initiatives and give constant attention to research and development to maintain state-of-the-art expertise and up-to-date equipment and technology. The fee structure should be adequate to achieve the objectives of the project and meet the expectations of the client. At the same time, the fee must generate a reasonable profit for the consultant so he can remain in business ready to serve the client with well trained, experienced staff and the latest in innovative approaches.

Professional Integrity: Mutual trust and integrity represent the oil in the machinery of the relationship between client and consultant. Without it the machine becomes inefficient, hot through friction and finally can come to a standstill. If absolute trust exists between the client and the consultant and both parties have integrity, and then the project will run more smoothly, the results will be better and both parties will be happier. These very factors of mutual trust and integrity are the reasons why there is repeated commission and consultants are commissioned by the same client again and again.

Quality Assurance System: The Employer/Client must check the adequacy of the Consultant's Quality Assurance System against the international norms and the following guidelines:

Clients/customers must expect that supplier of product or service can get it right first time, every time. This means getting the design, detailing and most important of all the performance aspects or fitness for purpose right in all disciplines. This in turn demands implementation of an effective quality system in the Design Office.

Further, it is essential that the quality system is flexible and alive as well as cost effective. It should be real system for the particular company and adapted to the specific project and not a copy of something somebody has produced. However, it is important to understand that no system will ever be effective and beneficial unless all those associated with its development and implementation is convinced the system will ultimately benefit the company. Furthermore, the system may fail from time to time during its implementation and the Senior Management must maintain enthusiasm to get it right first time, next time, by accepting the disappointments of any failure and learning a lesson from it.

In a project environment the design professional i.e. Architects, Civil and Structural Engineers, Services Engineers, etc. should be placed in the crucial decision making and advisory roles with the client on quality matters. If design, detailing and performance criteria for fitness for purpose are right, then there is a good chance that the desired (specified) quality will be achieved. Although the design engineering discipline may resolve most of the technical and economic issues on the quality front, but rest of the design discipline faces a more difficult task in getting the correct materials and components selection, effectively coordinated project information for quality appraisal and execution. For example, suppose each manufacturer's component may be produced in its total sense of fitness for purpose, but when assembled with other components or material may not be fully compatible with the planned quality attributes in that element of work.

There is another pitfall into which designers may fall and that is when the designer may think that desired quality is communicated through their designer details and drawings supported by the specification. There is a general tendency to reference codes and standards in the specifications which may not be readily available on a construction site or when general statements are made in the specifications, e.g., 'unless otherwise described the workmanship to be the best quality' (without qualifying the definition of best quality). In the quality efforts the biggest contribution the design team can make is review their 'modus-vivendi' and maintain necessary co-ordination with the other departments and deliver sound design engineering for the benefit of the Production Process and ultimately for the client.

Accordingly, the Client/Employer should seek information on all the above discussed matters by: (i) obtaining comprehensive written pre-qualification information from the consultant in a form appropriate for the assignment; (ii) interviewing senior personnel identified for the assignment; (iii) if necessary, visiting the premises of the consultants and examining systems and methods of work as well as hardware and software capabilities; (iv) where applicable, speaking to previous clients.

4.2 SELECTION PROCEDURE

The Employer/Client must adopt a selection procedure that allows the consultant to use creativity, innovativeness, experience, seasoned judgement and best practices in the best interest of the client in return for fair and adequate compensation, gives the best results. It must be always be remembered that in the scarce financial resources environment of today, the quest must be for the best possible solutions for the client and the end user. This requires the use of the appropriate technology, innovative solutions, the lowest life cycle cost, all executed with prudent resource utilisation, environmental sensitivity and sustainability. The end user deserves the best the consulting profession can deliver and that quality comes from top qualified firms at a competitive price.

Competition between consultants that results in the best quality of services is of benefit to the client and the public and in keeping with the philosophy of private enterprise. This competition, however, should be based on competence and qualifications. In an environment where investment money and loan funds are in short supply, it is in the interest of all concerned to focus on quality and best value for money.

4.3 TERMS OF REFERENCE (TOR)

Draft the terms of reference for the selection should include an assessment of the physical magnitude and resource requirements of the project. The required services can be identified under the following headings: (i) areas of expertise and categories of service; (ii) a statement of work defining the project; (iii) a time schedule ; (iv) regional factors such as geographic location, language, logistics, allowances, duration of commission; (v) type of contract proposed: (vi) a project budget.

4.4 PRE-QUALIFICATION

Make a list of consulting firms which appear to be qualified for the project. This is often referred to as the pre-qualification list. Names of possible consultants can be obtained through advertisement of invitation for "Expression of Interest" and/or from a number of sources including: (i) ACEI Directory of Members; (ii) persons or organizations that have employed consultants for similar projects by advertisement in the National Press for an "Expression of Interest" providing information on the firm relevant to the project.

4.5 PREPARE THE SHORT LIST

Draw up a short list of between three to five consulting firms which appear to be best qualified for the project, bearing in mind the factors, such as: (i) relevant experience; (ii) availability; (iii) capacity to complete the work; (iv) access to support resources; (v) past performance on client contracts; (vi) location of the firm's office in relation to the work; (vii) political, social and environment or sensitivity; and (viii) the desired security level.

4.6 CALL FOR REQUEST FOR PROPOSALS (RFP)

The Employer/client may at this stage invite the most suitable consultant to negotiate an agreement on a mutually agreed upon project scope, fee and contract terms. More formally he can write a letter to each of the firms on the short list and invite proposals. A request for proposals should contain as a minimum: (i) the statement of work, terms of reference and supporting documentation; (ii) financial proposal;(iii) submission or closing date; (iv) basis of evaluation; (v) a statement of information to be included in the proposal; and (vi) expected selection date.

Where appropriate, the request for proposal should also include the following elements which may have influence on the cost of consulting services: (i) methodology; (ii) alternatives to be considered; innovation invited; transfer of knowledge/technology, local participation and training; (iii) detailed target cost estimates for the project; and (iv) compliance with desired time schedule

The information required to include: (i) past experience with projects of a similar nature; (ii) details of organization, project control, financial control; (iii) size and responsibilities of staff; (iv) type of organization and managerial method proposed for executing the work; (v) quality assurance organization; (vi) knowledge of local condition; (vii) local resources; (viii) project methodology; (ix) availability of resources; (x) approach and commitment to technology transfer, if appropriate

Note: To assist the consultant in preparing a proper response to the proposal, the client should encourage the consultant to evaluate the scope of work by visiting the site and by meeting with the client.

4.7 ASSESSMENT OF PROPOSALS

Once the proposals are received, the client should systematically evaluate and rank each proposal against the basis for selection outlined in the request for proposal. This process helps to maintain the integrity of the selection process and can involve: (i) formation of a selection committee; (ii) a weighting or score for each criteria; (iii) independent evaluation of firms by each member of the selection committee; (iv) individual score sheets being collated and (v) a documented record of the selection process being retained.

Employers/clients may be assisted in this evaluation process by an independent consultant.

Note: If the project size and complexity warrants it, the client can include in the evaluation interviews of key consultant team members, visits to consultant's premises, discussions with consultant's past clients and project(s) end users and inspections of past projects.

4.8 VALUE ANALYSIS/COST EFFECTIVENESS

By and large, the consultant's fees range between one and two percent. However, the correct selection of a top-qualified consultant has major impact on the overall project costs. The decisions made by the consultant in the first five percent of their involvement with a project, have the highest leverage on the life cycle cost of the project. Since life cycle cost impacts between excellent and marginal design can easily exceed the consultant's total fee, it makes no sense to select the consultant on the basis of lowest fee. In an environment where investment money and loan funds are in short supply, it is in the best interest of Employer/client to focus on quality and deliver value. It must always be remembered that quality-based selection does not involve consultants preparing costly priced proposals which have the effect of escalating the overall cost of consulting services. It must always be kept in mind that one or two percent more spent on design costs can save up to ten or fifteen percent of the project cost.

4.9 FORMS OF AGREEMENT

When drawing up the contract for consulting engineering services both the client and the consultant should protect their interests, by using the model Conditions of Engagement documents produced by FIDIC. This is highly recommended as important instrument for reaching a fair and sound agreement between the client and the consultant.

Chapter 5

REVIEW OF DESIGN AND TECHNICAL DOCUMENTS

The review may involve the checking and verification of detailed calculations or more simply require the reviewer to follow through the design process to verify that appropriate assumptions and standards have been used and the conclusions reached are sound in general engineering terms, and are consistent with the design process followed. It must be borne in mind that a review is not an opportunity to displace a designer or consultant from his commission, prove that the reviewer is a more competent consulting engineer, or redesign a project to standards or on a basis that the reviewer may consider more appropriate as such practice is highly unethical, but it must be objective and beneficial.

Accordingly, the terms of engagement of the reviewer must be in writing and quite explicit as to the extent or the level of review required whilst defining the level of liability that the reviewer will assume. For example, the work of the reviewer should not extend to assume the designer's responsibility, an action which is contrary to the code of ethics and could also incur unintended liability.

In the event that the review recommends modifications to a design then the proposed amendment must only be implemented and documented by the original designer. Where a review is arranged or required by a third party (as against in-house review), it is more appropriate that party ensures that the original designer knows of the review and accepts, and has confidence in, the reviewer.

Where it is the client who engages the reviewer, the client must also notify the original designer about the engagement. If the original designer states that he/she does not have confidence in the reviewer; he/she should provide reasons which ought to be acceptable and accountable and all related communication must done in writing and should be disclosed to all parties; i.e., the client or the third party, the original designer and the reviewer.

When a review is anticipated from the beginning of the project the client (or its consultant) must inform the original designer of the proposed review process at the outset, i.e. before the commencement of the design related activities. Since, mutual trust is a key for successful review the person whose work is being reviewed should understand that the process is a positive one rather than a threatening one. Furthermore, whenever possible the reviewer should discuss their draft findings with the original designer before issuing a final report, thereby eliminating any chance of misunderstandings and unnecessary resentment.

It is of paramount importance that the scope of work/services of the reviewer which should be written into the consultant agreement, which should include, but not limited to the following: (i) the purpose of the review; (ii) the scope and depth of the review; (iii) who is entitled to view and to rely on the report and under what circumstances (sometimes there can be confidentiality issues, etc.); (iv) confirmation that a courtesy copy of the report will be provided to the original designer; (v) qualifying statements as to the extent of work done and not done, the reliance on information provided by others, matters requiring further investigation, and a clear statement of any assumptions made; (vi) liability carried by the reviewer; and any disclaimers. In this context it should be noted that signing the compliance certificate must not be done by the reviewer as that responsibility is vested in the original designer.

To avoid any misunderstanding at a later date, the reviewer must accept responsibility to understand fully, all the circumstances surrounding the original design brief, particularly where there appears to be a difference between the reviewer and the original designer. If practical to have a discussion at this stage between the reviewer and the designer, as such discussion often brings out issues that may not have been made clear in the brief for the review.

Note When the review is required as part of a regulatory/statutory process, the reviewer will be required to submit some form of producer statement (design review certificate), which will normally attract some liability.

The professional, ethical, contractual and legal responsibility of the reviewer undertaking the review cannot be over-emphasized and the reviewer should approach this task in the knowledge that: (a) properly conducted, a review is a positive contribution to high standards of engineering (and in so doing, can enhance the image of the profession); (b) for this reason, the name of the reviewer should appear in any review report or document as a technical advisor or similar; (c) for the review to be constructive and helpful to the designer and the client, it must be conducted sensitively and in an atmosphere of trust with full disclosure of facts and opinions; (d) the reviewer should uphold the code of ethics of the industry, which include specific obligations relating to the criticism of the work of another consulting engineer including the responsibility (whenever possible) to advise the original consultant that the review is being done.

A professional review is a process that is instituted to ensure that the end result of a design or investigation meets particular standards, is comprehensive, and has not over-looked potentially critical issues. It may cover part or all of a designer/consulting engineer's services and will generally be checking that recognized or specified processes of investigation, design, reporting construction monitoring or project administration have been performed satisfactorily and correctly.

In this respect it is vital that the scope and depth of the review is well defined. It may include some or all of the following: (i) Review of concepts, inputs and assumptions. (ii) Review of load paths or processes. (iii) Review of computer/analysis inputs. (iv) Detailed analysis/design check of primary elements (including numerical checking). (v) Review of drawings/documentation to confirm interpretation of design/analysis. (vi) Duplicate/parallel independent analysis.

A review, by and large, can be considered in four categories: (i) An in-house review or overview by a colleague or superior; (ii) A review as part of a statutory or regulatory process; (iii) An independent review of a project at the request of a client or his consultant; and (iv) A review as a result of a failure or disaster (this may be in anticipation of litigation and has special requirements). These categories having specific aspects are briefly discussed herein below:

In-house review: The in-house review often forms part of an organization's quality control or quality assurance program. The designer should be offered constructive advice which will be respected and acted upon from an early stage of the process, before a commitment and/or inappropriate course of action is taken. Differences may occur in interpretation of codes or standards, or the level of conservatism that is appropriate. Such matters can be brainstormed and any agreement or difference of opinion should be recorded as part of the review notes, keeping in mind that the reviewer is not automatically correct.

Review as part of a statutory process: A consulting engineer (reviewer), independent of the designer's firm, is engaged to review the work of the designer. This can vary from an in-depth design review to an expression of an opinion on design principles. It is, however, very most important to define the brief closely. A good brief will set out the task clearly, including the level of checking and review which the commissioning organization requires. The reviewer should be able fulfill the brief without unnecessary criticism of the design being reviewed. The reviewer should neither offer remedies or solutions to deficiencies in the design, nor offer alternative solutions when the original design is sufficient.

The guideline principles include: (i) If a consultant accepts an engagement to review another consulting engineer's work it should be on the understanding that they are permitted full rights of discussion with the designer. (ii) The reviewer should notify the designer (in writing) of such involvement. Both parties should be prepared to discuss the review frankly, and professionally. ii) A reviewer should exercise discretion, tact and restraint in the role of a reviewer, and ensure that the review is carried out in a climate of mutual confidence and understanding. (iv) A reviewer should not comment on the choice of the design or suggest alternative designs, but comment only on the validity and satisfactory compliance with the relevant codes/standards, statutory requirements and the law.

(v) A reviewer should consider the consequences of any issues raised in a review report such as it may affect risks and costs incurred to the owner or to the public, the reputation and livelihood of the designer and, the good standing of the industry itself. If the reviewer considers that the designer's work is seriously at fault, the matter should be discussed in the first instance with the designer to make every endeavor to resolve the matter. Independent, opinion should be sought, if deemed necessary. (vi) The reviewer should be aware that unnecessary delays could mean loss of revenue to the owner and may lead to a complaint being laid. Professional reviews should always be done promptly, and any issues resolved as a matter of urgency.

Independent review of a major project; Independent appraisals or reviews are at the invitation of a public or local authority, private client or another consulting engineer. They may include engagements as an expert witness in a court of law or other tribunal. The purpose of such a review is to provide an objective view of the project to assist the designer who is bound to be much involved with detail, and may find it difficult to view the work objectively. Best results are obtained when the reviewer is involved from the start and acts as part of the overall project team. To this end the designer should be involved in the selection of the reviewer(s).

The guideline principles include: (i) The reviewer should advise the client that they wish to advise the original designer of their appointment as reviewer, and wish to be free to approach the other consulting engineer to discuss the design and design philosophy, if the other consulting engineer is agreeable to such discussion. (ii) Formal lines of communication throughout the review process should be stated in express terms, along with careful definition of the scope, limitations of the review and liabilities of the reviewer. (iii) The reviewer should then notify the other consulting engineer in writing of the appointment to review. Before expressing an opinion, the reviewer should make every endeavor to obtain full knowledge of the facts, either by discussion of all aspects of the design philosophy and terms of commission with the designer, or by other suitable means.

(iv) The reviewer should avoid as far as practicable, intrusion of personal concepts and direct the review to the adequacy of the design; as would be expected in meeting normally accepted standards. (v) To this, the designer must remain responsible for the design and the reviewer must be satisfied with design principles and assumptions and adequacy of the functional and safety objectives of the project. (vi) Although a reviewer should not attempt to take over or usurp the design or impose their own solutions, they may, if involved from the start in a review of this type, be involved in review of the selection of the option chosen for the solution of the problem. Likewise the reviewer should not, unless the client insists, undertake numerical checking but should be satisfied by the designer that design quality assurance is being applied by the designer.

(vii) Where construction involves important field confirmations or decisions, these should be identified and be reviewed in the field. Similarly, where operational performance and surveillance are embodied in final proof of design, these aspects should also be reviewed. (viii) If the reviewer and the designer differ about the relative merits of two effective solutions (usually of different degrees of conservatism and cost), then the client should be briefed so that the client can make the ultimate choice. (ix) Members should avoid being placed in the position of giving an opinion or decision as to negligence which is the province of the courts alone. (x) If an engagement is not made for the purpose of appearing as an expert witness, the engagement should be accepted only on the understanding that the reviewer will not later accept engagement as expert witness by any party to a claim against the designer/consulting engineer whose work was reviewed and in relation to the project reviewed. (xi) A member is engaged to review the work of another consulting engineer shall not accept a commission to design or supervise remedial works except in circumstances where the further engagement does not compromise the code of ethics of the national Member Association or of FIDIC.

Review of a disaster or failure: Even if the reviewer's brief is restricted to an opinion on the causes of the failure, the question of blame or liability is bound to arise. The reviewer must above all be fair and objective and not be swayed by the benefit of hindsight. It requires a conscious effort on the part of the reviewer to judge the matter from the standards of reasonable care and skill, current at the time that the designer/consulting engineer's work was executed, which could be many years before the failure. The reviewer, after completing their report should discuss all the items of the report with the original consulting engineer, provide changes on the report where appropriate and only after that should submit the report to the client.

The reviewer should be careful to limit observations and conclusions to those which can be supported by the factual evidence when carrying out such a review. Where the reviewer expresses an opinion it must be made clear that the opinion is the opinion of the reviewer only and that there may be circumstances that could change that opinion and should not make judgment about the possible negligence of another consulting engineer. That is a legal matter for a court to decide, even though identification of the cause of the failure may well imply negligence. It must be understood that the job of a reviewer is to assist the court in its understanding of the technical issues.

Recommendations for corrective or remedial work do not form part of a review. Any such work is a separate engagement entered into only when the original designer's engagement has been formally terminated or modified appropriately. (It is important that the reviewer understand the role and scope of the original consulting engineer and can only comment on what another competent consulting engineer might have done - this is the test of negligence - often, the reviewer of a disaster is an "expert", whose skills may exceed those of a reasonably competent consulting engineer, and the expert would possibly have done something completely differently - this does not mean the original designer/consulting engineer has been negligent or is incompetent). The guidelines given (ix –xi) under independent review, also apply to review in the case of failure.

Chapter 6

VALUE MANAGEMENT/VALUE ENGINEERING IN CONSTRUCTION PROCESS

6.1 VALUE MANAGEMENT (VM) PROCESS

Value Management, by and large, is regarded as the strategic whole of the process with other techniques such as value planning, value engineering, and value analysis are the tools being used to complement the whole VM process, see diagram below.

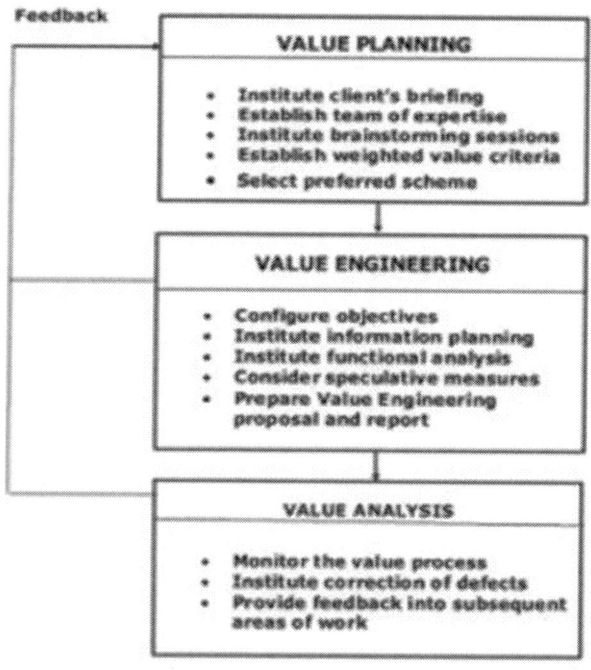

Value Management Process

Value planning is a range of techniques applied in assisting the decision making process regarding the selection of a particular design proposal This is undertaken during the early part of a project usually before the decision to build or at the outline/ conceptual design stage. The objectives of value planning part of VM process are to: to involve the client and all key stakeholders at the feasibility and concept stage; to improve the effectiveness of the client brief; and to assist the client to define what is good value.

In this context the term value engineering is a range of techniques applied during the detailed design stages of the project to reduce unnecessary costs in the design elements by testing them against the clients' objectives, i.e. by identifying and separating wants from the needs and effect saving in costs where ever possible.

Value Analysis is a range of techniques and sub-processes that would be carried out at the completion of the project and is effectively a review of the project to provide data and to establish whether the clients' objectives were met and to identify lessons learnt for future projects.

6.2 STAKEHOLDER MANAGEMENT – ROLE OF STAKEHOLDERS AND FACILITATORS

The principal roles of a stakeholder include: (1) to promote project objectives; and (2) to reach a consensus view. The key elements of stakeholder management include: (a) to define stakeholders i.e. project owner, designers, utilities; and end users, etc.; (b) to define a facilitator; (c) to involve all key stakeholders and to rely on full their full involvement; (d) to adopt an approach which is both practical and vigorous; and (e) to aim at whole cost solutions rather than specific functional costs.

The principal roles of a facilitator include: (i) to advise and guide the Vale management process; (ii) to provide a high level of inter-personal skills to consolidated different views of the team; and (iii) to act as a catalyst towards creative, effective and practical solutions. The role of Facilitator in Value Management process is shown below.

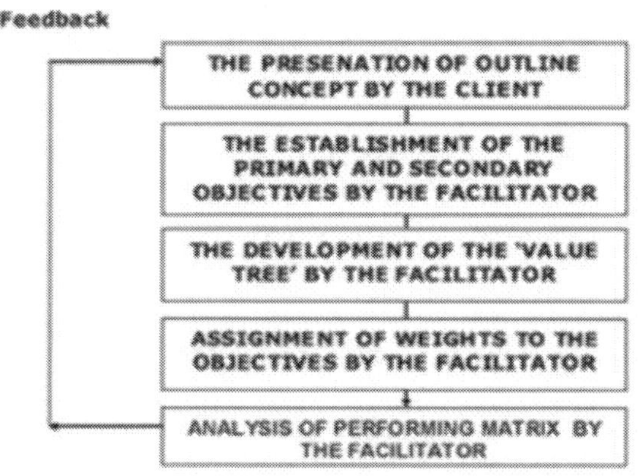

Role of Facilitator in VM Process

Note: In the UK construction industry, Value Management is widely accepted as an important tool in the management of projects as it provides a mechanism for integration to improve communication and information flow.

The framework for managing the total construction process is affected by three interlocking component, namely: (i) organizational framework, (ii) the procurement strategy, and (iii) the legal framework that brings the parties together. See below:

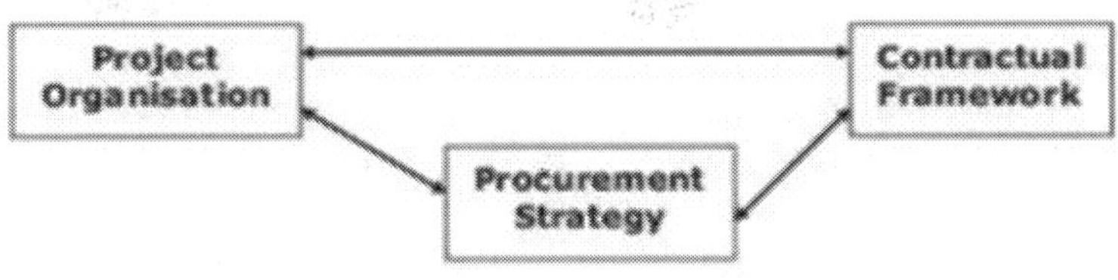

Framework for Managing Projects

6.3 PRINCIPAL OBJECTIVES OF VALUE MANAGEMENT

The principal objectives of the Value Management process include: (i) to involve the client and all key stakeholders at the feasibility, studies, and conceptual design stages; (ii) to improve the effectiveness of the client's brief; and (iii) to assist the client to define 'what is good value for money invested in the project'.

6.4 PRINCIPAL BENEFITS OF VALUE MANAGEMENT

The principal benefits of the Value Management include:

- clarification of the brief separating needs from wants can be achieved;
- (ii) the project's needs are verified and duly supported by date;
- (iii) the project's objectives are clearly expressed;
- (iv) improved performance through efficiency savings can be achieved;
- (v) all outline proposals are evaluated and selected on the basis of defined performance criteria and value for money invested in the project;
- (vi) alternative designs, solutions or locations can be identification and proactively considered;
- (vii) alternative construction methods can be identified and adopted;

- (viii) staff through multi-disciplinary teamwork can be empowered and developed;
- (ix) service and/ or product quality can be enhanced;
- (x) risks are identified in a structured way and can be adequately dealt with;
- (xi) additional functions that improve the outcomes of the project can be identified;
- (xii) staff morale, commitment and relationships can be improved;
- (xiii) the project program is rationalized prior to implementation stage;
- (xiv) decision making process is made proactive and rational;
- (xv) decision making process is accountable with shared responsibilities;
- (xvi) a high risk that the eventual construction will not meet all the stakeholders requirement is evaluated and avoided; and
- (xvii) a significant long-term benefits, both in terms of functionality and whole-life cost, are achieved.

In conclusion we can say that VM provides assurance to the project owner/client that a structured review is carried out by testing against possible alternatives confirming that the project is well designed and meets all the expectations of all parties having interest in the project i.e. the client, designers, project manager, contractor, end users, etc.

6.5 RISKS ASSOCIATED WITH VALUE MANAGEMENT

There are potential risks that must be guarded against. They can be managed effectively if recognized, identified and dealt with. These risks might include: (a) the exercise undertaken too late for changes to be effective; (b) inadequate information causing incorrect assumptions; (c) insufficient participation by stakeholders; (d) insufficient time allocated for the process; (e) inadequate support by senior management; and (f) unskilled facilitator using improper application of the methodology.

6.6 VALUE MANAGEMENT IN THE DESIGN PROCESS

The VM in the design process is shown below:

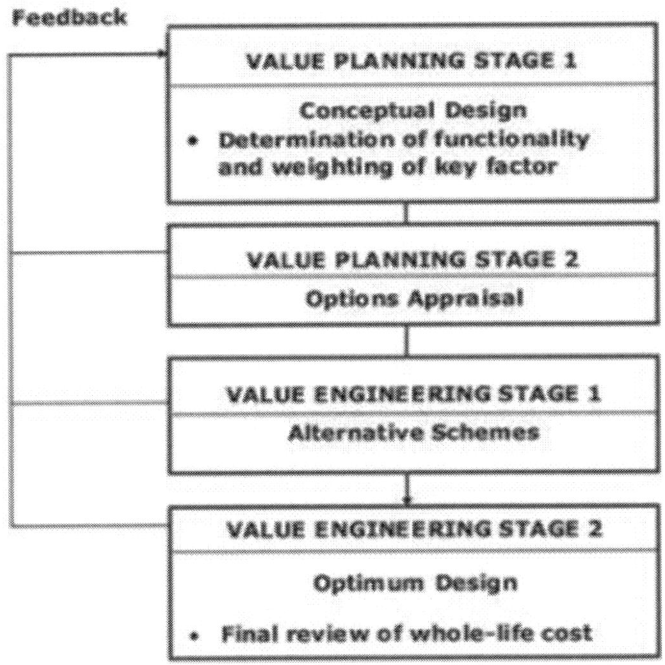

Stages of VM in Design Process

Chapter 7

PRE-CONSTRUCTION CONTRACT MANAGEMENT

7.1 PRE-QUALIFICATIONS AND SELECTION OF TENDERERS

Under some procurement procedures, the selection of tenderers may usefully be divided into two parts. First, if candidates do not meet certain basic requirements they can be excluded from participating in the tendering process. The selection can then be narrowed down further according to other permitted criteria. For example, candidates can often be excluded from tender lists when they have been convicted of a criminal offence or grave misconduct concerning professional conduct on matters such as health and safety.

Since the preparation of bids requires a substantial investment of effort and money, the pre-qualification or short-listing of contractors guarantees that the bid will not be rejected in the evaluation stage of the bids. The preparatory work for pre-qualification as well as the subsequent processing by owners is greatly facilitated by the use of standard forms.

The aim of pre-qualification is to establish a list of capable (qualified and competent) firms which appear suitable to provide the required works whilst ensuring that proper competition is maintained. The number of firms to be invited to compete should normally be in the range of three to seven.

Requiring a previous track record excludes possible new entrants and makes the procurement less competitive, but is essential to ensure appropriate capability. The overall objective of prequalification is to receive from suitably qualified firms proposals that respond to all requirements at a reasonable cost to the Engineer and/or the Owner/Employer. Pre-qualification will not guarantee of quality, but it at least excludes those who are obviously less likely to execute the contract successfully.

7.2 CALL FOR TENDERS

A key feature of project delivery is the selected procurement procedure, where suppliers are invited to submit a tender offer or a proposal (occasionally qualification information, or a response to a request for information). Procurement includes the ways in which these tenders or proposals (or information submissions) are treated.

The owner is seeking the best-value for money, or the most economically advantageous offer, namely: the optimum combination of whole life costs and quality (or fitness for purpose) to meet requirements having due regard to propriety and regularity. A request for proposals is used when the owner seeks a solution to resolve a problem, but is not sure how to achieve it. It is not an offer, and only contemplates an offer. Similarly, the receipt of a proposal is not an acceptance, so it does not result in a contract.

A call for tenders is used when owners know exactly what services they want, and are looking for the best value for money offer, and not simply the lowest price.

Tendering is the formal and detailed exercise of using a particular source selection to ensure delivery of a project which generally has a relatively high value and/or the specification is detailed or complex, and/or special terms and conditions may apply.

Bidding is based on a bid package ready for advertisement or distribution to selected contractors. Bid documents must be comprehensive and of an appropriate technical quality and clearly defining scope and quality of the work required.

The owner receives and evaluates bids, and selects and appoints a contractor using a fair, competent and transparent system. FIDIC's Guidelines for the Quality of Construction provide examples of the recommended non-price evaluation of tenders and a non-price tender assessment method that ensures project quality, and the procedure/recommendation therein should be followed.

7.3 TENDERING PROCESS

7.3.1 Introduction

In all dealings with suppliers and potential suppliers, responsible department should do their best to preserve the highest standards of honesty, integrity, impartiality and objectivity. In particular, responsible department should do their best to: (a) be fair, efficient, firm and courteous; (b) publicize procurement contact points and make available as much information as suppliers need to respond to the bidding process; (c) notify the outcome of bids promptly and, within the bounds of commercial confidentiality, to debrief winners and losers on request on the outcome of the bidding process to facilitate better performance on future occasions; (d) achieve the highest professional standards in the management of contracts; and (e) respond promptly, courteously and efficiently to suggestions, enquiries and complaints.

7.3.2 The Content of Tendering Process

The content of tendering process should include, but not limited to, the following:

1. Determine sufficient time for tender period
2. Issue tender invitation and tender documents to tenderers enclosing label and specific date time and address for return
3. Deal with tenderers queries promptly - and advise all other tenderers of information given
4. Place all tenders received in the tender box
5. Sort tenderers by name or preferably by price and assign a unique tender number to each
6. List tenders received, not received, on tender summary sheet
7. Prepare clear, consistent and comprehensive tender documents
8. Facilitate any site visits required by tenderers
9. List tender number, opening date, name and price in tender record book.

7.3.3 Competitive Bidding

The basic structure of the bidding process consists of the formulation of detailed plans and specifications of a project based on the objectives and requirements of the owner, and the invitation of qualified contractors to bid for to execute the project. The definition of a qualified contractor usually calls for a minimal evidence of financial stability and previous experience. In the private sector, the owner has considerable latitude in selecting the bidders, ranging from open competition to the restriction of bidders to a few favoured contractors. In the public sector, the rules are carefully set down to place all qualified contractors on an equal footing for competition, and strictly enforced to prevent unethical or illegal actions by public officials and possible collusion among contractors.

Detailed plans and specifications are usually prepared by an architectural/ engineering firm which oversees the bidding process on behalf of the owner. The final bids are normally submitted on either a lump sum or unit price basis, as stipulated by the owner in the conditions of contract. A lump sum bid represents the total price for which a contractor offers to complete a project according to the detailed plans and specifications. Unit price bidding is used in projects for which the quantity of materials or the amount of labor involved in some key tasks is particularly uncertain.

In such cases, the contractor is permitted to submit a list of unit prices for those tasks, and the final price used to determine the lowest bidder is based on the lump sum price computed by multiplying the quoted unit price for each specified task by the corresponding quantity in the owner's estimates for quantities. However, the total payment to the winning contractor will be based on the actual quantities multiplied by the respective quoted unit prices. If the competitive tender is based on price, then true competition will no doubt be based on efficient allocation of resources.

7.3.4 Types of Competitive Bidding

In the construction industry there are generally only two types of competitive bidding these are 'Open Bidding' or 'Sealed Bid':

Open Bidding: This is mainly used in the commercial or private sector and consists of an iterative process of negotiation with the client, where each contractor independently negotiates a contract price with the client until the client accepts a final bid from one of them when he believes that bid meets all of his criteria.

Sealed Bids: With this method each contractor is allowed to submit one bid and the client selects the bid which he believes meets with his objectives for the project, where each bid must be submitted on a specified date and before a specified time. This method relies on the client providing detailed information in the form of a Bill of Quantities, specification and drawings so that all contractors are bidding on the same basis.

7.4 RECEIVING AND EVALUATING TENDER DOCUMENTS

7.4.1 Receiving Tender Documents

Information relating to the evaluation of Tenders must not be disclosed to tenderers or any other persons - not officially concerned with such process until information on Contract award is communicated to all tenderers From the time of Tender opening to the time of Contract award, if any tenderer wishes to contact the Employer on any matter related to the tendering process, it should do so in writing. If any attempt by a tenderer to influence improperly the Employer in the evaluation of the Tenders or Contract award decisions, its Tender may result in the rejection.

The Employer may, at its discretion, in order to assist in the examination, evaluation, and comparison of the Tenders and qualification of the tenderers, ask any tenderer for a clarification of its Tender allowing a reasonable time for response. If any clarification submitted by a tenderer that is not in response to a request by the Employer, it shall not be considered by the Employer. The Employer's request for clarification and the response shall be in writing. No change in the prices or substance of the Tender shall be sought, offered, or permitted, except to confirm the correction of arithmetic errors discovered by the Employer in the evaluation of the Tenders. In case a tenderer does not provide clarifications of its Tender by the date and time set in the Employer's request for clarification, its Tender may be rejected.

The Employer's determination of a Tender's responsiveness is to be based on the contents of the Tender itself and a substantially responsive Tender is one that meets the requirements of the Tender Document without material deviation, omission, or reservation. In this reference: "Deviation" is a departure from the requirements specified in the Tender Document; "Omission" is the failure to submit part or all of the information or documentation required in the Tender Document; whilst "Reservation" is the setting of limiting conditions or withholding from complete acceptance of the requirements specified in the Tender Document.

A material deviation, omission, or reservation is one that, (a) if accepted, would: affect in any substantial way the scope, quality, or performance of the Requirements or limit in any substantial way, inconsistent with the Tender Document, the Employer's rights or the tenderer's obligations under the proposed Contract; and/or (b) if rectified, would unfairly affect the competitive position of other tenderers presenting substantially responsive Tenders. The Employer must examine the technical aspects of the Tender in particular, to confirm that all requirements have been met without any material deviation, omission, or reservation.

If a Tender is not substantially responsive to the requirements of the Tender Document, it shall be rejected by the Employer and may not subsequently be made responsive by correction of the material deviation, omission or reservation. However, provided that a Tender is substantially responsive, the Employer may waive any quantifiable nonconformity in the Tender that do not constitute a material deviation, omission, or reservation.

7.4.2 Evaluation and Comparison of Tender

The Employer must use the prescribed Evaluation and Qualification Criteria or methodologies. Provided that the Tender is substantially responsive, the Employer must correct arithmetical errors and if a tenderer does not accept the correction of errors, its Tender deemed be declared non-responsive.

For the evaluation and comparison purposes the Employer must adjust the Tender prices using the prescribed criteria and methodology. If in the opinion of the Employer the Tender which results in the lowest Evaluated Tender Price, is seriously unbalanced or front loaded or substantially below the Employer's estimates, the Employer may require the tenderer to produce detailed price analyses for any or all items of the Bill of Quantities, to demonstrate the internal consistency of those prices with the methods and schedule proposed. After evaluation of the price analyses, taking into consideration the schedule of estimated Contract payments, the Employer may require that the amount of the performance security be increased at the expense of the tenderer to a level sufficient to protect the Employer against financial loss in the event of default of the successful tenderer under the Contract.

The Employer must determine to its satisfaction whether the tenderer that is selected as having submitted the lowest evaluated and substantially responsive Tender meets specified the qualifying criteria. Such determination must be based upon an examination of the documentary evidence of the tenderer's qualifications submitted by the tenderer. An affirmative determination must be a prerequisite for award of the Contract to the tenderer, whilst a negative determination must result in disqualification of the Tender, in which event the Employer shall proceed to the next lowest evaluated Tender to make a similar determination of that tenderer's qualifications to perform satisfactorily.

The capabilities of the manufacturers and subcontractors proposed in its Tender to be used by the lowest evaluated tenderer for identified major items of the Requirements will also be evaluated for acceptability in accordance with the prescribed criteria and methodologies. Their participation should be confirmed with a letter of intent between the parties, as needed. Should a manufacturer or subcontractor be determined to be unacceptable, the Tender will not be rejected, but the tenderer will be required to substitute an acceptable manufacturer or subcontractor without any change to the Tender price?

Note: The Employer reserves the right to accept or reject any tender, and to annul the Tendering process and reject all Tenders at any time prior to contract award, without thereby incurring any liability to tenderers. In case of annulment, all Tenders submitted and specifically, Tender securities, must be promptly returned to the tenderers.

7.5 AWARD OF CONTRACT

The Employer must award the Contract to the tenderer whose offer has been determined to be the lowest evaluated Tender and is substantially responsive to the Tender Document, provided further that the tenderer is determined to be qualified to perform the Contract satisfactorily.

Prior to the expiration of the period of Tender validity, the Employer must notify the successful tenderer, in writing, that its Tender has been accepted and such notification of ward deemed to be binding until a formal contract is prepared and executed.

At the same time, the Employer must also notify all other tenderers of the results of the Tendering. After publishing of the award, unsuccessful tenderers may request in writing to the Employer for a debriefing seeking explanations on the grounds on which their Tenders were not selected. The Employer must promptly respond in writing to any unsuccessful tenderer who, after Publication of contract award, requests a debriefing.

Promptly upon notification, the Employer must send the successful tenderer the Contract Agreement. Within twenty-eight (28) days of receipt of the Contract Agreement, the successful tenderer must sign, date, and return the same to the Employer. Upon the successful tenderer's furnishing of the signed Contract Agreement and Performance Security, the Employer will discharge its tender security.

Within twenty-eight (28) days of the receipt of notification of award from the Employer, the successful tenderer must furnish the performance security in accordance with the conditions of contract, using for that purpose the Performance Security Annex to the Particular Conditions - Contract Forms, or another form acceptable to the Employer. If the performance security furnished by the successful tenderer is in the form of a bond, it must be issued by a bonding or insurance company that has been determined by the successful tenderer to be acceptable to the Employer. A foreign institution providing a bond must have a correspondent financial institution located in the Employer's Country where the project is being executed.

Failure of the successful tenderer to submit the above-mentioned Performance Security or sign the Contract shall constitute sufficient grounds for the annulment of the award and forfeiture of the tender security. In that event the Employer may award the Contract to the next lowest evaluated tenderer whose offer is substantially responsive and is determined by the Employer to be qualified to perform the Contract satisfactorily.

Chapter 8

CONSTRUCTION MANAGEMENT AGREEMENT UNDER FIDIC CONTRACTS

FIDIC Client / Consultant Model Services Agreement Fourth Edition 2006 includes: General Conditions; Particular Conditions; and Appendices 1, 2, 3 and 4. The terms of the White Book have been prepared by FIDIC and are recommended for general use for the purposes of pre-investment and feasibility studies, designs and administration of construction and project management, where proposals for such services are invited on an international basis. They are equally adaptable for domestic agreements. In their preparation it was recognised that while there are numerous clauses which will be generally applicable there are some provisions which must necessarily vary to take account of the circumstances and locality in which the Services are to be performed.

The drafters of the White Book are predominately engineers who within this form sought to create conditions of agreement that would span the life cycle of an engineer's or consultant's involvement. Accordingly the document is suitable for use during: (i) pre-investment and feasibility studies; (ii) the design phase; and (iii) the administration of a contract. The White Book incorporates the same financial protection as afforded to contractors in that the consultant too can ask the Client (as opposed to the Employer) if it has the ability to pay the Consultant's fees. In a similar vein, and maybe not surprising to some, the White Book limits the consultant's responsibilities, and therefore liabilities, to "exercise reasonable skill, care and allegiance in the performance of his obligations under the Agreement".

This limitation is further qualified since nothing else in the agreement, or any legal requirement of the Country or any other jurisdiction can impose a greater risk upon the consultant. Thus the consultant/engineer has a limited risk that, it is suggested, is not in accord with the thoughts of employers and contractors alike.

In the White Book, the clauses of general application have been grouped together and are referred to as General Conditions. They are intended for incorporation as printed in the documents comprising the Agreement. The General Conditions are linked with the Particular Conditions by the corresponding numbering of the clauses, so that General Conditions and Particular Conditions together comprise the conditions governing the rights and obligations of the parties. Where other material is to be incorporated into a Contract of Appointment, care must be taken to ensure consistency both in the use of terminology and the allocation of duties and obligations.

The FIDIC White Book represents the basic form of a Contract of Appointment between a Client and his Consultant. It is intended to cover the minimum requirements of a typical appointment contract. Additional or amended clauses may be required in the Particular Conditions to address particular project and commercial issues between the parties. The drafters of the White Book are predominately engineers who within this form sought to create conditions of agreement that would span the life cycle of an Engineer's or Consultant's involvement. Accordingly the document is suitable for use during: pre-investment and feasibility studies; the design phase; and the administration of a contract. As with FIDIC contracts there are both general and particular conditions of contract which combined set out the scope of the consultant's work, payment terms and the like.

The White Book incorporates the same financial protection as afforded to contractors in that the consultant too can ask the Client (as opposed to the Employer) if it has the ability to pay the Consultant's fees. In a similar vein, the White Book limits the consultant's responsibilities, and therefore liabilities, to "exercise reasonable skill, care and allegiance in the performance of his obligations under the Agreement". This limitation is further qualified since nothing else in the agreement, or any legal requirement of the Country or any other jurisdiction can impose a greater risk upon the consultant. Thus the Consultant/Engineer has a limited risk.

Chapter 9

SELECTION OF FIDIC FORM OF CONTRACT

9.1 INTRODUCTION

The selection of contract type to be used for a construction project is made by the owner, acting upon the advice of his Engineer and his legal advisor. The selection must meet the owner Objectives and takes into account the constraints that might relate to the project. Consultants and contractors should be fully informed by the project objectives and constraints. The scope and the nature of the project will primarily affect the selection of type of contract.

9.2 SELECTION OF APPROPRIATE FORM OF CONTRACT

For Relatively small value, short construction time or involving simple or repetitive work: If the price for the contract is relatively small, say under US$ 500,000, or the construction time is short, say less than 6 months, or the work involved is relatively simple or repetitive - dredging work might be a good example: then consider using the **Short Form of Contract**, which is a completely new FIDIC Book specially prepared for such projects. It does not matter whether the design is provided by the Employer (or his Engineer/Architect if he has one) or by the Contractor. It also does not matter whether the project involves construction, electrical, mechanical, or other engineering work.

For Larger or more complex projects: We need to find the answer to the following questions:

First: Is the Employer (or the Engineer) going to do most of the design? As in traditional projects, e.g., infrastructure, buildings, hydropower, etc., the Employer did nearly all the design (perhaps not construction details, reinforcement, etc.) **(The Red Book)**, and the Engineer administered the Contract, monitored the construction work and certified payment and the Employer was kept fully informed, could make variations, etc. and with payment according to bills of quantities or lump sums for approved work done. If this is what is wanted - choose the Conditions of Contract for Construction for Building and Engineering Works Designed by the Employer **(The Construction Contract)**, which effectively updates and supercedes the existing Red Book from 1987.

Note: In 2005, FIDIC licenced the Multilateral Development Banks (MDB) to use the MDB Harmonised Edition of the Construction Contract for projects funded by the banks. The MDB Construction Contract mainly incorporates Particular Conditions to the Red Book that was used by the World Bank in its Standard Bidding Documents before it and the other MDBs adopted the Harmonised Edition.

Second: Is the Contractor going to do most of the design? As in traditional projects, e.g., electrical and mechanical works, including erection on site (The Yellow Book) the Contractor (or Supplier) did the majority of the design, e.g., the detail design of the plant or equipment, so that the plant met the outline or performance specification prepared by the Employer, and in the relatively more recent design-build and turnkey type projects the Contractor also did the majority of the design, not only of plant projects but also of various infrastructure and other types of projects, and the project was required to fulfill the "Employer's Requirements", i.e., an outline or performance specification prepared by the Employer (The Orange Book), and the Engineer (Employer in the Orange Book) administered the Contract, monitored the manufacture and erection on site or construction work and certified payment, and with payment according to achieved milestones generally on a lump sum basis.

If this is what is wanted - choose the Conditions of Contract for Plant and Design-Build for Electrical and Mechanical Plant and for Building and Engineering Works Designed by the Contractor **(Plant and Design-Build Contract)** which effectively updates and supercedes both the existing Yellow Book from 1987 and the Orange Book from 1995.

Third: Is it a Privately Financed (or Public/Private Financed) Project of BOT or similar type where the Concessionaire takes total responsibility for the financing, construction and operation of the Project? Here the Concessionaire (the "Employer") probably requires to have a contract with the construction Contractor, i.e., an EPC (Engineer, Procure, Construct) Contract, where the Contractor takes total responsibility for the design and construction of the infrastructure or other facility, and where there is a higher degree of certainty that the agreed contract price and time will not be exceeded.

Also, the Employer does not wish to be involved in the day-to-day progress of the work, provided the end result meets the performance criteria he has specified; and the parties concerned (e.g., sponsors, lenders and the Employer) are willing to see the Contractor paid more for the construction of the Project in return for the Contractor bearing the extra risks associated with enhanced certainty of final price and time.

If this is what is wanted - choose the Conditions of Contract for EPC/Turnkey Projects (**EPC/Turnkey Contract**) - the FIDIC Book suitable for this purpose.

Also for the EPC/Turnkey Contract further selections are considered for the following questions.

(1) Is it a Process Plant or a Power Plant (or a factory or similar) where the Employer - who provides the finance - wishes to implement the Project on a Fixed-Price Turnkey Basis? Then the Employer wishes the Contractor to take total responsibility for the design and construction of the process or power facility and hand it over ready to operate "at the turn of a key", and the Employer wishes a higher degree of certainty that the agreed contract price and time will not be exceeded and the Employer wishes - or is used to - the Project being organised on a strictly two party approach, i.e. without an "Engineer" being involved.

Also, the Employer does not wish to be involved in the day-to-day progress of the construction work, provided the end result meets the performance criteria he has specified, and the Employer is willing to pay more for the construction of his Project (than would be the case if the Conditions of Contract for Plant and Design-Build were used) in return for the Contractor bearing the extra risks associated with enhanced certainty of final price and time.

If this is what is wanted - choose the Conditions of Contract for EPC/Turnkey Projects **(EPC/Turnkey Contract)**.

(2) Is it an Infrastructure Project (e.g., road, rail link, bridge, water or sewage treatment plant, transmission line, even dam or hydropower plant) or similar where the Employer - who provides the finance - wishes to implement the Project on a Fixed-Price Turnkey Basis? Then the Employer wishes the Contractor to take total responsibility for the design and construction of the infrastructure facility, and the Employer wishes a higher degree of certainty that the agreed contract price and time will not be exceeded, except that if underground works in uncertain or difficult ground conditions are likely then the risk of unforeseen ground conditions should be borne by the Employer (and the provisions of the Plant and Design-Build Conditions in this respect - Sub-Clause 4.12 - would be appropriate)

Also, the Employer wishes - or is used to - the Project being organised on a strictly two party approach, i.e. without an "Engineer" being involved, and the Employer does not wish to be involved in the day-to-day progress of the construction work, provided the end result meets the performance criteria he has specified, and the Employer is willing to pay more for the construction of his Project (than would be the case if the Conditions of Contract for Plant and Design-Build were used) in return for the Contractor bearing the extra risks associated with enhanced certainty of final price and time.

If this is what is wanted - choose the Conditions of Contract for EPC/Turnkey Projects **(EPC/Turnkey Contract)**.

(3) Is it a Building Project where the Employer wishes to have his building(s) constructed on a Fixed-

Price Turnkey Basis generally complete with all furniture, fittings and equipment? In the case of a building or building development Project, the Employer or his Architect may have done some or most of the design, but - with suitable modification regarding design responsibility - the Conditions of Contract for EPC/Turnkey Projects **(EPC/Turnkey Contract)** may be chosen.

Chapter 10

THE OBLIGATIONS OF THE EMPLOYER UNDER THE CONSTRUCTION CONTRACTS

10.1 RIGHT OF ACCESS TO THE SITE

It is Obligation of the Employer to give the Contractor right of access to the Contractor to execute the Works.

Clause 2.1 Right of Access to site of Red Book reads:

Clause 2.1 Right of Access to the Site

The Employer shall give the Contractor right of access to, and possession of, all parts of the Site within the time (or times) stated in the Appendix to Tender. The right and possession may not be exclusive to the Contractor. If, under the Contract, the Employer is required to give (to the Contractor) possession of any foundation, structure, plant or means of access, the Employer shall do so in the time and manner stated in the Specification. However, the Employer may withhold any such right or possession until the Performance Security has been received.

**If no such time is stated in the Appendix to Tender, the Employer shall give the Contractor right of access to, and possession of, the Site within such times as may be required to enable the Contractor to proceed in accordance with the programme submitted under Sub-Clause 8.3 [Programme].*

If the Contractor suffers delay and/or incurs Cost as a result of a failure by the Employer to give any such right or possession within such time, the Contractor shall give notice to the Engineer and shall be entitled subject to Sub-Clause 20.1 [Contractor's Claims] to: (a) an extension of time for any such delay, if completion is or will be delayed, under Sub-Clause 8.4 [Extension of Time for Completion], and (b) payment of any such Cost plus reasonable profit, which shall be included in the Contract Price.

After receiving this notice, the Engineer shall proceed in accordance with Sub-Clause 3.5 [Determinations] to agree or determine these matters.

However, if and to the extent that the Employer's failure was caused by any error or delay by the Contractor, including an error in, or delay in the submission of, any of the Contractor's Documents, the Contractor shall not be entitled to such extension of time, Cost or profit.

The Employer is required to give the Contractor right of access to, and possession of, all parts of the Site within a prescribed time, which is to be stated in Red Book Appendix to Tender. For example, if, under the Contract, the Employer is required to give (to the Contractor) possession of any foundation, structure, plant or means of access, the Employer must do so in the time and manner stated in the Specification.

The possession of, the Site must be timely as required to enable the Contractor to proceed without disruption in accordance with the programme submitted as per the contract provisions. Unless otherwise stated therein, the Contractor will be entitled to occupy all of the Site from the end of the prescribed period of time, but the second sentence of the Sub-Clause states that other parties may also have right of access to, and possession of, the Site. The work to be carried out by these other parties should be described in the tender documents, so that tenderers may anticipate the consequences.

Under Red Book the second paragraph specifies that, if no such prescribed time is so stated, the Employer is required to make the Site available within the times required to enable the Contractor to proceed as shown in the programme submitted under Sub-Clause 8.3. This provision prevents the Employer's obligations being dependent upon a post-contract document.

Sub-Clause 2.1 does not entitle the Contractor to an access route suitable for his transport, except to the extent that a "means of access" under its third sentence may have been specified elsewhere in the Contract. Under Sub-Clause 4.15, the Contractor is deemed to have satisfied himself on this matter, subject to the same extent (if any) that a "means of access" is specified. In other words, the practical difficulties in getting to and from the Site are to be solved by the Contractor. For example, if the Site is totally surrounded by land owned by third parties, the Contract should clarify how the Contractor is to be granted right of access across their lands.

If the Contractor suffers delay and/or incurs Cost as a result of a failure by the Employer to give any such right or possession within such time, the Contractor must give notice to the Engineer and will be entitled subject to: (a) an extension of time for any such delay, if completion is or will be delayed, and (b) payment of any such Cost plus profit, which will be included in the Contract Price. After receiving this notice, the Engineer must proceed in to agree or determine these matters in accordance with the contract provisions.

In a case, if and to the extent that the Employer's failure was caused by any error or delay by the Contractor, including an error in, or delay in the submission of, any of the Contractor's Documents, the Contractor will not be entitled to such extension of time, Cost or profit. Remember that non-availability of the

Site constitutes a substantial failure of the Employer and entitles the Contractor to terminate the Contract under clause 16.2 (d) of Red Book. The Contractor may also need to carry out work on the additional/working areas referred to in Sub-Clause 4.23 Contractor's Operation on Site. The Employer is not responsible for these areas, which do not become part of the Site. For example, the Contractor may need to arrange for the provision of additional areas from which to obtain natural materials or he may need to arrange for the provision of working areas on which to prefabricate parts of the Works before transporting them to the Site.

10.2 PERMITS, LICENCES OR APPROVAL

It is obligation of the Employer to provide reasonable assistance to the Contactor to secure permits, licences or approval from the authorities of the country where works to be executed.

Clause 2.2 Permits, Licences or Approval of Red Book Book read:

2.2 Permits, Licences or Approval

The Employer shall (where he is in a position to do so) provide reasonable assistance to the Contractor at the request of the Contractor: (a) by obtaining copies of the Laws of the Country which are relevant to the Contract but are not readily available; and (b) for the Contractor's applications for any permits, licences or approvals required by the Laws of the Country: (i) which the Contractor is required to obtain under Sub-Clause 1.13 [Compliance with Laws], (ii) for the delivery of Goods, including clearance through customs, and (iii) for the export of Contractor's Equipment when it is removed from the Site.

Under the law of the Country, permits, licences or approvals may be required for the Works, such as for any Contractor's design regulations, imports and exports. For some of these matters, the Contractor may need reasonable assistance from the Employer in the preparation and submission of his applications. This "reasonable assistance" may, for example, comprise authentication of the Contractor's application documentation, but it would not be reasonable for the Contractor to expect the Employer to do anything which the Contractor can do himself. Sub-Clause 2.2 follows the general provisions contained in Compliance with Laws Sub-Clause 1.13(b), but Country-specific requirements may need to be specified in the Particular Conditions.

In order to encourage tenderers and also minimise delay to the project, the Employer should apply for any essential licences which can be procured prior to inviting tenders. Tenderers may be reluctant to incur expense in the preparation of their tenders if they are uncertain whether statutory requirements can be satisfied, and there may also be time-related constraints. The Employer, however, has no obligations under Sub-Clause 2.2 unless and until he receives the Contractor's request, which must be in writing in accordance with Sub-Clause 1.3. The Employer does not then become liable in any way for the success or otherwise of the applications. Sub-Clause 2.2 does not relieve the Contractor from his responsibilities under Compliance with Laws Sub-Clause 1.13 or otherwise, provided the Employer provides the reasonable assistance requested.

10.3 EMPLOYER'S PERSONNEL

It is obligation of the Employer to assure that all his personnel act with due respect and professionalism towards the Contractor's personnel on equal footing and not to show any superiority towards them.

Clause 2.3 Employer Personnel FIDIC Red Book read:

2.3 Employer Personnel

The Employer shall be responsible for ensuring that the Employer's Personnel and the Employer's other contractors on the Site: (a) co-operate with the Contractor's efforts under Sub-Clause 4.6 [Co-operation]; and (b) take actions similar to those which the Contractor is required to take under subparagraphs (a), (b) and (c) of Sub-Clause 4.8 [Safety Procedures] and under Sub- Clause 4.18 [Protection of the Environment].

The Employer's Personnel includes Engineer, his representative and his project management team. They are required to cooperate with the Contractor's co-ordination efforts, and to take certain actions in respect of safety procedures. The work to be carried out by these other contractors should be described in the tender documents, and aspects such as co-ordination and safety may need to be specified in the contract.

10.4 EMPLOYER'S BUDGET (FINANCIAL ARRANGEMENTS)

It is obligation of the Employer that Funding for Project budget has adequately arranged prior to signing of the Contract. Clause 2.4 Employer's Financial Arrangement of Red Book reads:

Clause 2.4 Employer's Financial Arrangement

The Employer shall submit, within 28 days after receiving any request from the Contractor, reasonable evidence that financial arrangements have been made and are being maintained which will enable the Employer to pay the Contract Price (as estimated at that time) in accordance with

Clause 14 [Contract Price and Payment]. If the Employer intends to make any material change to his financial arrangements, the Employer shall give notice to the Contractor with detailed particulars.

The Employer is required to provide evidence of his financial arrangements when requested, and may also benefit from providing it when inviting tenders. The Employer has no obligation under Sub-Clause 2.4 unless and until he receives the Contractor's request, which must be in writing in accordance with Sub-Clause 1.3. Although no mention is made of the period between receiving the evidence and issuing the next request, the Contractor would not be able to rely upon the consequences of a further request being issued within an unreasonably short period. However, it would be reasonable to issue a request when the estimated final Contract Price had increased above the amount substantiated by the evidence which the Employer had submitted previously. Typically, a Variation would increase the estimated final Contract Price.

The evidence is required to demonstrate the Employer's ability to pay the Contract Price, which typically would be the estimated final Contract Price at the time of the request but excluding the effect of adjustments which have not yet become applicable. For example, it would usually be unreasonable to add a contingency to allow for the possibility of a future event resulting in an adjustment under Sub-Clause 13.7 Adjustment for Changes in Legislation. Although future adjustments under Sub-Clause 13.8 Adjustment for Changes in Cost could be assumed to continue at the same adjustment multiplier "Pn" as that for the current month, the Contractor may not be able to rely upon an alleged failure by the Employer if his evidence only failed to substantiate an amount calculated using adjustment multipliers which increase each month, due to inflation.

The evidence is required to demonstrate the Employer's ability to pay in accordance with Clause 14, including the periods for payment under Sub-Clause 14.7 Payment. The form of the evidence depends upon the sources of the Employer's finances, and may also (in due course) depend upon the extent to which payments may not have been made in accordance with Clause 14. If the Employer is a governmental authority, the evidence may be in the public domain, in which case the request under Sub-Clause 2.4 may be no more significant than a request under Sub-Clause 2.2. If an international financial institution is providing part of the Contract Price, as a loan or a grant, it should have no difficulty providing evidence of these financial arrangements, and it may be prepared to support the Contractor's request for evidence of the other financial arrangements which will enable the Employer to pay the other parts of the Contract Price.

If the Employer anticipates that (because of the Contract's duration, for example) he will not be able to submit evidence in respect of the whole Contract Price, he would presumably have limited his obligations by an appropriate amendment in the Particular Conditions. He may even consider it necessary to delete Sub-Clause 2.4, especially if he expects tenderers to make their own financial arrangements. Tenderers would be entitled to be concerned at such deletion of this Sub-Clause, especially if the Employer had been unable to replace it by some other form of assurance. Sub-Clause 16.1 Contractor's Entitlement to suspend Work entitles the Contractor (after 21 days' notice) to suspend work, or reduce the rate of work, if the Employer fails to submit the evidence requested under Sub-Clause 2.4. Termination under Sub-Clause 16.2 provides the ultimate remedy.

10.5 EMPLOYER'S CLAIMS

The Employer is obliged to give notice to the Contractor, if he thinks that he has a claim against the Contractor.

Clause 2.5 Employer's Claims of Red Book read as follow:

Clause 2.5 Employer's Claims

If the Employer considers himself to be entitled to any payment under any Clause of these Conditions or otherwise in connection with the Contract, and/or to any extension of the Defects Notification Period, the Employer or the Engineer shall give notice and particulars to the Contractor. However, notice is not required for payments due under Sub-Clause 4.19 [Electricity, Water and Gas], under Sub-Clause 4.20 [Employer's Equipment and Free-Issue Material], or for other services requested by the Contractor.

The notice shall be given as soon as practicable after the Employer became aware of the event or circumstances giving rise to the claim. A notice relating to any extension of the Defects Notification Period shall be given before the expiry of such period. The particulars shall specify the Clause or other basis of the claim, and shall include substantiation of the amount and/or extension to which the Employer considers himself to be entitled in connection with the Contract. The Engineer shall then proceed in accordance with Sub-Clause 3.5 [Determinations] to agree or determine (i) the amount (if any) which the Employer is entitled to be paid by the Contractor, and/or (ii) the extension (if any) of the Defects Notification Period in accordance with Sub-Clause 11.3 [Extension of Defects Notification Period].

**This amount may be included as a deduction in the Contract Price and Payment Certificates. The Employer shall only be entitled to set off against or make any deduction from an amount certified in a Payment Certificate, or to otherwise* *claim against the Contractor, in accordance with this Sub-Clause.*

Note: In the Silver Book the last paragraph marked * above is replaced with the following Paragraph:

The Employer may deduct this amount from any moneys due, or to become due, to the Contractor. The Employer shall only be entitled to set off against or make any deduction from an amount due to the Contractor, or to otherwise claim against the Contractor, in accordance with this Sub-Clause or with sub-paragraph (a) and/or (b) of Sub-Clause 14.6 [Interim Payments].

This Sub-Clause prescribes the procedure to be followed by the Employer if he considers himself to be entitled to any payment under or in connection with the Contract; or he considers himself to be entitled to an extension of the Defects Notification Period under Sub-Clause 11.3. Notice is to be given as soon as practicable, except in respect of any services which the Contractor requested because he would then not need to be notified. No time period is specified for notices relating to payment, but the applicable Laws may do so. A notice relating to an extension must be given before the relevant Defects Notification Period expires. If the Employer fails to give the notice before such Period expires, he cannot claim an extension under Sub-Clause 11.3 thereafter. The notice shall be given in writing (Sub-Clause 1.3) and shall be listed in the progress report under Sub-Clause 4.21(f). Red Book 1.3 states that, when a notice is issued by the Engineer or the Employer, a copy shall be sent to the other.

The Contractor may not need to respond to the notice, other than to acknowledge receipt under Sub-Clause 1.3(a). He should not regard the notice as an aggressive act which must be rebutted, but merely as an act which enables him to be aware of the Employer's intention to claim. Sub-Clause 4.21(f) requires progress reports to list all notices which have been given under Sub-Clauses 2.5 and 20.1.

Although the Contractor should respond to the notice if he is aware of factual errors in the notice, the absence of any rebuttal should not be taken as any indication of agreement. Particulars may be given at any time, but excessive delay in their submission may be construed as an indication that the Employer will not be proceeding with the notified claim. In order to be effective, the particulars should include the basis of the claim, with relevant Clause number(s), and detailed substantiation of the extension and/or payment being claimed. The claim then becomes subject to the procedure prescribed in Sub-Clause 3.5.

Under Red Book 3.5, the Engineer endeavours to agree and settle the claim, failing which he is required to make a fair determination. If the claim included an extension to the Defects Notification Period, the extension then becomes binding for the purposes of Clause 11, subject to the procedures in Clause 20 for the resolution of any dispute. In the case of a payment having been claimed, the Engineer may include it as a deduction in Payment Certificates.

Under Sub-Clause 14.7, the Employer is required to pay the amount certified (namely, incorporating this deduction), but is not entitled to make any further deduction. If the Employer considers himself to be entitled to any payment under or in connection with the Contract, he is thus required to follow the procedure prescribed in Sub-Clause 2.5, and is not entitled to withhold payment whilst awaiting the outcome of these procedures.

In FIDIC Red Book, Sub-Clause 2.5 requires the Employer to adhere to a claims procedure, which is specified with less precision than the procedure imposed on the Contractor (who may be more familiar with preparing claims than many Employers). It was considered that, if the Employer had to give notice within a specified period calculated from the date when the Employer was aware of the event Personnel should have been aware of a default by the Contractor, thus unfairly relieving the Contractor of liability or circumstance giving rise to his claim, such date might be regarded as being when observant Employer's Personnel should have been aware of a default by the Contractor, thus unfairly relieving the Contractor of liability.

10.6 NOMINATED SUBCONTRACTORS

10.6.1 Introduction:

Clause 5 of Red Book includes basic provisions which should only be invoked with a degree of caution. Generally, the Contractor should be given reasonable freedom to decide (subject to Sub-Clause 4.4) what parts of the Works he wishes to subcontract, and to whom. The Contractor's freedom to subcontract may be restricted other than by invoking Clause 5: (i) If there are particular restrictions related to the manufacturer of certain items of Plant or Materials, the Specification may refer to the named manufacturer without making him a nominated Subcontractor. (ii) If the Employer wishes to ensure that a part of the Works is executed by a specialist company and not by the Contractor himself, the Specification may list acceptable potential Subcontractors, and/or tenderers could be invited to specify their chosen Subcontractors in a Schedule.

For avoidance of doubt, the Specification or Schedule may also state that the Subcontractor is not a nominated Subcontractor under this Clause. (iii) If the Employer wishes to ensure that part of the project is designed and executed by a specialist company, and/or wishes to participate (either directly or through the Engineer) in the choice of plant to be provided by such company, a separate contract may be less problematic than a nominated subcontract. In accordance with the second sentence of Sub-Clause 4.4, the Contractor is responsible for the acts or defaults of each nominated Subcontractor. The Employer and Engineer should not deal directly with a nominated Subcontractor (or with any Subcontractor) but should only deal with the Contractor (unless he agrees otherwise).

The following apparent advantages of instructing the employment of a nominated Subcontractor may be persuasive, namely that the Employer and/or Engineer: (i) can choose the specialist company: as noted above, this can be achieved other than by nomination; (ii) can participate in the choice of plant: again, this can be achieved other than by nomination, and the need to discuss technical matters through the Contractor often causes problems; and/or (iii) can avoid participation in co-ordination of the interface between the nominated Subcontractor's and the Contractor's works: this apparent advantage is frequently not achieved in practice, because the Contractor may incur Cost as a result of the requirements for co-ordination, and the Contractor may have been unaware of them and/or of the terms of the subcontract when he priced his Tender (which thus excluded such Cost).

10.6.2 Definition of "nominated Subcontractor"

Clause 5.1 Definition of "nominated Subcontractor" of Red Book read as follows:

5.1 Definition of "nominated Subcontractor"

In the Contract, "nominated Subcontractor" means a Subcontractor: (a) who is stated in the Contract as being a nominated Subcontractor, or (b) whom the Engineer, under Clause 13 [Variations and Adjustments], instructs the Contractor to employ as a Subcontractor.

Sub-Clause 5.1 defines two types of nominated Subcontractor, without implying that any Subcontractors will be nominated: (a) The Contract may specify the named specialist company to be appointed for a particular part of the Works; in which case it should also specify coordination and other requirements, and the terms of the proposed subcontract. (b) The Engineer may instruct the Contractor to employ a named specialist company; typically under Sub-Clause 13.3 (as a Variation), under Sub- Clause 13.5 (in respect of a Provisional Sum), or under Sub-Clause 13.6 (as daywork).

10.6.3 Objection to Nomination

Clause 5.2 Objection to Nomination of the Read Book read as follows:

5.2 Objection to Nomination

The Contractor shall not be under any obligation to employ a nominated Subcontractor against whom the Contractor raises reasonable objection by notice to the Engineer as soon as practicable, with supporting particulars. An objection shall be deemed reasonable if it arises from (among other things) any of the following matters, unless the Employer agrees to indemnify the Contractor against and from the consequences of the matter: (a) there are reasons to believe that the Subcontractor does not have sufficient competence, resources or financial strength; (b) the subcontract does not specify that the nominated Subcontractor shall indemnify the Contractor against and from any negligence or misuse of Goods by the nominated Subcontractor, his agents and employees; or (c) the subcontract does not specify that, for the subcontracted work (including design, if any), the nominated Subcontractor shall: (i) undertake to the Contractor such obligations and liabilities as will enable the Contractor to discharge his obligations and liabilities under the Contract, and (ii) indemnify the Contractor against and from all obligations and liabilities arising under or in connection with the Contract and from the consequences of any failure by the Subcontractor to perform these obligations or to fulfil these liabilities.

Some of the other problems which can arise, in addition to those mentioned in the above comments on Clause 5, are indicated in the matters described in the sub-paragraphs of Sub-Clause 5.2. If the Contractor wishes to object to the nomination, he must do so promptly, describing all the grounds on which his objections are based.

The grounds need not be restricted to those described in the sub-paragraphs, although they list the most likely grounds for objection under a CONS contract. The grounds listed in these sub-paragraphs may also be relevant to objections raised under Sub-Clause 4.5 of a P&DB or EPCT contract, but may not be the most likely grounds.

The Sub-Clause provides the Employer with a possible resolution of the objection, namely indemnification. The Engineer is not authorised to issue such indemnities on behalf of the Employer. If the Contractor does not object to the nomination, or if his objections are resolved by indemnification and/or negotiations between the Parties and the prospective Subcontractor, the Contractor must comply with the instruction in accordance with Sub-Clauses 3.3 and 5.1(b).

10.6.4 Payments to nominated Subcontractors

Clause 5.3 Payments to nominated Subcontractors of Red Book read as follows:

5.3 Payments to nominated Subcontractors

The Contractor shall pay to the nominated Subcontractor the amounts which the Engineer certifies to be due in accordance with the subcontract. These amounts plus other (a) charges shall be included in the Contract Price in accordance with subparagraph, (b) of Sub-Clause 13.5 [Provisional Sums], except as stated in Sub-Clause 5.4 [Evidence of Payments].

Sub-Clause 13.5(b) states that the Contractor shall be paid the actual amounts which he pays to the nominated Subcontractor plus a percentage for the Contractor's overheads and profit. The Engineer is required to certify such actual amounts as are due to be paid to the Subcontractor. These certificates may be in the form of a letter incorporating the following words: "We hereby certify that the amount of ... is due to be paid to ... in respect of his application for payment..."

10.6.5 Evidence of Payments

Clause 5.4 Evidence of Payments of Red Book read as follows:

5.4 Evidence of Payments

Before issuing a Payment Certificate which includes an amount payable to a nominated Subcontractor, the Engineer may request the Contractor to supply reasonable evidence that the nominated Subcontractor has received all amounts due in accordance with previous Payment Certificates, less applicable deductions for retention or otherwise. Unless the Contractor: (a) submits this reasonable evidence to the Engineer, or (b) (i) satisfies the Engineer in writing that the Contractor is reasonably entitled to withhold or refuse to pay these amounts, And (ii) submits to the Engineer reasonable evidence that the nominated Subcontractor has been notified of the Contractor's entitlement, then the Employer may (at his sole discretion) pay, direct to the nominated Subcontractor, part or all of such amounts previously certified (less applicable deductions) as are due to the nominated Subcontractor and for which the Contractor has failed to submit the evidence described in sub-paragraphs (a) or (b) above. The Contractor shall then repay, to the Employer, the amount which the nominated Subcontractor was directly paid by the Employer.

The Engineer should not normally request evidence of previous payments, unless he has reason to believe that the Contractor is in default under the subcontract. The nominated Subcontractor may feel that, since he was selected and nominated by (or on behalf of) the Employer, he should be entitled to seek the support of the Employer or Engineer in respect of any disagreements which he is having with the Contractor. However, the Employer may have originally opted for nomination with the intention of minimising any dealings with the Subcontractor.

The Engineer has no stated duty to request the evidence of previous payments. The nominated Subcontractor is not a party to the Contract, so he is not entitled to rely upon its provisions. However, he may be entitled to certain rights under the applicable law, particularly if specific undertakings were given to the Subcontractor to encourage him to enter into the subcontract. Such undertakings should be honoured, and should have been copied to the tenderers for the main Contract.

If the Engineer requests the evidence of previous payments to a nominated Subcontractor, he must do so sufficiently in advance of issuing a Payment Certificate.

The Contractor must be allowed a reasonable time to present the documents described in sub-paragraph (a) or (b), and the Engineer will need time to review these documents and issue a Payment Certificate within the time specified in Clause 14. If the Contractor fails to provide the documents described in sub-paragraph (a) or (b) of Sub-Clause 5.4, the Employer is entitled to pay the Subcontractor directly.

There is no obligation to do so, unless (as mentioned above) specific undertakings were given. Payment is at the Employer's (not the Engineer's) discretion. The Engineer should therefore consult the Employer before requesting the Contractor to provide the reasonable evidence. If the Employer elects to pay the Subcontractor directly, he should ensure that the procedure set out in this Sub-Clause is adhered to. In accordance with Sub-Clause 2.5: (i) the Employer or the Engineer should give prompt notice to the Contractor of the amount which the Employer directly paid, and (ii) "This amount may be included as a deduction in the Contract Price and Payment Certificates." If the procedures specified in Sub-Clauses 2.5 and 5.4 are not adhered to, the Employer may not be entitled to this deduction.

CHAPTER 11

EMPLOYER'S PERSONNEL (FOR COSTRUCTION SUPERVISION, MANAGEMENT AND CONTROL) WITH PARTICULAR REFERENCE TO FIDIC CONTRACTS

11.1 EMPLOYER'S PERSONNEL

It is obligation of the Employer to assure that all his personnel act with due respect and professionalism towards the Contractor's personnel on equal footing and not to show any superiority towards them. Clause 2.3 Employer Personnel FIDIC Red Book, Yellow Book and Silver Book read:

2.3 Employer Personnel

The Employer shall be responsible for ensuring that the Employer's Personnel and the Employer's other contractors on the Site: (a) co-operate with the Contractor's efforts under Sub-Clause 4.6 [Co-operation]; and (b) take actions similar to those which the Contractor is required to take under subparagraphs (a), (b) and (c) of Sub-Clause 4.8 [Safety Procedures] and under Sub- Clause 4.18 [Protection of the Environment].

The Employer's Personnel includes Red Book and Yellow Book's Engineer, his representative and his project management team or Silver Book's Employer's Representative, and his staff. They and contractors are required to cooperate with the Contractor's co-ordination efforts, and to take certain actions in respect of safety procedures. The work to be carried out by these other contractors should be described in the tender documents, and aspects such as co-ordination and safety may need to be specified in the contract.

11.2 THE ENGINEER

11.2.1 Engineer's Duties and Authority

The clause 3.1 Engineer's Duties and Authority in FIDIC Red Book and read as follows:

3.1 Engineer's Duties and Authority

The Employer shall appoint the Engineer who shall carry out the duties assigned to him in the Contract. The Engineer's staff shall include suitably qualified engineers and other professionals who are competent to carry out these duties. The Engineer shall have no authority to amend the Contract. The Engineer may exercise the authority attributable to the Engineer as specified in or necessarily to be implied from the Contract. If the Engineer is required to obtain the approval of the Employer before exercising a specified authority, the requirements shall be as stated in the Particular Conditions. The Employer undertakes not to impose further constraints on the Engineer's authority, except as agreed with the Contractor.

However, whenever the Engineer exercises a specified authority for which the Employer's approval is required, then (for the purposes of the Contract) the Employer shall be deemed to have given approval. Except as otherwise stated in these Conditions: (a) whenever carrying out duties or exercising authority, specified in or implied by the Contract, the Engineer shall be deemed to act for the Employer; (b) the Engineer has no authority to relieve either Party of any duties, obligations or responsibilities under the Contract; and (c) any approval, check, certificate, consent, examination, inspection, instruction, notice, proposal, request, test, or similar act by the Engineer (including absence of disapproval) shall not relieve the Contractor from any responsibility he has under the Contract, including responsibility for errors, omissions, discrepancies and non-compliances.

Under Red Book or Yellow Book, the Employer is required to appoint the "Engineer", who is to be named in the Appendix to Tender. The Engineer does not represent the Employer for all purposes. The Engineer is not authorised to amend the Contract, but he is deemed to act for the Employer as stated in sub-paragraph (a). The role of the Engineer is thus not stated to be that of a wholly impartial intermediary, unless such a role is specified in the Particular Conditions. If Engineer is an independent consulting engineer who is to act impartially.

If the Employer wishes to impose constraints on the Engineer's authority, these constraints must be listed in the Particular Conditions, so as to avoid having to seek the Contractor's agreement to further constraints. Under Sub-Clause 1.3, the Employer's approval (of the Engineer exercising a specified authority) shall be in writing and shall not be unreasonably withheld or delayed. When deciding which constraints to list in the Particular Conditions, the Employer should take account of the likelihood of the Contractor being entitled to recover the additional costs he incurs whilst the Engineer awaits the Employer's written approval.

However, when the Contractor receives an Engineer's communication for which the Employer's prior approval was required, the Contractor is not entitled to query whether it was approved. For the purposes of the Contract, the Employer is deemed to have given approval. For the purposes of the Engineer's agreement with the Employer, whether the Employer actually approved is a matter of fact, and acting without approval may be a breach of this consultancy agreement.

Sub-paragraph (b) states that the Engineer has no authority to relieve either Party of any duties, obligations and responsibilities except as otherwise stated in the Contract. The main exception is the authority to instruct Variations, because they may include omission of any work, as described in Red Book 13.1(d). Finally, sub-paragraph (c) states that various actions of the Engineer do not relieve the Contractor from any responsibility under Red Book or Yellow Book.

11.2.2 Delegation by the Engineer

Red Book Clause 3.2 Delegation by the Engineer read as follows:

3.2 Delegation by the Engineer

The Engineer may from time to time assign duties and delegate authority to assistants, and may also revoke such assignment or delegation. These assistants may include a resident engineer, and/or independent inspectors appointed to inspect and/or test items of Plant and/or Materials. The assignment, delegation or revocation shall be in writing and shall not take effect until copies have been received by both Parties. However, unless otherwise agreed by both Parties, the Engineer shall not delegate the authority to determine any matter in accordance with Sub-Clause 3.5 [Determinations].

Assistants shall be suitably qualified persons, who are competent to carry out these duties and exercise this authority, and who are fluent in the language for communications defined in Sub-Clause 1.4 [Law and Language] Each assistant, to whom duties have been assigned or authority has been delegated, shall only be authorised to issue instructions to the Contractor to the extent defined by the delegation. Any approval, check, certificate, consent, examination, inspection, instruction, notice, proposal, request, test, or similar act by an assistant, in accordance with the delegation, shall have the same effect as though the act had been an act of the Engineer. However: any failure to disapprove any work, Plant or Materials shall not constitute approval, and shall therefore not prejudice the right of the Engineer to reject the work, Plant or Materials; (b) if the Contractor questions any determination or instruction of an assistant, the Contractor may refer the matter to the Engineer, who shall promptly confirm, reverse or vary the determination or instruction.

Under Red Book, the Engineer has a major role in the administration of the Contract, particularly with respect to issuing Variations and Payment Certificates, and reviewing any Contractor's Documents. When examining the tender documents and considering the role of the Engineer, tenderers may take account of such matters as: (i) the Engineer's technical competence and reputation, particularly in relation to reviewing Contractor's Documents; (ii) the degree of independence indicated by the status of the appointed Engineer, namely whether he is an independent consulting engineer,; and (iii) the practical consequences of any constraints on the Engineer's authority.

The Contractor shall only take instructions from the Engineer, or from an assistant to whom the appropriate authority has been delegated under this Clause. If an instruction constitutes a Variation, Clause 13 [*Variations and Adjustments*] shall apply. The Contractor shall comply with the instructions given by the Engineer or delegated assistant, on any matter related to the Contract. These instructions shall be given in writing.

11.2.3 Instructions of the Engineer

Clause 3.3 Instructions of the Engineer of the Red Book reads as follows:

3.3 Instructions of the Engineer

The Engineer may issue to the Contractor (at any time) instructions and additional or modified Drawings which may be necessary for the execution of the Works and the remedying of any defects, all in accordance with the Contract. The Contractor shall only take instructions from the Engineer, or from an assistant to whom the appropriate authority has been delegated under this Clause. If an instruction constitutes a Variation, Clause 13 [Variations and Adjustments] shall apply.

The Contractor shall comply with the instructions given by the Engineer or delegated assistant, on any matter related to the Contract. Whenever practicable, their instructions shall be given in writing. If the Engineer or a delegated assistant: (a) gives an oral instruction; (b) receives a written confirmation of the instruction, from (or on behalf of) the Contractor, within two working days after giving the instruction, and (c) does not reply by issuing a written rejection and/or instruction within two working days after receiving the confirmation, then the confirmation shall constitute the written instruction of the Engineer or delegated assistant (as the case may be).

Under Red Book, the Contractor executes the Works in accordance with the Engineer's instructions, and with designs which have been carried out by (or on behalf of) the Employer. The Engineer is empowered to issue instructions, and the Contractor is generally obliged to comply.

It may even be necessary for immediate oral instructions to be given, although they should be avoided wherever possible, so detailed procedures are specified for an instruction which is not immediately confirmed in writing. The procedures require prompt confirmation or denial of an alleged oral instruction, in order that its validity or invalidity can be established as soon as practicable.

11.2.4 Replacement of the Engineer

Under Red Book clause 3.4 Replacement of the Engineer read as follows:

3.4 Replacement of the Engineer

If the Employer intends to replace the Engineer, the Employer shall, not less than 42 days before the intended date of replacement, give notice to the Contractor of the name, address and relevant experience of the intended replacement Engineer. The Employer shall not replace the Engineer with a person against whom the Contractor raises reasonable objection by notice to the Employer, with supporting particulars.

Having studied these matters, tenderers may not want the Employer to be able to replace the Engineer, at least not without good reason. By contrast, Employers understandably consider that there should be no restriction imposed on replacing the Engineer, whom the Employer has appointed to administer the Contract.

Sub-Clause 3.4 provides a fair and reasonable compromise between the conflicting desires of the Parties. If the Employer intends to replace the Engineer, the Contractor must receive 42 days' notice, which must include details of the replacement Engineer's experience which is relevant to the duties and authority he would have in respect of the Works. In order to prevent the Employer appointing an unsuitable replacement Engineer, the Contractor should notify the Employer of the "reasonable objection" as soon as possible during the period of 42 days. If the objection is reasonable, the Employer "shall not replace the Engineer ..." Supporting particulars are to accompany the notice of the Contractor's "reasonable objection". What would suffice as a "reasonable objection" depends upon the circumstances, including the representations originally made to the tenderers, the details of the replacement Engineer's experience, and the duties.

11.2.5 Determinations

In Red Book clause 3.5 Determinations read as follows:

3.5 Determinations

Whenever these Conditions provide that the Engineer shall proceed in accordance with this Sub-Clause 3.5 to agree or determine any matter, the Engineer shall consult with each Party in an endeavour to reach agreement. If agreement is not achieved, the Engineer shall make a fair determination in accordance with the Contract, taking due regard of all relevant circumstances.

The Engineer shall give notice to both Parties of each agreement or determination, with supporting particulars. Each Party shall give effect to each agreement or determination unless and until revised under Clause 20 [Claims, Disputes and Arbitration].

Under Red Book, the Engineer first consults with each Party, separately and/or jointly, and endeavours to achieve the agreement of both Parties (not, it should be noted, just the Engineer's agreement with one Party). If the agreement of both Parties cannot be achieved within a reasonable time, the Engineer is then required to make a "fair determination in accordance with the Contract". The Engineer's determination is not required to be made impartially, unless such a requirement is stated in the Particular Conditions. However, he should carry out this duty in a professional manner, utilising his "suitably qualified engineers and other professionals" mentioned in Sub-Clause 3.1.

The Engineer is then required to notify both Parties of his determination, which is binding upon them unless and until revised under the dispute resolution procedures in Clause 20. In practice, the Engineer may first make an interim determination(s), indicating his intention to review it when further particulars are presented to him, and meanwhile including the appropriate adjustment in Interim Payment Certificates. Although an interim determination may nevertheless be referable to the DAB directly without further delay, it is usually preferable, if further particulars become available, for the Engineer to review his previous determination.

Under the Red Book and Yellow Book Contracts, the Engineer will be in control of project on behalf of the Employer and will carry out the duties assigned to him in the contract in accordance with contract provisions whilst some of the duties he will delegate to his representative (resident engineer) and his staff of the project will include competent qualified engineers, inspectors and other professionals (i.e. contract administrators, lab technicians, surveyors, clerks of works, quantity surveyors, etc.). The Engineer will have no authority to change or otherwise amend any terms of the contract. The Engineer, however, may issue to the Contractors at any time during the period of contract instructions and additional or modified drawings which may be necessary for the execution of the Works and remedying any defective work in accordance with the contract provisions. The Contractor will not take instruction from anyone other than the Engineer (or from assistant(s) to whom the appropriate authority is delegated by the Engineer).

Engineer's Duties and Authority: The clause 3.1 Engineer's Duties and Authority in FIDIC Red Book and Yellow Book read as follows:

3.1 Engineer's Duties and Authority

The Employer shall appoint the Engineer who shall carry out the duties assigned to him in the Contract. The Engineer's staff shall include suitably qualified engineers and other professionals who are competent to carry out these duties. The Engineer shall have no authority to amend the Contract. The Engineer may exercise the authority attributable to the Engineer as specified in or necessarily to be implied from the Contract. If the Engineer is required to obtain the approval of the Employer before exercising a specified authority, the requirements shall be as stated in the Particular Conditions. The Employer undertakes not to impose further constraints on the Engineer's authority, except as agreed with the Contractor.

However, whenever the Engineer exercises a specified authority for which the Employer's approval is required, then (for the purposes of the Contract) the Employer shall be deemed to have given approval. Except as otherwise stated in these Conditions: (a) whenever carrying out duties or exercising authority, specified in or implied by the Contract, the Engineer shall be deemed to act for the Employer; (b) the Engineer has no authority to relieve either Party of any duties, obligations or responsibilities under the Contract; and (c) any approval, check, certificate, consent, examination, inspection, instruction, notice, proposal, request, test, or similar act by the Engineer (including absence of disapproval) shall not relieve the Contractor from any responsibility he has under the Contract, including responsibility for errors, omissions, discrepancies and non-compliances.

Under Red Book or Yellow Book, the Employer is required to appoint the "Engineer", who is to be named in the Appendix to Tender. The Engineer does not represent the Employer for all purposes. The Engineer is not authorised to amend the Contract, but he is deemed to act for the Employer as stated in sub-paragraph (a). The role of the Engineer is thus not stated to be that of a wholly impartial intermediary, unless such a role is specified in the Particular Conditions. If Engineer is an independent consulting engineer who is to act impartially.

If the Employer wishes to impose constraints on the Engineer's authority, these constraints must be listed in the Particular Conditions, so as to avoid having to seek the Contractor's agreement to further constraints. Under Sub-Clause 1.3, the Employer's approval (of the Engineer exercising a specified authority) shall be in writing and shall not be unreasonably withheld or delayed. When deciding which constraints to list in the Particular Conditions, the Employer should take account of the likelihood of the Contractor being entitled to recover the additional costs he incurs whilst the Engineer awaits the Employer's written approval.

However, when the Contractor receives an Engineer's communication for which the Employer's prior approval was required, the Contractor is not entitled to query whether it was approved. For the purposes of the Contract, the Employer is deemed to have given approval. For the purposes of the Engineer's agreement with the Employer, whether the Employer actually approved is a matter of fact, and acting without approval may be a breach of this consultancy agreement.

Sub-paragraph (b) states that the Engineer has no authority to relieve either Party of any duties, obligations and responsibilities except as otherwise stated in the Contract. The main exception is the authority to instruct Variations, because they may include omission of any work, as described in Red Book 13.1(d). Finally, sub-paragraph (c) states that various actions of the Engineer do not relieve the Contractor from any responsibility under Red Book or Yellow Book.

Delegation by the Engineer: Red Book and Yellow Book Clause 3.2 Delegation by the Engineer read as follows:

3.2 Delegation by the Engineer

The Engineer may from time to time assign duties and delegate authority to assistants, and may also revoke such assignment or delegation. These assistants may include a resident engineer, and/or independent inspectors appointed to inspect and/or test items of Plant and/or Materials. The assignment, delegation or revocation shall be in writing and shall not take effect until copies have been received by both Parties. However, unless otherwise agreed by both Parties, the Engineer shall not delegate the authority to determine any matter in accordance with Sub-Clause 3.5 [Determinations].

Assistants shall be suitably qualified persons, who are competent to carry out these duties and exercise this authority, and who are fluent in the language for communications defined in Sub-Clause 1.4 [Law and Language] Each assistant, to whom duties have been assigned or authority has been delegated, shall only be authorised to issue instructions to the Contractor to the extent defined by the delegation. Any approval, check, certificate, consent, examination, inspection, instruction, notice, proposal, request, test, or similar act by an assistant, in accordance with the delegation, shall have the same effect as though the act had been an act of the Engineer. However: any failure to disapprove any work, Plant or Materials shall not constitute approval, and shall therefore not prejudice the right of the Engineer to reject the work, Plant or Materials; (b) if the Contractor questions any determination or instruction of an assistant, the Contractor may refer the matter to the Engineer, who shall promptly confirm, reverse or vary the determination or instruction.

Under Red Book or Yellow Book , the Engineer has a major role in the administration of the Contract, particularly with respect to issuing Variations and Payment Certificates, and reviewing any Contractor's Documents. When examining the tender documents and considering the role of the Engineer, tenderers may take account of such matters as: (i)- the Engineer's technical competence and reputation, particularly in relation to reviewing Contractor's Documents; (ii)- the degree of independence indicated by the status of the appointed Engineer, namely whether he is an independent consulting engineer,; and (iii)- the practical consequences of any constraints on the Engineer's authority.

The Contractor shall only take instructions from the Engineer, or from an assistant to whom the appropriate authority has been delegated under this Clause. If an instruction constitutes a Variation, Clause 13 [*Variations and Adjustments*] shall apply. The Contractor shall comply with the instructions given by the Engineer or delegated assistant, on any matter related to the Contract. These instructions shall be given in writing.

Instructions of the Engineer: Clause 3.3 Instructions of the Engineer of the Red Book reads as follows:

3.3 Instructions of the Engineer

The Engineer may issue to the Contractor (at any time) instructions and additional or modified Drawings which may be necessary for the execution of the Works and the remedying of any defects, all in accordance with the Contract. The Contractor shall only take instructions from the Engineer, or from an assistant to whom the appropriate authority has been delegated under this Clause. If an instruction constitutes a Variation, Clause 13 [Variations and Adjustments] shall apply.

The Contractor shall comply with the instructions given by the Engineer or delegated assistant, on any matter related to the Contract. Whenever practicable, their instructions shall be given in writing. If the Engineer or a delegated assistant: (a) gives an oral instruction; (b) receives a written confirmation of the instruction, from (or on behalf of) the Contractor, within two working days after giving the instruction, and (c) does not reply by issuing a written rejection and/or instruction within two working days after receiving the confirmation, then the confirmation shall constitute the written instruction of the Engineer or delegated assistant (as the case may be).

Clause 3.3 Instructions of the Engineer of the Yellow Book reads as follows:

3.3 Instructions of the Engineer

The Engineer may issue to the Contractor (at any time) instructions which may be necessary for the execution of the Works and the remedying of any defects, all in accordance with the Contract. The Contractor shall only take instructions from the Engineer, or from an assistant to whom the appropriate authority has been delegated under this Clause. If an instruction constitutes a Variation, Clause 13 [Variations and Adjustments] shall apply.

The Contractor shall comply with the instructions given by the Engineer or delegated assistant, on any matter related to the Contract. These instructions shall be given in writing.

Under Red Book, the Contractor executes the Works in accordance with the Engineer's instructions, and with designs which have been carried out by (or on behalf of) the Employer. The Engineer is empowered to issue instructions, and the Contractor is generally obliged to comply. It may even be necessary for immediate oral instructions to be given, although they should be avoided wherever possible, so detailed procedures are specified for an instruction which is not immediately confirmed in writing. The procedures require prompt confirmation or denial of an alleged oral instruction, in order that its validity or invalidity can be established as soon as practicable.

Under Yellow Book, the Contractor provides Plant and executes any other Works in accordance with his own design, although P&DB 17.3(g) indicates that there may be certain elements of the design which were issued to the Contractor by (or on behalf of) the Employer. The Engineer is empowered to issue instructions, but Yellow Book 13.1(ii) anticipates the possibility of an instruction prejudicing the Contractor's responsibility for the design of the Works. In order to lessen the likelihood of instructions being misunderstood, oral instructions are invalid and ineffective.

Replacement of the Engineer: Under Red Book and Yellow Book clause 3.4 Replacement of the Engineer read as follows:

3.4 Replacement of the Engineer

If the Employer intends to replace the Engineer, the Employer shall, not less than 42 days before the intended date of replacement, give notice to the Contractor of the name, address and relevant experience of the intended replacement Engineer. The Employer shall not replace the Engineer with a person against whom the Contractor raises reasonable objection by notice to the Employer, with supporting particulars.

Having studied these matters, tenderers may not want the Employer to be able to replace the Engineer, at least not without good reason. By contrast, Employers understandably consider that there should be no restriction imposed on replacing the Engineer, whom the Employer has appointed to administer the Contract.

Sub-Clause 3.4 provides a fair and reasonable compromise between the conflicting desires of the Parties. If the Employer intends to replace the Engineer, the Contractor must receive 42 days' notice, which must include details of the replacement Engineer's experience which is relevant to the duties and authority he would have in respect of the Works. In order to prevent the Employer appointing an unsuitable replacement Engineer, the Contractor should notify the Employer of the "reasonable objection" as soon as possible during the period of 42 days. If the objection is reasonable, the Employer "shall not replace the Engineer ..." Supporting particulars are to accompany the notice of the Contractor's "reasonable objection". What would suffice as a "reasonable objection" depends upon the circumstances, including the representations originally made to the tenderers, the details of the replacement Engineer's experience, and the duties.

Determinations: In Red Book and Yellow Book clause 3.5 Determinations read as follows:

3.5 Determinations

Whenever these Conditions provide that the Engineer shall proceed in accordance with this Sub-Clause 3.5 to agree or determine any matter, the Engineer shall consult with each Party in an endeavour to reach agreement. If agreement is not achieved, the Engineer shall make a fair determination in accordance with the Contract, taking due regard of all relevant circumstances.

The Engineer shall give notice to both Parties of each agreement or determination, with supporting particulars. Each Party shall give effect to each agreement or determination unless and until revised under Clause 20 [Claims, Disputes and Arbitration].

Under Red Book or Yellow Book, the Engineer first consults with each Party, separately and/or jointly, and endeavours to achieve the agreement of both Parties (not, it should be noted, just the Engineer's agreement with one Party). If the agreement of both Parties cannot be achieved within a reasonable time, the Engineer is then required to make a "fair determination in accordance with the Contract". The Engineer's determination is not required to be made impartially, unless such a requirement is stated in the Particular Conditions. However, he should carry out this duty in a professional manner, utilising his "suitably qualified engineers and other professionals" mentioned in Sub-Clause 3.1.

The Engineer is then required to notify both Parties of his determination, which is binding upon them unless and until revised under the dispute resolution procedures in Clause 20. In practice, the Engineer may first make an interim determination(s), indicating his intention to review it when further particulars are presented to him, and meanwhile including the appropriate adjustment in Interim Payment Certificates. Although an interim determination may nevertheless be preferable to the DAB directly without further delay, it is usually preferable, if further particulars become available, for the Engineer to review his previous determination.

11.2.5 Employer's Representative

The Silver Book clause 3.1 Employer's Representative read as follows:

3.1 Employer's Representative

The Employer may appoint an Employer's Representative to act on his behalf under the Contract. In this event, he shall give notice to the Contractor of the name, address, duties and authority of the Employer's Representative.

The Employer's Representative shall carry out the duties assigned to him, and shall exercise the authority delegated to him, by the Employer. Unless and until the Employer notifies the Contractor otherwise, the Employer's Representative shall be deemed to have the full authority of the Employer under the Contract, except in respect of Clause 15 [Termination by Employer].

If the Employer wishes to replace any person appointed as Employer's Representative, the Employer shall give the Contractor not less than 14 days' notice of the replacement's name, address, duties and authority, and of the date of appointment.

Silver Book 3.1 entitles the Employer to appoint the "Employer's Representative", although there is no obligation to do so. If no such appointment is made, it becomes even more essential for the Employer to notify the Contractor of the name of the person authorised to sign as the Employer. Employer's Representative, who may be an independent consulting engineer, is expected to fully represent the Employer. The Employer may therefore have no need to constrain his Representative's authority, although he is fully entitled to do so.

The Employer thus may, or may not, notify the Contractor of an Employer's Representative. If the Employer does so notify, he may (or may not) notify the Contractor of the appointee's duties and authority, including any limitations.

Unless and until the Contractor is notified by the Employer: (i) of the appointee's name and address, there will be no "Employer's Representative" as defined in the Contract; (ii) of the appointee's duties and authority, he/she will be deemed to have the full authority of the Employer except in respect of Clause 15 (this exception was included in the General Conditions in order to allow for the probability of the appointee being an independent consulting engineer); and (iii) that a previously notified appointee has ceased to be the Employer's Representative, he/she continues as Employer's Representative under the Contract.

Silver Book 3.1 omits the sub-paragraphs contained in CONS 3.1 and P&DB 3.1, for the following reasons: (a) Silver Book 1.1.2.4 states that the Employer's Representative acts on behalf of the Employer (without Red' or Yellow Book's exception of anything otherwise stated); (b) 3.1 states that, unless and until the Employer notifies otherwise, the Employer's Representative is deemed to have the full authority of the

Employer (except for Clause 15), and therefore does have the same authority as the Employer to relieve the Contractor from obligations under the Contract; an (Silver Book 3.3(a) refers to communications, either from the Employer's Representative or from an assistant, not relieving the Contractor from responsibility.

Other Employer's Personnel: Silver Book clause 3.2 reads as follow:

3.2 Other Employer's Personnel

The Employer or the Employer's Representative may from time to time assign duties and delegate authority to assistants, and may also revoke such assignment or delegation. These assistants may include a resident engineer, and/or independent inspectors appointed to inspect and/or test items of Plant and/or Materials. The assignment, delegation or revocation shall not take effect until a copy of it has been received by the Contractor.

Assistants shall be suitably qualified persons, who are competent to carry out these duties and exercise this authority, and who are fluent in the language for communications defined in Sub-Clause 1.4 [Law and Language].

Dedicated Persons: In the Silver Book Sub-clause 3.3 delegated Persons provide:

3.3 Delegated Persons

All these persons, including the Employer's Representative and assistants, to whom duties have been assigned or authority has been delegated, shall only be authorised to issue instructions to the Contractor to the extent defined by the delegation. Any approval, check, certificate, consent, examination, inspection, instruction, notice, proposal, request, test, or similar act by a delegated person, in accordance with the delegation, shall have the same effect as though the act had been an act of the Employer. However: (a) unless otherwise stated in the delegated person's communication relating to such act, it shall not relieve the Contractor from any responsibility he has under the Contract, including responsibility for errors, omissions, discrepancies and non-compliances; (b) any failure to disapprove any work, Plant or Materials shall not constitute approval, and shall therefore not prejudice the right of the Employer to reject the work, Plant or Materials; and (c) if the Contractor questions any determination or instruction of a delegated person, the Contractor may refer the matter to the Employer, who shall promptly confirm, reverse or vary the determination or instruction.

Many assistants may need to be appointed, including resident engineer(s) and other professional staff on the Site, and inspectors on the Site and/or to visit manufacturers' works. Some of these persons may need to have authority delegated to them in accordance with Sub-Clause 3.2, so that they can be fully effective. Delegation and revocation do not take effect until copies have been passed to the Parties, and therefore cannot be retrospective. The Employer should ensure that there are sufficient assistants, and that they comply with the criteria in the second paragraph of Sub-Clause 3.2. They are all included within the definition of "Employer's Personnel".

Silver Book 3.3 refers to the Employer's Representative and to his/her assistants. Whenever he/she or an assistant acts in accordance with a delegated power, the act has the same effect as though it had been performed by the Employer. Under Silver Book 3.3(a), these acts performed (in effect) by the Employer shall not relieve the Contractor from any responsibility, unless otherwise stated in the communication relating to such act. Therefore, an approval or consent under the Contract, given in accordance with a delegated power, has the same effect as it would have had if it had been given by the Employer. If it is written in terms which clearly relieve the Contractor from a responsibility under the Contract, the Contractor is entitled to rely upon it as though it had been given by the Employer.

However, irrespective of Silver Book's relief from responsibility in respect of approvals and consents given by the Employer's Representative or his/her assistants, the right to reject Plant, Materials, design or workmanship under Silver Book 7.5 is wholly unaffected if: (i)- approval or consent was only given by a person to whom the relevant authority had not been delegated; (ii)- approval or consent was only given orally, which is not in accordance with Sub-Clause 1.3; or (iii)- no approval (or disapproval) or consent has been given. The Contractor may be dissatisfied with an assistant's determination or instruction. For example, the determination might have been disapproval or an opinion of non-compliance, or might have been given under Sub-Clause 3.5.

Determination: In The Silver Book clause 3.5 Determinations read as follows:

3.5 Determinations

Whenever these Conditions provide that the Employer shall proceed in accordance with this

Sub-Clause 3.5 to agree or determine any matter, the Employer shall consult with the Contractor in an endeavour to reach agreement. If agreement is not achieved, the Employer shall make a fair determination in accordance with the Contract, taking due regard of all relevant circumstances.

The Employer shall give notice to the Contractor of each agreement or determination, with supporting particulars. Each Party shall give effect to each agreement or determination, unless the Contractor gives notice, to the Employer, of his dissatisfaction with a determination within 14 days of receiving it. Either Party may then refer the dispute to the DAB in accordance with Sub-Clause 20.4 [Obtaining Dispute Adjudication Board's Decision].

If the Contractor is dissatisfied with a determination or instruction which had been given by an assistant or by Employer's Representative, he may refer the matter to the Employer , who shall confirm, reverse or vary the determination or instruction. The consequences of the reversal or variation are not stated, because they depend upon the nature of the determination or instruction and on the actual events, particularly any events which were influenced by, or took account of, the determination or instruction.

Under Silver Book, to "proceed in accordance with Sub-Clause 3.5 to agree or determine", the extension and financial compensation. The Engineer or Employer does not "proceed in accordance with Sub-Clause 3.5" only once in respect of each claim. He does so in stages, as further particulars are submitted under Sub-Clause 20.1, until the extension and financial compensation are finally agreed or determined. Under Sub-Clause 1.3, determinations shall be in writing, and shall not be unreasonably withheld or delayed.

Under Silver Book, the Contractor is firstly consulted by the Employer, or by the Employer's Representative (if any) unless he/she has no such delegated authority. If the agreement of both Parties cannot be achieved within a reasonable time, the Employer is then required to make, and to notify the Contractor of, the Employer's "fair determination in accordance with the Contract". The Parties must give effect to such determination, unless the Contractor issues a notice of dissatisfaction within 14 days (in which case the determination is of no effect).

Irrespective of whether the Contractor issues a notice of dissatisfaction, he may invoke the dispute resolution procedures in Clause 20. In order for the Employer to be able to rely upon a communication as being a determination under Sub-Clause 3.5, and to require the Contractor to give effect to it unless notice of dissatisfaction is given, the Contractor must be aware that it is such a communication. In other words, the determination should state that it is made under Sub-Clause 3.5, so that the Contractor is aware of its consequences under Silver Book 3.5. If it is unclear whether the Employer's communication is a determination under Sub-Clause 3.5, he may not be able to rely upon it as such.

Under Silver Book 14.7(b), the Employer's obligation is stated as being to pay the amount which "is due", subject to Sub-Clause 2.5 but irrespective of the Employer's notice under Silver Book 14.6 and irrespective of any non-binding determinations under Silver Book 3.5. This amount due may incorporate reductions to which the Employer is entitled, having claimed compensation from the Contractor in accordance with Sub-Clause 2.5 and having received no notice of dissatisfaction. If the Contractor notifies dissatisfaction with the Employer's determination under the last paragraph of Silver Book 3.5: (i)- the determination is of no effect, and the Employer cannot rely upon it as entitling him to recover such compensation; (ii)- he must still pay the amount which "is due", irrespective of the Employer's own determination under Sub-Clause 3.5; and (iii)- the answer to the question as to what amount "is due" may be determined by reference to the provisions on which the Employer based his claim, either by agreement or under the dispute resolution procedures described in Clause 20. For example, the DAB may decide the amount which was due, having been informed of the (lesser or greater) amount actually paid by the Employer. If the DAB decides that the Employer had paid less than the amount which was due under Silver Book 14.7(b), the Contractor would be entitled to financing charges under Silver Book 14.8.

Chapter 12

COMMENCEMENT OF CONSTRUCTION WORK UNDER FIDIC CONTRACTS

The "Commencement Date" is the date on which the Time for Completion commences (i.e. project calendar starts). The Contractor is required to commence the execution of the Works as soon as practicable thereafter. No period is specified within which he has to commence, because of the practical difficulties in defining what constitutes commencement.

It may be necessary to add further information regarding the arrangements for giving the Contractor possession of the Site in accordance with Sub-Clause 2.1. The Employer should not enter into the Contract until he expects to be able to comply with Sub-Clause 2.1. The Contractor cannot start work on the Site until possession has been given under Sub-Clause 2.1. The period of 42 days is specified because one or both of the Parties usually prefers an early Commencement Date.

Clause 8.1 Commencement of Work of Red Book Provides:

8.1 Commencement of Work

The Engineer shall give the Contractor not less than 7 days' notice of the Commencement Date. Unless otherwise stated in the Particular Conditions, the Commencement Date shall be within 42 days after the Contractor receives the Letter of Acceptance.

The Contractor shall commence the execution of the Works as soon as is reasonably practicable after the Commencement Date, and shall then proceed with the Works with due expedition and without delay.

Clause 8.1 Commencement of Work of Yellow Book provides:

8.1 Commencement of Work

The Engineer shall give the Contractor not less than 7 days' notice of the Commencement Date. Unless otherwise stated in the Particular Conditions, the Commencement Date shall be within 42 days after the Contractor receives the Letter of Acceptance.

The Contractor shall commence the design and execution of the Works as soon as is reasonably practicable after the Commencement Date, and shall then proceed with the Works with due expedition and without delay.

Clause 8.1 Commencement of Work of Silver Book provides:

8.1 Commencement of Work

Unless otherwise stated in the Contract Agreement: (a) the Employer shall give the Contractor not less than 7 days' notice of the Commencement Date; and (b) the Commencement Date shall be within 42 days after the date on which the Contract comes into full force and effect under Sub- Clause 1.6 [Contract Agreement]. The Contractor shall commence the design and execution of the Works as soon as is reasonably practicable after the Commencement Date, and shall then proceed with the Works with due expedition and without delay.

Failure to notify the Commencement Date in accordance with Sub-Clause 8.1 would constitute a breach of the Contract, the effect of which would depend upon the magnitude of the failure and applicable Laws. For example, if the notified Commencement Date were only a few days after the six weeks had expired, the Contractor might only be entitled to relatively small financial compensation, and not to termination. The importance of the last sentence of Sub-Clause 8.1 should not be overlooked.

Except as otherwise specified in the Particular Conditions of Contract, the Commencement Date will be the date at which the following precedent conditions have all been fulfilled and the Engineer's (in Red Book and Yellow Book) or Employer (in Saver Book) notification recording the agreement of both Parties on such fulfilment and instructing to commence the Work is received by the Contractor, which include, but not limited to: (a) signature of the Contract Agreement by both Parties, and if required, approval of the Contract by relevant authorities of the Country; (b) delivery to the Contractor of reasonable evidence of the Employer's Financial arrangement (project budget); (c) except if otherwise specified in the Contract Data, effective access to and possession of the Site given to the Contractor together with such permission(s) as required for the commencement of the Works; (d) receipt by the Contractor of the Advance provided that the corresponding bank guarantee has been delivered by the Contractor: all in accordance with the contract provisions.

The Contractor will commence the execution of the Works as soon as is reasonably practicable after the Commencement Date, and then proceed with the Works with due expedition with sufficient resources and without delay.

Notwithstanding extensions to the Time for Completion, particularly for delays which only affect part of the Works, the Contractor has to proceed expeditiously. This may, depending on the circumstances, oblige him to complete other parts (which were not affected by a delay which entitled him to an extension of time) before the expiry of the extended Time for Completion. However, the circumstances may give rise to practical difficulties in defining what constitutes "due expedition", particularly if the Employer considers himself entitled to termination under Sub-Clause 15.2(c).

Chapter 13

PROGRAMME OF CONSTRUCTION WORKS UNDER FIDIC CONTRACTS

13.1 PROGRAMME UNDER FIDIC CONTRACTS

Clause 8.3 Programme of Red Book read as follows:

Clause 8.3 Programme

The Contractor shall submit a detailed time programme to the Engineer within 28 days after receiving the notice under Sub-Clause 8.1 [Commencement of Works]. The Contractor shall also submit a revised programme whenever the previous programme is inconsistent with actual progress or with the Contractor's obligations. Each programme shall include: (a) the order in which the Contractor intends to carry out the Works, including the anticipated timing of each stage of design (if any), Contractor's Documents, procurement, manufacture of Plant, delivery to Site, construction, erection and testing; (b) each of these stages for work by each nominated Subcontractor (as defined in Clause 5 [Nominated Subcontractors]); (c) the sequence and timing of inspections and tests specified in the Contract; and (d) a supporting report which includes: (i) a general description of the methods which the Contractor intends to adopt, and of the major stages, in the execution of the Works, and (ii) details showing the Contractor's reasonable estimate of the number of each class of Contractor's Personnel and of each type of Contractor's Equipment, required on the Site for each major stage.

Unless the Engineer, within 21 days after receiving a programme, gives notice to the Contractor stating the extent to which it does not comply with the Contract, the Contractor shall proceed in accordance with the programme, subject to his other obligations under the Contract. The Employer's Personnel shall be entitled to rely upon the programme when planning their activities.

The Contractor shall promptly give notice to the Engineer of specific probable future events or circumstances which may adversely affect the work, increase the Contract Price or delay the execution of the Works. The Engineer may require the Contractor to submit an estimate of the anticipated effect of the future event or circumstances, and/or a proposal under Sub-Clause 13.3 [Variation Procedure].

If, at any time, the Engineer gives notice to the Contractor that a programme fails (to the extent stated) to comply with the Contract or to be consistent with actual progress and the Contractor's stated intentions, the Contractor shall submit a revised programme to the Engineer in accordance with this Sub-Clause.

Clause 8.3 Programme of Yellow Book read as follows:

Clause 8.3 Programme

The Contractor shall submit a detailed time programme to the Engineer within 28 days after receiving the notice under Sub-Clause 8.1 [Commencement of Works]. The Contractor shall also submit a revised programme whenever the previous programme is inconsistent with actual progress or with the Contractor's obligations. Each programme shall include: (a) the order in which the Contractor intends to carry out the Works, including the anticipated timing of each stage of design, Contractor's Documents, procurement, manufacture, inspection, delivery to Site, construction, erection, testing, commissioning and trial operation, (b) the periods for reviews under Sub-Clause 5.2 [Contractor's Documents] and for any other submissions, approvals and consents specified in the Employer's Requirements; (c) the sequence and timing of inspections and tests specified in the Contract; and (d) a supporting report which includes: (i) a general description of the methods which the Contractor intends to adopt, and of the major stages, in the execution of the Works, and (ii) details showing the Contractor's reasonable estimate of the number of each class of Contractor's Personnel and of each type of Contractor's Equipment, required on the Site for each major stage.

Unless the Engineer, within 21 days after receiving a programme, gives notice to the Contractor stating the extent to which it does not comply with the Contract, the Contractor shall proceed in accordance with the programme, subject to his other obligations under the Contract. The Employer's Personnel shall be entitled to rely upon the programme when planning their activities.

The Contractor shall promptly give notice to the Engineer of specific probable future events or circumstances which may adversely affect the work, increase the Contract Price or delay the execution of the Works. The Engineer may require the Contractor to submit an estimate of the anticipated effect of the future event or circumstances, and/or a proposal under Sub-Clause 13.3 [Variation Procedure].

If, at any time, the Engineer gives notice to the Contractor that a programme fails (to the extent stated) to comply with the Contract or to be consistent with actual progress and the Contractor's stated intentions, the Contractor shall submit a revised programme to the Engineer in accordance with this Sub-Clause.

Clause 8.3 Programme of Silver Book read as follows:

Clause 8.3 Programme

The Contractor shall submit a time programme to the Employer within 28 days after the Commencement Date. The Contractor shall also submit a revised programme whenever the previous programme is inconsistent with actual progress or with the Contractor's obligations. Unless otherwise stated in the Contract, each programme shall include: (a) the order in which the Contractor intends to carry out the Works, including the anticipated timing of each major stage of the Works; (b) the periods for reviews under Sub-Clause 5.2

[Contractor's Documents]; (c) the sequence and timing of inspections and tests specified in the Contract; and (d) a supporting report which includes: (i) a general description of the methods which the Contractor intends to adopt for the execution of each major stage of the Works, and (ii) the approximate number of each class of Contractor's Personnel and of each type of Contractor's Equipment for each major stage.

Unless the Employer, within 21 days after receiving a programme, gives notice to the Contractor stating the extent to which it does not comply with the Contract, the Contractor shall proceed in accordance with the programme, subject to his other obligations under the Contract. The Employer's Personnel shall be entitled to rely upon the programme when planning their activities.

The Contractor shall promptly give notice to the Employer of specific probable future events or circumstances which may adversely affect or delay the execution of the Works. In this event, or if the Employer gives notice to the Contractor that a programme fails (to the extent stated) to comply with the Contract or to be consistent with actual progress and the Contractor's stated intentions, the Contractor shall submit a revised programme to the Employer in accordance with this Sub-Clause.

The Employer's Personnel will, however, be bound by any constraints contained in the Contract (the periods for reviews under Yellow Book 5.2, for example), and the programme may (or may not) be suitable for calculating an extension of time. The Employer's Personnel are stated to be entitled to rely upon the programme and they may, for example, need to arrange for certain people to be available when particular parts of the Works are being executed, or when particular Contractor's Documents are to be submitted for review.

The third paragraph in the clause requires the Contractor to give notice of probable future events which may adversely affect the Works, and particularly those which may increase the actual time required for completion. Note that it is the actual time which is referred to as being affected, not the Time for Completion to which the Contractor is entitled, so the obligation to notify includes events other than those listed in Sub-Clause 8.4. Anticipation of future problems is an important part of project management. Similarly, the Employer's Personnel should keep the Contractor informed of these probable future events, it being in the Employer's interest to ensure that the Contractor is fully aware of them. There is no statement to this effect in the General Conditions, because an inadvertent failure might then be construed as excusing delayed completion. Under the second and the last sentences of Sub-Clause 8.3, the Contractor should revise the programme whenever the previous programme is inconsistent with: (i) actual progress (which may be either behind or ahead of the current version of the programme); (ii) the Contractor's obligations (accelerated completion would be consistent with such obligations), or (iii) his stated intentions.

The Contractor is required to submit a detailed time programme to the Engineer (Employer under Silver Book), by and large, within 28 days after receiving the notice of *Commencement of Works*. The Contractor is also required to submit a revised programme whenever the previous programme is inconsistent with actual progress or with the Contractor's obligations. Each programme to include: (i) The order in which the Contractor intends to carry out the Works, including the anticipated timing of each stage of design (if any), Contractor's Documents, procurement, manufacture of Plant, delivery to Site, construction, erection and testing. (ii) Each of these stages for work by each nominated Subcontractor. (iii) The sequence and timing of inspections and tests specified in the Contract. And (v) a supporting report which includes: (a) a general description of the methods which the Contractor intends to adopt, and of the major stages, in the execution of the Works, and (b) details showing the Contractor's reasonable estimate of the number of each class of Contractor's Personnel and of each type of Contractor's Equipment, required on the Site for each major stage.

By and large, under FIDIC Contracts, unless the Engineer (Employer under Silver Book), within 21 days after receiving a programme, gives notice to the Contractor stating the extent to which it does not comply with the Contract, the Contractor is required to proceed in accordance with the programme, subject to his other obligations under the Contract. This program is a working document for the Employer's Personnel who may rely upon the programme when planning their activities. If, at any time, the Engineer (Employer under Silver Book) gives notice to the Contractor that a programme fails (to the extent stated) to comply with the Contract or to be consistent with actual progress and the Contractor's stated intentions, the Contractor is required to submit a revised programme to the Engineer (Employer under Silver Book) in accordance in accordance with the contract provisions.

13.2 PROGRAMME AND FOLLOW-UP AND UPDATING SCHEDULE

Clause 8.3 Programme of Red Book has been discussed in detail under 4.3.1 above. An experienced contractor will always prepare an up-to-date programme regardless it will be required under FIDIC Red Book/Yellow Book by the Engineer to monitor progress, and under all Books by Employer's Personnel to plan their activities. However, the Sub-Clause 8.3 does not empower them to give or withhold approval to the programme, only to notify the extent to which it does not comply with the Contract. Therefore, neither Party can misuse the programme in order to achieve an unfair advantage over the other Party. Whenever there is major change occurs when may likely to delay the completion date, it is imperative that schedule is updated and resources adjusted to keep the progress of the project on track.

Since there is no approval, therefore: (i) approval cannot be wrongfully withheld unless and until the programme incorporates a constraint which was not envisaged in the Contract; and (ii) if the Contractor wrongfully submits an over-optimistic programme or supporting report (in terms of productivity, for example), there will be no approved programme or report to be used thereafter for the unquestionable validation of a claim for extension of time. It would not be reasonable for obligations to be imposed on the Employer by reason of a document which was prepared after the Contract became effective and to which consent was not required to be given, and was not given.

Chapter 14

GENERAL ASPECTS OF CONTRACTS MANAGEMENT AND ADMINISTRATION OF CONSTRUCTION PHASE

Contract management is managing the construction contracts with the principal aim to obtain the product as agreed in the contract and achieve value for money and may also involve aiming for continuous improvement in performance over the life of the contract. The foundations of contract management are, however, laid much before contract award in the detailed project report (DPR) stage of the procurement process.

The word contract can be defined in short as an agreement between the parties enforceable under the law. A contract is a legally binding agreement between the parties identified in the agreement to fulfil all the terms and conditions outlined in the agreement. A prerequisite for the enforcement of a contract, amongst other things, is the condition that all the parties to the contract accept the terms of the claimed contract. One who is in charge of the project is known as the Employer. One who agrees to execute or perform is known as the Contractor.

On International construction projects including construction projects under FIDIC Contracts, contract has a specific meaning and scope. The Contract means the Contract Agreement, the Letter of Acceptance, the Letter of Tender, these Conditions, the Specification, Bill of Quanties, the Drawings, the Schedules, Contract Data, and the further documents (if any) which are listed in the Contract Agreement or in the Letter of Acceptance as defined in the General Conditions. The terms and conditions of the contract should also include many mechanisms, such as, but not limited to; contractor bonus, liquidated damages; time period; means to measure items executed; price adjustment procedures; variation/change control procedures; foreclosure; termination; and all the other formal mechanisms that enable a contract to be implemented.

Under FIDIC contract the Parties or ordained (The Employer and the Contractor) to enter into a Contract Agreement within **28 days** after the Contractor receives the Letter of Acceptance, unless the Particular Conditions establish otherwise, whilst the Contract Agreement must be based upon the form annexed to the Particular Conditions. It also requires that the costs of stamp duties and similar charges (if any) imposed by law in connection with entry into the Contract Agreement must be borne by the Employer.

There are, however certain constraints that must be observed. For example Assignment, which dictates that neither Party shall assign the whole or any part of the Contract or any benefit or interest in or under the Contract with a proviso that either Party: (a) may assign the whole or any part with the prior agreement of the other Party, at the sole discretion of such other Party; and (b) may, as security in favour of a bank or financial institution, assign its right to any moneys due, or to become due, under the Contract.

Performance Security or Security Deposit is the amount to be paid by the contractor to the Employer before signing of contract as a security against performance. The amount varies from 5 % to 10 % of the estimated cost put to tender. This security can be furnished in form of a bank guarantee in the prescribed form.

Some contracts provide for mobilisation advance to the contractor @ 5 % of the contract amount against a bank guarantee in the prescribed form. These advances are paid at the beginning of the contract or commencement of the work. The purpose is to provide cash to the contractor for initial infrastructure required to be created to take up the actual construction work. The Employer shall make an advance payment, at a stipulated interest for mobilisation and cash flow support, when the Contractor submits a guarantee in accordance with the contract. The total advance payment, the number and timing of instalments (if more than one), and the applicable currencies and proportions, shall be as stated in the Contract Data.

Unless and until the Employer receives this guarantee, or if the total advance payment is not stated in the Contract Data, then no advance shall be payable. If there is a provision for advance payment in the contract then the Engineer shall deliver to the Employer and to the Contractor an Interim Payment Certificate for the advance payment or its first instalment after receiving a Statement under the provisions for [Application for Interim Payment Certificates]) and after the Employer receives (i) the Performance Security in accordance with the provision for [Performance Security] and (ii) a guarantee in amounts and currencies equal to the advance payment. This guarantee shall be issued by an entity and from within a country approved by the Employer, and shall be in the form approved by the Employer.

The Contractor must ensure that the guarantee is valid and enforceable until the advance payment has been repaid, but its amount shall be progressively reduced by the amount repaid by the Contractor as indicated in the Payment Certificates. If the terms of the guarantee specify its expiry date, and the advance payment has not been repaid prior to the expiry date, the Contractor shall extend the validity of the guarantee until the advance payment has been repaid.

Major projects, regardless they are predominantly building, civil engineering, chemical engineering, electrical engineering, mechanical engineering, or any combination, are, by and large, complex. With the increasing complexity of contract conditions, it is becoming increasingly important for them to be based upon a standardised form of contract with which the contracting parties and financial institutions are familiar. The contracting parties, by and large, will react favourably to such a standardised form of contract, which should lessen the likelihood of unsatisfactory performance, increased costs and disputes. If the contract is to be based on standard conditions of contract, tenderers should not need to make financial provision for unfamiliar contract conditions. Furthermore, the widespread use of standard conditions facilitates the training of personnel in contract management, reducing the need for them having to work with ever-changing contract conditions.

At the inception stage of a project of any major construction project, procurement options should be reviewed and a decision made as to the most appropriate option available and the procurement of project should include the determination of the appropriate procurement strategy, with decisions being reached on the matters such as: the works to be executed under contract (often called "contract packaging"); the extent of design to be provided to, or to be carried out by, the contractor; and lump-sum, measure-and-value, cost-plus or other basis for determining the final contract price.

For a large project, decisions on the number and scope of contracts may be critical to the success of the project to meet the triple constraint criteria. Having a large number of contracts may give the Employer more control than under a single contract for the entire project, and may be more economic by maximising competitive pricing. But nevertheless, these advantages may be offset by a greater extent of co-ordination risk borne by the Employer.

For each contract, the party responsible for the design will develop the design during the detailed design stage and if the design is carried out by (or on behalf of) the Employer, he will have a much greater control over the details. But by this approach problems may arise on occasions from the division of responsibility between designer and constructor. On the other hand if the construction Contractor is responsible for the design, he will wish to develop it in his own interests, subject to any constraints in the Contract and also the Employer will have less control over the design than he would have if he was responsible for providing the design himself. Also under Contractor-design, the contract price would typically have been tendered on a lump-sum basis, so any change in cost (increase or decrease) to the Contractor resulting from design development will be the Contractor's risk and would not be passed on to the Employer.

Under FIDIC Red Book, design is the responsibility of the Employer, except to the extent that Contractor-design is specified in the Contract. The Specification must therefore clearly state which (if any) parts of the Works shall be designed by the Contractor, and should also specify the appropriate criteria with which these parts shall comply. If most of the Works are to be designed by the Contractor, Red Book would usually be considered inappropriate and more suited in Yellow Book.

Under Yellow Book or Silver Book, design is the responsibility of the Contractor and he will wish to economise, in terms of his costs, which may be at the expense of compromising on quality. Therefore, it is essential consideration for the Employer to have in-house (or procures) expert technical services, in order to ensure that his requirements are elaborated in the tender documents and are achieved in practice. If expertise is unavailable, problems may arise, particularly in respect of the need for variations. Accordingly, under a contract for Contractor-design: (i) variations should be instructed as varied requirements with which the Contractor's design must comply, and not as a varied design instructed by (or on behalf of) the Employer; and (ii) - the costs and other consequences of variations should be agreed in advance, so as to minimise disputes. In practice, however, these aspects can make Contractor-design appear somewhat rigged. Also Contractor-design is typically less amenable to variations initiated by the Employer, compared with Red Book' Employer-design where the designer is independent of the Contractor.

Furthermore Contractor-design prevents the Employer from having a close involvement in the design process, it does enable him to have the benefits of (i) lump-sum pricing; (ii) the Contractor's undivided liability for the works (including design); and (iii) the potential savings (in cost and time) due to a degree of overlap of design and construction. This overlap of design and construction may (or may not) lessen the total period between the commencement of the preparation of tender documents and the completion of construction, because the saving may be offset by the lack of continuity of the design processes during the pre-contract stages (unlike under Red Book' Employer-design, design development should continue uninterrupted). Accordingly, procurement should commence with strategic decisions on contract packaging and, for each contract, on the allocation of design responsibility and on the basis for determining the contract price.

Tenderers for a construction contract need to study hydrological and sub-surface data, to the extent that this data is relevant to the particular type of works, in order to plan and estimate the costs of the excavation and other works. Under Red Book contract, this is the primary use of this data, which the Employer makes available under but under Yellow Book and Silver Book contract, and also in the case of a Red Book contract which includes a significant element of Contractor-design, tenderers will require additional relevant data on hydrological, sub-surface and other conditions on the Site in order to design and determine the details of the works for which costs are to be estimated. Tenderers for Contractor-design works require as much data as that required by the Employer's designer under Red Book. They may require even more data, because the Employer's designer would co-ordinate the pre-tender sub-surface investigations to suit the specific location's requirement.

In contrast, when the Employer arranges for pre-tender investigations in order to obtain the data needed by the tenderers' designers, he may find it difficult to anticipate their preferred locations. Tenderers require considerable data for the preparation of tenders for Silver Book contract, under which the Contractor assumes much greater risks than under a Red Book or Yellow Book contract.

If the risk of sub-surface conditions is significant, taking account of the type of works, it may be in the Employer's interests for the contract to allocate this risk to the Employer, either by amending Silver Book 4.12 or by using Yellow Book. Similarly, if other Silver Book-only risks are significant, the Employer should carefully consider the consequences of allocating them to the Contractor. FIDIC's publication of Silver Book does not constitute any indication of its suitability for a particular set of circumstances.

Accordingly, selection of the appropriate Book (two Books for Contractor-design: Yellow Book and Silver Book) requires important decisions to be made on procurement strategy. The important consideration is that tender documents need to be drafted with care, particularly in respect of quality, tests and performance criteria for Contractor-design contracts. If tender documents are deficient, the Employer may pay an very high price for unacceptable works. The Employer must therefore ensure that adequate resources are allocated to the skilled tasks of drafting the technical and commercial aspects of the tender documents, and of analysing the tenderers' proposals followed by preparation of adequate prequalification Documentation

In practice it has been found that, particularly for contracts which include Contractor-design, prequalification of tenderers is particularly desirable. It enables the Employer to establish the competence of a known number of companies and joint ventures who are subsequently invited to tender. Restricting tendering to a pre-determined number encourages the better qualified entities to tender in the knowledge that they have a reasonable chance of success. Procedures for the prequalification of prospective tenderers may, however, be imposed by the applicable laws of the country, or by the requirements of the financial institutions who will be providing funds for the project. In particular, they may not permit any limit on the number of prequalified tenderers.

By and large , the Employer initiates the prequalification stage of the project, by publishing advertisements which either (i) contain all the necessary information on the project and on how applicants should apply for prequalification; or (ii) describe how to obtain a document which contains all this prequalification information.

Such information should include: (a) information on the prequalification procedure, including qualification criteria and any relevant policies which the Employer may have (on joint ventures, on the intended number of prequalified tenderers, and/or on preference for local firms, for example); (b) instructions on the language and content of each application for prequalification (completion of FIDIC's "Standard prequalification forms for contractors", for example) and on the time and place for its submission; and (c) information on the contract (and on the project of which it forms part, if any), including the names of the Employer and the Engineer or Employer's Representative, location of site, description of works, anticipated time programme, contract law and language, form of contract (i.e., name of FIDIC's Book), source of finance, currencies of payment, and any other unusual features or constraints.

Other information on the contract may also be included, such as the Employer's intentions regarding securities and price escalation provisions. However, the Employer may not have reached decisions on these matters before inviting applications for prequalification. Primarily, prospective applicants need sufficient information to assess their interest in submitting tenders. They do not need to assess various other matters which only become relevant when they receive all the tender documents.

The Employer should therefore, in his own interests and unless he is not permitted to do so, limit both the number of prequalified tenderers and the extent of the details which they are required to submit with their tenders. The prequalification information should ideally indicate the number of firms and joint ventures which are expected to be prequalified. This number should be determined carefully, taking account of the requirements of any financial institution providing funds for the project, and of the work required for the preparation of a compliant tender. Whereas six to eight tenderers might be appropriate for an uncomplicated CONS contract, four or five might be preferable for Contractor-designed works, and three might suffice for complex turnkey works.

Having analysed the applications, the Employer should notify each applicant whether it has been prequalified to tender for the Contract. Notice should be given as soon as the Employer has reached his decision on the applications, and should not await the completion or issue of the tender documents. If issue of the tender documents seems likely to be delayed, the prequalified prospective tenderers should be notified accordingly, so that they can plan the future activities of their estimating teams. Tenders should not be invited until the Employer has obtained the necessary financing, or has advised prospective tenderers of the financial situation so that they are aware of the outstanding financing arrangements.

When invited to tender, each tenderer may be able to discover the number (and possibly abilities) of the competing tenderers. If so, he may compare the benefits of being awarded the contract with his estimated tendering costs and chance of success. These costs may be substantial for Contractor-designed Works, particularly if the Employer requests tenderers to submit extensive details of their designs.

When tender documents have been prepared and project funding arrangements have been finalised, the Employer should write Letter of Invitation to each tenderer and invite him to submit a Tender, which includes information which may not be available when the tender documents were prepared, and which the example forms of Instructions therefore refer to as being specified in the Invitation. The other documents issued to prospective tenderers will, by and large include: (a) Instructions to Tenderers, including descriptions of the compliance criteria for tenders and of the procedures for submitting and evaluating them, which become irrelevant when the Employer accepts a Tender. The Instructions specify the procedures to be followed until the Employer either enters into a Contract or advises tenderers that the Employer does not intend to do so.

Such procedures include, for example, those for a joint site visit (if any) and for the preparation, submission, opening and evaluation of Tenders. Also, the Instructions should define what will comprise a responsive The Instructions to Tenderers could be based upon FIDIC's example form. Instructions should define what will comprise a responsive Tender requirements which are directed to the tenderers and are superseded by the award of the Contract. Letter of Tender should be based upon the Example Form at the end of each Book.

Tender Documentation to include: Specification; and Drawings (for Red Book Contract and. Employer's Requirements, which may include some drawings (for Yellow Book and silver Book); Information and data on hydrological and sub-surface conditions at the Site, studies on environmental impact, and reports on any other investigations initiated by the Employer. The Contractor's obligations should be stated in clear unambiguous terms, and not in such a way that the application of opinion or judgement is necessary. Vague phrases, which tenderers would find difficult to understand to the precision necessary for pricing e.g. specifying the use of "up-to-date technology"), should be avoided.

For Contractor-design, the Employer may wish to encourage the tenderer to propose solutions complying with requirements which the Employer can only describe in subjective terms. If the Employer wishes to include subjective requirements, they should only be stated in the Instructions to Tenderers. Each tenderer can then propose solutions as part of his Tender. It is then these solutions in the Tender which (unlike the subjective requirement in the Instructions to Tenderers) will form part of the Contract.

In order to manage tendering procedures effectively, it may be advisable for one person to be appointed (by the Employer, Engineer or Employer's Representative) as tendering co-ordinator, responsible for: (i) despatching the tender documents to each prospective tenderer; (ii) ensuring that each tenderer has formally acknowledged receipt of the tender documents (iii) managing the site inspection, having ensured that tenderers have received details of the arrangements: the tendering co-ordinator should prepare an agenda, appropriate supplementary briefing information for the visitors, and a record of the visit; (iv) receiving and responding to queries from prospective tenderers, such as:: (a) a question which could have been asked by any tenderer to all tenderers; (b) a question which relates solely to the tenderer's particular proposals for carrying out the contract (for example, regarding the acceptability in principle of a possible alternative design) should be regarded as confidential and answered to the enquiring tenderer only, the other tenderers not being advised; (c) if amendments need to be made to the Tender Documents, the tendering coordinator should issue to prospective tenderers an Addendum to Tender Documents, and ensure that each tenderer has formally acknowledged receipt.

After receiving and analysing the tenders, the successful tenderer will enter into contract with the Employer. Unsuccessful tenderers will retain the copyright of their designs and the Employer must return their designs, without copies being retained and without releasing details to the successful tenderer, i.e. the Contractor.

Chapter 15

SUPERVISION, MANAGEMENT AND CONTROL OF CONSTRUCTION IN GENERAL

It is, however, vital to build a contract that identifies clearly the obligations of the parties (contractor and the employer). For example, the contract must be built on a firm formal and legal foundation whilst it should be flexible, to accommodate changes, variations etc.

Good contract management goes much further than ensuring that the agreed terms of the contract are being met. For example, since there will always be some friction between the different perspectives and approach of employer and contractor, good contract management must strive to resolve or minimise such friction and achieve the completion of the project on time, every time as envisaged in the contracts. Good Contract management consists of the full and proper fulfilment of roles and responsibilities. The main task areas are site management, adherence to specifications, and contract administration.

One of the chief reasons for project delays is poor contract management, and any or all of the following may happen: (i) Parties fail to understand their obligations and responsibilities. (ii) There is inaction and/or misinterpretation at the implementing level, with too many issues being referred to top management for decisions. (iv) Progress is slow and the inability to proceed forward gets compounded. (v) The expected product specifications are not realised.

There are also several reasons why organizations fail to manage contracts successfully. For example, some possible reasons include: (a) Poorly drafted contracts. (b) Inadequate resources assigned to contract management. (c) Project team and the contractor team lacking skills and or experience. (d) Inexperienced people being put in place causes personality clashes. (e) Contents, responsibilities and obligations of the contract are not well appreciated and understood. (f) Inadequate delegation of authority and /or responsibility, resulting in financial decisions not being taken in time. (g) Failure to monitor and manage retained responsibilities due to external interference and pressures from stakeholders.

In the International construction, many organizations are moving towards building constructive relationships with contractors for the benefit of both parties, which is the key to successful project management. In this context, the factors that are essential for good contract management, include but not limited to: (a) Good preparation of bid document, e.g. a detailed estimate, project report of the work helps create a clear output-based specification. Proper eligibility criterion effective evaluation procedures and selection will ensure that the contract is awarded to the right person. (b) The right contract form, e.g. since the contract is the foundation for the project implementation, it should include aspects such as obligations of the parties, the quality assurance of items required, and defect liability period, as well as procedures for variations and dispute resolution.

Above all, a good contract management practice is proactive aiming to anticipate and respond to project needs. For example, if contracts are not well managed from the employer side, any or all of the following may happen: (i) the contractor is likely to neglect the quality, resulting in substandard product that is not durable and structurally unsafe; (ii) decisions are not taken at the right time – or not taken at all; (iii) that leads to delays in payment, approvals - leading to claims; and time and cost overrun; etc.

Good project preparation and the right contract are essential foundations for effective contract management and contract administration. Contract administration handles the formal governance of the contract and changes to the contract documentation, which are inevitable. In long term contracts, where interdependency between employer and contractor is inevitable, it is in the interests of both parties to make the relationship work smoothly and together with a unified approach all these areas must be managed successfully.

It must always be understood that the four key factors for success are: trust; good communication; honesty; and recognition of mutual aims. Accordingly, management structures for the contract need to be designed these factors built-in and to facilitate effective implementation and staff involved must at all levels show their commitment to it approach. Information flows and proper communication should be stipulated at the beginning of a contract, and maintained throughout contract period. There should be set procedures for raising issues and resolving disputes, so that they are dealt with as early as possible and at the appropriate level in the organization.

I have used this approach whilst assigned as the Engineer's representing on Constructional project of Central Lancashire New Town development and I am having pride in stating that I successfully completed more that 35 contracts and none of the contract went into dispute. I always considered the contractor as part of my team. I worked on three fundamental principle, namely: Be Firm; Be Fair; and Be Reasonable and with the application of these principles, I not only achieved success of all my projects on triple constraint (within budget, within time schedule, and within quality parameters) but exceeding on all these also earned the respect of top management of both my employer as well as management of all my contractors. I always went an extra miles in discharging my roles in contracts management.

I made all my project decision proactively and without fear or undue favour. I recall once we received a Memorandum from British Government to the effect that prior we must seek prior approval from the government before committing to the addition expenditure on the project. I within taking notice of this memorandum and continued to make my project decisions. Whenever I felt that extra work is necessary to complete the project I did not hesitate to issue change order instruction, which was in my power, and subsequently got approval for that work. My counterparts took the memorandum literary and delayed the projects whilst getting approval and consequently there projects went into claims and disputes.

Regarding the principles of mutual trust and good communication I recall an incident, when I received a complaint from one of my contractor's management about one of my Clerks of Works that he interfered with the site work without the contractor asking for inspection and developed into argument with the contractor's personnel. I called the managing director of the contractor in my site office and gone through with him the detail of interference and explained that the Clerk of Works acted for the contractor's benefit and saved a lot of money for the contractor. The issue was that the Contractor was laying pipes in the duel trench and mistakenly laying fuel pipe above the surface water pipe which was illogical so the Clerk of Works interfered. I explained to the MD by showing him the drawing that if he would have waited until the job completed then inevitably the whole work would have been rejected thereby the contractor would have been forced to rework and that would have eaten his profit. The Managing Director not only apologised from the Clerk of Work but since that day onwards extensive trust and cooperation to the extent that few other contracts successfully completed with the same team with mutual trust.

Regarding principle of honesty, I recall an incident when on a day-work sheet I paid the contractor more than ten time the contractor asked for and it so happened that the Auditor raised this point with me by stating that he has first time come across such an action. In response to the Auditor's comment, I asked him that if I would have paid the contractor only 10% what he asked for, would that be on his list, his answer was in negative. Then I explained to him that such discrepancies only occur due to genuine mistake or oversight. I showed him progress photographs and explained that the work involved took three days to construct with plant and labour and the contractor also put 3 days timber hire charges whilst timber was there in place for more that 30 days therefore I corrected it and consequently it raised the value of the day-work sheet. The Auditor was so pleased and satisfied that he too went extra and within an hour I received a memorandum from him agreeing with the final account I submitted for audit.

Regarding recognition of mutual aims, I adopted a very fair and flexible approach. For example for interim payment certificate I used to call the Contractor's project manager with his QS in my office and go through interim account and agreeing what to pay and what not to pay and subsequently I was receiving interim accounts which I was certifying for payment with no red marking and or correction as it was pre-agreed. My counterparts were handing this responsibility to their QSs and they were making many changes thereby developing arguments during progress meetings. With my approach there were no arguments and my project went smoothly without any hassle. I was working on the principle that since the contractor work is always (up to 2 months) in hand, therefore to cut his interim account provide no benefit to the Employer, but on the contrary it helps the completion of the projects. It was also my practice to help my contractors to release payment earlier, than the usual practice of releasing payment on last specified day, to help their cash-flow, upon receiving requests from the management of the contractors.

Regarding being Firm, I never paid the contractor on his plea that they are losing money because of bad rate put in the contract by the estimator but strictly what he was entitled to under the contract and never compromised on the quality or works. I was however flexible in approving the substituted material provided it was better than the specified one because to me specification is minimum standard of quality.

Together with good contract management, a good contract administration is the key to the success of the projects. Contract administration, the formal governance of the contract, includes such tasks as: contract maintenance and change control; charges and cost monitoring; variation order process and payment procedures; management reporting; etc. Accordingly, the importance of contract administration to the success of the contract, and to the relationship between employer and contractor, should not be underestimated. For example, clear administrative procedures will ensure that the parties to the contract understand **who does what, when, and how.** The contract documentation itself must continue to accurately reflect the arrangement, and changes to it as per stipulated procedures, and carefully controlled. Responsibility for authorising different types of variations will often rest with top management, and documented internal procedures should reflect this.

Contract administration will require appropriate resourcing and the responsibility falls on the contract manager to provide such resources. It is important that all members of the team deal promptly with contract administration tasks, during the various stages of the contract implementation. Some typical procedures that combine to make up contract administration include, but not limited to: (i) Contract document maintenance and variation/change control; (ii) Cost monitoring; (iii) Variation/change ordering procedures; (iv) Payment procedures; Project funding procedures; (v) Planning and resource management; (vi) Management reporting; (vii) Project Asset management. It should be borne in mind that additional administrative procedures may also be needed.

These procedures will need to be designed to reflect the specific works in the contract so that contractual relationships evolve and must respond to changes in the work environment. It follows that in response to changing requirements, the contract document itself must be capable of evolving efficiently and effectively, through formal change control procedures and by mutual consent. Rather than relying on informal arrangements, It is preferable to update documentation as changes occur.

To keep the contract documentation up to date is an important activity, and should be entrusted to an experienced person i.e. document control manager. The effort required may be minimised by prescribing the formats for variation/change order, interim payments etc. The contract must clearly stipulate provisions to enable required changes and pricing mechanism within agreed parameters. Without needing to change the contract documentation or conditions, procedures should be established to keep the contract documentation up to date and to ensure that all documents relating to the contract are consistent. For a large or complex contract, however, some form of change control procedure is needed.

Applying document management principles involves: (i) Identifying all relevant documentation (including contract clauses and schedules, procedures manuals etc); (ii) Change control, variation procedures, and ensuring no changes are made without appropriate authorisation from the competent authorities; (iii) Recording the status of every document (current/historic, draft/final); (iv) Ensuring consistency across various documents.

The supervision of the project needs to be handled by an experienced team of persons or experts of relevant fields. For infrastructure contracts, there is a practice to invite bids from consultants with relevant experience. The bid document for the consultancy services typically comprise Terms of Reference (TOR), standard conditions of consultancy contract, period of completion, payment schedule etc. The TOR includes the type of personnel to be appointed by the consultant for the job and their qualifications, experience, period on the project (man-months) etc.

The role of the supervision consultant is very crucial for the contract management and completion of the project. Apart from the day-to-day supervision, the Project Management Consultant (PMC) has to carry out documentation of the contract and the project. Generally, the entire correspondence with the Contractor is made through the PMC. It is therefore important to have a capable, qualified and experienced PMC on the job who understands the various provisions of the contract. FIDIC has also published "Client-Consultant Agreement (White Book) Guide" 2nd Ed. This document can be used with project specific changes.

The exact monitoring requirements and methodology will depend on the nature of the contract and the project to be completed. There are some standard practices that can apply. These include, but not limited to: (i) Monitoring the contractor's performance against the specific targets and milestones laid down in the contract i.e. a particular milestone being reached in stipulated time. (ii) Inspection of completed work or random sample checks. (iii) The contractor providing information and reports on his own performance. (iv) Regular review meetings held between the Employer and contractor. (v) Recording complaints received from client, specific systems may need to be set up where a good complaints or customer satisfaction procedure like ISO 9000 can be prescribed.

In standard contracts, the Contractor is expected to institute a quality assurance system to demonstrate compliance with the requirements of the Contract. The system should be in accordance with the details stated in the Contract. The Engineer must be entitled to audit any aspect of the system. Details of all procedures and compliance documents must be submitted to the Engineer for information before each design and execution stage is commenced. When any document of a technical nature is issued to the Engineer, evidence of the prior approval by the Contractor himself should be apparent on the document itself. Compliance with the quality assurance system, however, must not relieve the Contractor of any of his duties, obligations or responsibilities under the Contract.

Construction programme in simple words is the activity chart of the contractor as to how he intends to complete the project within the prescribed time schedule. The contractor has to submit the Construction Programme immediately on commencement of the contract. The periodic review will indicate the status of the project as well as how contractor is performing. The monitoring of Construction Programme will also help the Engineer and the Employer to take timely, corrective measures. The contractor has to revise and submit the Construction Programme if deemed necessary as per the provisions of the contract. The Engineer may ask for modifications in the programme if found necessary. The approved programme becomes the basis for the performance evaluation and project monitoring. The contractor has to submit the cash-flow, equipment, manpower details to the Engineer for evaluation of the Construction Programme. The Engineer's decision in the Construction Programme is final and binding on the contractor.

The progress of the contract is monitored with reference to the approved contraction programme. Generally, monthly progress reports are to be prepared by the Contractor and submitted to the Engineer (Employer in Silver Book Contract) in multiple copies.

The first report must cover the period up to the end of the first calendar month following the Commencement Date. Reports must be submitted monthly thereafter, each within 7 days after the last day of the period to which it relates. Reporting should continue until the Contractor has completed all work.

Each report should typically include: (a) Charts and detailed descriptions of progress, including each stage of design (if any), Contractor's Documents, procurement, manufacture, delivery to Site, construction, erection and testing; and including these stages for work by each nominated Subcontractor. (b) Photographs showing the status of manufacture and of progress on the Site. (c) For the manufacture of each main item of Plant and Materials, the name of the manufacturer, manufacture location, percentage progress, and the actual or expected dates of: (i) commencement of manufacture,(ii) Contractor's inspections, (iii) tests, and (iv) shipment and arrival at the Site. (d) Details described in contract. (e) copies of quality assurance documents, test results and certificates of Materials. (f) list of notices given under contract [Employer's Claims] and notices given under contract [Contractor's Claims]. (g) safety statistics, including details of any hazardous incidents and activities relating to environmental aspects and public relations. (h) Comparisons of actual and planned progress, with details of any events or circumstances which may jeopardise the completion in accordance with the Contract, and the measures being adopted to overcome delays.

Effective control ensures that both parties fulfil their contractual obligations. The contract manager must record, co-ordinate and communicate what is and has happened with the contract. This information can then be used for forward planning and any future contracts likely to be undertaken. A skill that is required for effective control is the ability to identify problems that require corrective action. The types of problems that might occur include: (i) Unsatisfactory performance. (ii) Misunderstanding the requirement. (iii) Inadequate channels of communication. (iv) Changes to the contract, brought about by unexpected requirements.

Contract control involves actively keeping the contractor's performance to the required standard. Participation by both parties is needed if this is to be successful, to enable any problems to be quickly identified and resolved. If monitoring indicates that a contractor's performance has deteriorated, action will need to be taken as per contract provisions. The nature of the action, however, will depend upon the level of the under-performance or shortfall. If regular monitoring is effectively carried out, problems will be identified early and the degree of any disruption from the target and corrective action will be minimised.

In every contract there is a provision for the extension of the time for completion of the project for reasons beyond the control of the contractor. The contractor, however, has to continuously report to the engineer delays occurring in the project, which entitles him for extension of time for completion. The Engineer must assess and determine the admissible extension to the contractor due to these delays. The Engineer shall satisfy that the delays are beyond the control of the contractor and he is entitled to the extension as per the provisions of the contract. In that case the Engineer shall notify the contractor and the Employer, the certificate of extension of time for completion.

The Contractor shall be entitled subject to contract provisions to an extension of the time for completion if and to the extent that completion for the purposes of contract taking-over of the works or sectional completion is or will be delayed by any of the following causes: (a) Variation (unless an adjustment to the Time for Completion has been agreed under the contract's Variation Procedure) or other substantial change in the quantity of an item of work included in the Contract. (b) Cause of delay giving an entitlement to extension of time under contract conditions. (c) Exceptionally adverse climatic conditions. (d) Unforeseeable shortages in the availability of personnel or Goods caused by epidemic or governmental actions. Or (e) Any delay, impediment or prevention caused by or attributable to the Employer, the Employer's Personnel, or the Employer's other contractors.

If the Contractor considers himself to be entitled to an extension of the Time for Completion, the Contractor shall give notice to the Engineer in accordance with the provisions of the contract. When determining each extension of time under the contract, the Engineer shall review previous determinations and may increase, but shall not decrease, the total extension of time.

Liquidated damage is the predetermined amount to be paid by the contractor to the Employer for the delays in completion of the project or achievement of a stipulated milestone. A milestone is the pre-decided stage of the project to be completed by the contractor in the prescribed period as per contract. Non-achievement of a stipulated milestone will render contractor liable to pay the stipulated liquidated damages to the Employer unless the period is extended.

The liquidated damages are prescribed in the contract, as an amount to be paid per day or per week. This amount, payable by the contractor, is generally deducted from the interim payments due to the contractor. It needs to be noted that this is not a source of revenue to the Employer, or a penalty to the contractor in the strict sense. It is an estimated predetermined damage to be paid by the contractor to the Employer on failure of performance like non-achievement of stipulated milestone in the contract.

A successful arrangement requires a mutual commitment to adapting to changing circumstances. Reasons for change during contracts can come from a range of sources, both internal and external. Whatever the reasons, it is important to realise the implications of change for the contract and all parties involved. There could be implications or concerns in areas such as continuing value for money, and the possibility of moving beyond the original scope of the requirement. Change is easier to deal with when preparations are made. Not every possibility can be foreseen and planned for, but it is desirable that the contract includes some flexibility as well as the necessary procedures for handling changes.

A properly managed change can be a good opportunity to alter or improve the project, prompted by: (i) Significant revisions to the corporate strategy and/or/ corporate objectives of either party. (ii) Developments, changes in technology. (iii) Public demand. (iv) Change in the requirements of the Employer. (v) Changes in local legislations or development plans etc. (vi) Financial or other restraints.

The importance of understanding the implications of change from the perspective of both parties cannot be overemphasised as change to a contractual arrangement affects the scope, and thus the viability of the contract, for either or both parties. To an extent, both parties are taking a calculated risk when they enter long term contract arrangements that the cumulative effect of change over the term will balance out for both. Joint planning of change is vital if risks are to be minimised. It is essential that both parties have realistic expectations of what the contract will deliver at the outset.

Changes are always easier to manage when they are planned. Even where they occur without warning, it is often possible to foresee what might happen and plan for what can be done. According to the type of contract, the contractor may be closely involved in planning the changes, or may even be entirely accountable for them. Changes will always need to be negotiated with the contractor by the Engineer.

In all cases, it is likely that there will be consequent changes, leading to a contract variation that will need to be negotiated with the contractor. Key principles of this re-negotiation are that: the contract(s) should have provisions for such change; and the employer should always be aware of the possibility of the contractor seeking to increase their profitability. Therefore, solutions and the associated costs proposed by the contractor should always be rigorously audited by the expert for best value. Change control procedures should be included in the contract.

The respective roles and responsibilities of both parties in the change control process must be clearly identified, along with the procedures for raising, evaluating, costing and approving change requests. A change control procedure should apply to all changes, although there may be certain delegated or shortened procedures available in defined circumstances – such as delegated budget tolerance levels within which a contract manager or the Engineer would not have to seek senior management approval. However, flexibility needs to be built into this procedure to deal with issues such as emergencies.

A change control procedure should provide a clear set of steps and clearly allocated responsibilities covering: requesting changes; assessment of impact; prioritisation and authorisation; agreement with contractor; control of implementation; documentation of change assessments and variation orders.

Responsibility for authorising different types of change will often rest with competent authorities, and documented internal procedures should reflect this. In particular, changes to the overall contract, such as changes to prices outside the scope of agreed price variation mechanisms, must have senior management approval. In many cases, it will be possible to delegate limited powers to authorise minor changes using agreed processes. Appropriate structures need to be established, with representatives of both employer and contractor management, for reviewing and authorising change requests.

The Contractor must not make any alteration and/or modification of the Permanent Works, unless and until the Engineer instructs or approves a Variation. The Contractor may, at any time, submit to the Engineer a written proposal which will, if adopted, (i) accelerate completion, (ii) reduce the cost to the Employer of executing, maintaining or operating the Works, (iii) improve the efficiency or value to the Employer of the completed Works, or (iv) otherwise be of benefit to the Employer. The proposal shall be prepared at the cost of the Contractor and shall include the items listed in the contract [Variation Procedure]. If a proposal, which is approved by the Engineer, includes a change in the design of part of the Permanent Works, then unless otherwise agreed by both Parties: (a) The Contractor shall design this part. (b) Contractor's General Obligations shall apply. (c) If this change results in a reduction in the contract value of this part, the Engineer shall proceed in accordance with the contract [Determinations] to agree or determine a fee, which shall be included in the Contract Price. This fee shall be decided as per the provisions of the contract.

If this Sub-Clause applies, the amounts payable to the Contractor shall be adjusted for rises or falls in the cost of Labour, Goods and other inputs to the Works, by the addition or deduction of the amounts determined by the formulae prescribed in this Sub-Clause. To the extent that full compensation for any rise or fall in Costs is not covered by the provisions of this or other Clauses, the Accepted Contract Amount shall be deemed to have included amounts to cover the contingency of other rises and falls in costs.

The adjustment to be applied to the amount otherwise payable to the Contractor, as valued in accordance with the appropriate Schedule and certified in Payment Certificates, shall be determined from formulae for each of the currencies in which the Contract Price is payable. No adjustment is to be applied to work valued on the basis of Cost or current prices. The formulae shall be included in the contract with base indices for calculating the price adjustment. It may not always be possible to predict all variations. Changes to the requirements normally affect the cost and so will need to be recorded. It may be decided that during the course of the contract, a slight change to the requirement is needed due to external factors.

Changes to the contract may affect: The stipulated specifications; the quantity of items in BOQ; completion times or milestones. It will normally be the role of the contract manager to ensure that the need for any contract variation is recorded and is varied in line with the procurement procedures for variations. The variation must be clearly tied in with the main contract so a clear audit trail is possible.

The Contract should provide for the period, minimum amount of interim amount to be paid to the contractor. It should also provide for interest on delayed payments. It needs to be borne in mind that it is the responsibility of the Employer to make payment in time as this affects the cash flow of the contractor and in turn the performance and completion of the project.

Further the contract can also provide for interim payments to the contractor at prescribed interval for the work completed. Payment to the contractor should be made as prescribed and provided in the contract. Generally the Contractor shall submit a Statement in multiple copies to the Engineer after the end of each month, in a form approved by the Engineer. This bill shall indicate showing in detail the amounts to which the Contractor considers himself to be entitled, together with supporting documents.

Thereafter, the Engineer shall, within prescribed period after receiving a Statement and supporting documents, deliver to the Employer and to the Contractor an Interim Payment Certificate which shall state the amount which the Engineer fairly determines to be due, with all supporting particulars for any reduction or withholding made by the Engineer on the Statement if any. The Employer has to then make payment as per the certificate of the Engineer. The Employer should carry out some in-house checking so as to avoid in correct payment. As per the standard contract provisions all payments to the contractor are running or advance payments. Hence any over payment or mistake in payment can be rectified in the subsequent or the final bill.

Within the prescribed period after receiving the Performance Certificate, the Contractor shall submit, to the Engineer, multiple copies of a draft final statement with supporting documents showing in detail in a form approved by the Engineer:(a) the value of all work done in accordance with the Contract, and (b) any further sums which the Contractor considers to be due to him under the Contract or otherwise. If the Engineer disagrees with the draft final statement, the Contractor shall submit such further information as the Engineer may reasonably require within the prescribed period and shall make such changes in the draft as may be agreed between them. The Contractor shall then prepare and submit to the Engineer the final statement as agreed. This agreed statement is generally referred to as the "Final Statement".

However if, there is any dispute to the draft final statement, the Engineer shall deliver to the Employer an Interim Payment Certificate for the agreed parts of the draft final statement. Thereafter, if the dispute is finally resolved under the contract, the Contractor shall then prepare and submit to the Employer a Final Statement. When submitting the Final Statement, the Contractor shall submit a discharge, which confirms that the total of the Final Statement represents full and final settlement of all moneys due to the Contractor under the Contract. This discharge may state that it becomes effective when the Contractor has received the Performance Security and the outstanding balance of this total, in which event the discharge shall be effective on such date.

After receiving the Final Statement and discharge in accordance with the contract, the Engineer shall deliver, to the Employer and to the Contractor the Final Payment Certificate which shall state: The amount is finally due, and After giving credit to the Employer for all amounts previously paid by the Employer and for all sums to which the Employer is entitled, the balance (if any) due from the Employer to the Contractor or from the Contractor to the Employer, as the case may be.

If the Contractor has not applied for a Final Payment Certificate in accordance with the contract, the Engineer shall request the Contractor to do so. If the Contractor fails to submit an application within a prescribed period, the Engineer shall issue the Final Payment Certificate for such amount as he fairly determines to be due. The Employer shall not be liable to the Contractor for any matter or thing under or in connection with the Contract or execution of the Works, except to the extent that the Contractor shall have included an amount expressly for it: in the Final Statement; and also things arising after the issue of the Taking-Over Certificate.

If contractor defaults or there is a breach of contract the contract can be terminated. The typical provisions for the breach of contract are: If the Engineer certifies that the Contractor: (i) Repudiated the contract. (ii) Failed to commence or proceed with the work. (iii) Failed to comply with a notice. (iv) Persistently or flagrantly neglecting his obligations then employer can terminate the contract.

Typical provisions related to the termination of the contract are: (i) In the event of default contract can be terminated. (ii) Notice of termination issued by

Engineer after approval from Employer. (iii) Termination payments as per contract. (iv) Contractor expelled from site. (v) Work to be completed by other contractor.

If the contractor continually fails to perform, this may constitute a breach of contract. The severity of the failure and the cost to the Employer will need to be assessed. Legal advice may be required before any further action is considered. Although it is sometimes difficult to predict accurately where problems may arise, good contract management with regular dialogue between the contractor and employer will help to identify potential problems. This will enable problems to be dealt with swiftly and effectively and so prevent major disputes.

"Retention Money" means the accumulated retention moneys which the Employer retains under the contract". Retention money is the amount deducted, generally 5 % from interim payments for remedying the defects if any in the work. When the Taking-Over Certificate is issued for the Works, generally the Engineer shall certify the first half of the Retention Money for payment to the Contractor. If a Taking-Over Certificate is issued for a Section or part of the Works, a proportion of the Retention Money shall be certified and paid. This proportion shall be half (50%) of the proportion calculated by dividing the estimated contract value of the Section or part, by the estimated final Contract Price. Promptly after the latest of the expiry dates of the Defects Notification Periods, the outstanding balance of the Retention Money shall be certified by the Engineer for payment to the Contractor.

If a Taking-Over Certificate was issued for a Section, a proportion of the second half of the Retention

Money shall be certified and paid promptly after the expiry date of the Defects Notification Period for the Section. This proportion shall be half (50%) of the proportion calculated by dividing the estimated contract value of the Section by the estimated final Contract Price.

Handling problems concerning dispute resolution, whatever the nature of the problem, it is vital that: problems are recorded as they occur, in order to highlight any trends and to help in assessing overall performance and value for money; the contractor is notified of problems by an appropriate route and at an appropriate level; approaches to resolving problems are clear and documented; and escalation procedures are followed.

If a dispute cannot be resolved at the level where it arises, it will be necessary to involve a higher level of authority. This escalation process needs to be managed. Escalation procedures should allow for successive levels of response depending on the nature of the problem and the outcome of action taken at lower levels. The levels for escalation should match those of the interfaces established between contractor and customer. Every effort should be made to resolve the problem at the lowest practicable level. For more serious problems, the contract should specify the circumstances under which the organization would have the right to terminate the contract. The contract manager must consult senior management and contractual advisors as soon as this possibility arises.

The contract manager should collate information on the number and severity of problems, as well as the way they were resolved, during the life of the contract. This information will provide useful input to reviews. The contract manager should periodically arrange for a check on the financial viability of the contractor, as well as continually monitoring any changes in ownership of the contractor. Where potential problems are identified the contract manager should seek specialist advice as soon as possible. Normally, most problems should be resolved before they become major issues; contract managers on both sides should meet regularly to raise any issues promptly as they occur. In extreme cases, where agreement cannot be reached, the Employer and contractor should seek the assistance of mediators before resorting to legal action.

Handling problems/ Settlement of Disputes - Every standard contract document provides for the settlement of dispute between the parties to the contract. A provision comprises reference to the Engineer within a stipulated period. The Engineer has to give his decision within the prescribed period. On failure or dissatisfaction of the either party with the decision of the Engineer the dispute can be taken further or referred to the Appellate authorities stipulated in the contract. Where notice of dissatisfaction has been given under the contract, both Parties shall attempt to settle the dispute amicably before the commencement of arbitration.

Settlement of dispute should be the responsibility of the Advisory /steering committees, if provided for. If either party is not satisfied the dispute could be further referred to an Arbitrator to be nominated by the designated party. The Arbitrator so appointed then deals the dispute as per the Arbitration act. In some Government contracts, the provision of Arbitration is replaced by a hierarchical clause. The dispute is first referred to the Engineer and if the contractor is not satisfied by the decision of the Engineer the dispute is further referred to the Appellate Authorities/higher ups in the organization. The Arbitrator is supposed to give reasoned award within the stipulated time. The expenses towards arbitration are to be shared by the parties to the contract. The contractor has to continue to work during pending disputes.

However, unless both Parties agree otherwise, arbitration may be commenced on or after the day on which a notice of dissatisfaction and intention to commence arbitration was given, even if no attempt at amicable settlement has been made. Unless indicated otherwise in the Particular Conditions of contract, any dispute not settled amicably and in respect of which the Dispute Board (DB)"s decision (if any) has not become final and binding shall be finally settled by arbitration. Unless otherwise agreed by both Parties.

Some standard provisions of the Arbitration clause are reproduced for guidance- (a) the place of arbitration shall be the city where the headquarters of the appointed arbitration institution is located, (b) the arbitration shall be conducted in the language for communications defined in the contract [Law and Language], and (c) for contracts with domestic contractors, arbitration with proceedings conducted in accordance with the laws of the Employer's country.

The arbitrators shall have full power to open up, review and revise any certificate, determination, instruction, opinion or valuation of the Engineer, and any decision of the DB, relevant to the dispute. Nothing shall disqualify representatives of the Parties and the Engineer from being called as a witness and giving evidence before the arbitrators on any matter whatsoever relevant to the dispute.

Neither Party shall be limited in the proceedings before the arbitrators to the evidence, nor did arguments previously put before the DB, to obtain its decision, or to the reasons for dissatisfaction given in its notice of dissatisfaction. Any decision of the DB shall be admissible in evidence in the arbitration. Arbitration may be commenced prior to or after completion of the Works. The obligations of the Parties, the Engineer and the DB shall not be altered by reason of any arbitration being conducted during the progress of the Works. In the event that a Party fails to comply with a final and binding DB decision, then the other Party may, without prejudice to any other rights it may have, refer the failure itself to arbitration.

If a dispute arises between the Parties in connection with, or arising out of, the Contract or the execution of the Works and there is no DB in place, whether by reason of the expiry of the DB"s appointment or otherwise: provisions of Obtaining Dispute Board's Decision and Amicable Settlement shall not apply, and the dispute may be referred directly to arbitration

It is good practice at the completion of any contract to review and place on record what went well and what lessons can be learned for any future contracts. After completion of any contract, the contract manager is required to complete a Contractor Evaluation Report. This should include the following: (i) The outcome of the project. (ii) The extent to which the expected benefits (deliverables) were achieved. And (iii) The total cost (including full economic cost of in-house staff engaged on the project).

Dealing with the claims is another important role of construction management and control, which may also include count-claims against the contractor. If the Employer considers himself to be entitled to any payment under any Clause of these Conditions or otherwise in connection with the Contract, and/or to any extension of the Defects Notification Period, the Employer or the Engineer must give notice and particulars to the Contractor. The notice must be given as soon as practicable and no longer than 28 days after the Employer became aware, or should have become aware, of the event or circumstances giving rise to the claim. A notice relating to any extension of the Defects Notification Period shall be given before the expiry of such period.

The particulars must specify the Clause or other basis of the claim, and shall include substantiation of the amount and/or extension to which the Employer considers him to be entitled in connection with the Contract. The Engineer shall then proceed in accordance to agree or determine (i) the amount (if any) which the Employer is entitled to be paid by the Contractor, and/or (ii) the extension (if any) of the Defects Notification Period in accordance with the contract provisions This amount may be included as a deduction in the Contract Price and Payment Certificates. The Employer must only be entitled to set off against or make any deduction from an amount certified in a Payment Certificate, or to otherwise claim against the Contractor, in accordance with the contract provisions.

Chapter 16

SUPERVISION, MANAGEMENT AND CONTROL OF CONSTRUCTION PARTICULAR TO FIDIC CONTRACTS

16.1 COOPERATION, COORDINATION MEETING AND PROGRESS REPORTS

Regarding Cooperation and coordination Clause 4.6 of Red Book read as follow:

4.6 Co-operation

The Contractor shall, as specified in the Contract or as instructed by the Engineer, allow appropriate opportunities for carrying out work to: (a) the Employer's Personnel; (b) any other contractors employed by the Employer; and (c) the personnel of any legally constituted public authorities, who may be employed in the execution on or near the Site of any work not included in the Contract.

Any such instruction shall constitute a Variation if and to the extent that it causes the Contractor to incur Unforeseeable Cost. Services for these personnel and other contractors may include the use of Contractor's Equipment, Temporary Works or access arrangements which are the responsibility of the Contractor.

If, under the Contract, the Employer is required to give to the Contractor possession of any foundation, structure, plant or means of access in accordance with Contractor's Documents, the Contractor shall submit such documents to the Engineer in the time and manner stated in the Specification.

Clause 4.6 Co-operation of Yellow Book read as follow:

4.6 Co-operation

The Contractor shall, as specified in the Contract or as instructed by the Engineer, allow appropriate opportunities for carrying out work to: (a) the Employer's Personnel; (b) any other contractors employed by the Employer; and (c) the personnel of any legally constituted public authorities, who may be employed in the execution on or near the Site of any work not included in the Contract.

Any such instruction shall constitute a Variation if and to the extent that it causes the Contractor to incur Unforeseeable Cost. Services for these personnel and other contractors may include the use of Contractor's Equipment, Temporary Works or access arrangements which are the responsibility of the Contractor.

The Contractor shall be responsible for his construction activities on the Site, and shall coordinate his own activities with those of other contractors to the extent (if any) specified in the Employer's Requirements.

If, under the Contract, the Employer is required to give to the Contractor possession of any foundation, structure, plant or means of access in accordance with Contractor's Documents, the Contractor shall submit such documents to the Engineer in the time and manner stated in the Employer's Requirements.

Clause 4.6 Co-operation of Silver Book read as follow:

4.6 Co-operation

The Contractor shall, as specified in the Contract or as instructed by the Engineer, allow appropriate opportunities for carrying out work to: (a) the Employer's Personnel; (b) any other contractors employed by the Employer; and (c) the personnel of any legally constituted public authorities, who may be employed in the execution on or near the Site of any work not included in the Contract.

Any such instruction shall constitute a Variation if and to the extent that it causes the Contractor to incur Cost in an amount which was not reasonably foreseeable by an experienced contractor by the date for submission of the Tender. Services for these personnel and other contractors may include the use of Contractor's Equipment, Temporary Works or access arrangements which are the responsibility of the Contractor.

The Contractor shall be responsible for his construction activities on the Site, and shall coordinate his own activities with those of other contractors to the extent (if any) specified in the Employer's Requirements.

If, under the Contract, the Employer is required to give to the Contractor possession of any foundation, structure, plant or means of access in accordance with Contractor's Documents, the Contractor shall submit such documents to the Employer in the time and manner stated in the Employer's Requirements.

As stated in the second sentence of Sub-Clause 2.1, the Contractor may not have exclusive right of access to, and possession of, the Site. In addition to the Employer's Personnel, the Contractor must also allow the Employer's other contractors to carry out their work. Under Sub-Clause 2.3(a), the Employer is responsible for ensuring that his other contractors co-operate with the Contractor's efforts under this Sub-Clause 4.6.

It is preferable for the tender documents to describe the extent to which the Contractor will have to "allow appropriate opportunities" under Sub-Clause 4.6. If instructions are given under the first sentence of Sub-Clause 4.6, the Contractor is expected to have allowed in his Tender for the Cost which an experienced contractor could reasonably have foreseen. To the extent that the Cost was not reasonably foreseeable by an experienced contractor, taking account of the information available to tenderers, the instruction constitutes a Variation and Clause 13 applies.

Red Book omits the other Books' penultimate paragraph because it is usually impractical to require a Red Book Contractor to co-ordinate his activities with those of other contractors to an extent which is defined in the Contract and therefore which the Contractor can allow for in his Tender. The Contractor will nevertheless be responsible for most of his construction activities on the Site, but there may be a few exceptions where the Engineer is required to direct some such activities. These few exceptions are difficult to describe in general terms, so Red Book omits the entire paragraph.

16.2 DELAYS AND SUSPENSION OF WORKS

16.2.1 Extension of Time

Clause 8.4 Extension of Time for Completion of Red Book and Yellow Book read as follows:

8.4 Extension of Time for Completion

The Contractor shall be entitled subject to Sub- Clause 20.1 [Contractor's Claims] to an extension of the Time for Completion if and to the extent that completion for the purposes of Sub-Clause 10.1

*[Taking Over of the Works and Sections] is or will be delayed by any of the following causes: *(a) a Variation (unless an adjustment to the Time for Completion has been agreed under Sub- Clause 13.3 [Variation Procedure]) or other substantial change in the quantity of an item of work included in the Contract; (b) a cause of delay giving an entitlement to extension of time under a Sub-Clause of these Conditions; (c) exceptionally adverse climatic conditions; (d) Unforeseeable shortages in the availability of*

personnel or Goods caused by epidemic or governmental actions; or (e) any delay, impediment or prevention caused by or attributable to the Employer, the Employer's Personnel, or the Employer's other contractors on the Site.

If the Contractor considers himself to be entitled to an extension of the Time for Completion, the

Contractor shall give notice to the Engineer in accordance with Sub-Clause 20.1 [Contractor's Claims].

When determining each extension of time under Sub-Clause 20.1, the Engineer shall review previous determinations and may increase, but shall not decrease, the total extension of time.

Note: In the Yellow Book the item (a) marked * is replaced with the following text

(a) a Variation (unless an adjustment to the Time for Completion has been agreed under Sub- Clause 13.3 [Variation Procedure]),

Clause 8.4 Extension of Time for Completion of Silver Book and Yellow Book read as follows:

8.4 Extension of Time for Completion

*The Contractor shall be entitled subject to Sub- Clause 20.1 [Contractor's Claims] to an extension of the Time for Completion if and to the extent that completion for the purposes of Sub-Clause 10.1 [Taking Over of the Works and Sections] is or will be delayed by any of the following causes: *(a) a Variation (unless an adjustment to the Time for Completion has been agreed under Sub- Clause 13.3 [Variation Procedure]) or other substantial change in the quantity of an item of work included in the Contract; (b) a cause of delay giving an entitlement to extension of time under a Sub-Clause of these Conditions, or(c) any delay, impediment or prevention caused by or attributable to the Employer, the Employer's Personnel, or the Employer's other contractors on the Site.*

If the Contractor considers himself to be entitled to an extension of the Time for Completion, the Contractor shall give notice to the Employer in accordance with Sub-Clause 20.1 [Contractor's Claims]. When determining each extension of time under Sub-Clause 20.1, the Employer shall review previous determinations and may increase, but shall not decrease, the total extension of time.

Provisions for extension of time are for the benefit of both parties, the Contractor as well as Employer. For example, it benefits the Contractor by giving him more time if any of the listed events occurs and delays completion and protects the Employer. Sub-Clause 8.4 does not include a descriptive list of all events which can give rise to an extension. Sub-paragraph (b) refers to other Sub-Clauses which entitle the Contractor to extensions of time. Each of these other Sub-Clauses entitles the Contractor (usually in a sub-paragraph (a)) to "an extension of time ..., if completion is or will be delayed, under Sub-Clause 8.4". The phrase "completion... Unless the Contractor does not consider himself entitled to an extension of time(e.g., because "completion" will not be delayed), he is required to give the notice described in the first paragraph of Sub-Clause 20.1 (to which Sub-Clause 4.21(f) refers). Sub-Clause 20.1 specifies the procedure for agreement or determination of the extension of time, which is the same procedure as that for the agreement or determination of additional payments. However, Sub-Clause 8.4 and entitlements to extension of time do not themselves entitle the Contractor to additional payment.

Red Book/Yellow Book 1.3 requires the Contractor to send a copy of his notices to the Employer. Most of the Sub-Clauses to which sub-paragraph (b) of Sub-Clause 8.4 relates provide for the financial consequences, but Sub-Clause 8.5 is one exception. Under Red Book or Yellow Book, Sub-Clause 8.4(c) entitles the Contractor to an extension of time for climatic conditions which are "exceptionally adverse". In order to establish whether such climatic conditions occurred, under Silver Book, the Contractor is not entitled to an extension of time for climatic conditions, unless they constitute Force Majeure under Clause 19.

Although the Contractor may submit a proposal (under Sub-Clause 13.2(i)) which will "accelerate completion", or he may (under Sub-Clause 13.1) be requested to submit such a proposal, the General Conditions contain no provisions under which he may be instructed to achieve completion before the Time for Completion expires, including extensions due under Sub-Clause 8.4. If the Employer wishes this to be achieved, the Parties should endeavour to reach agreement.

16.2.2 Delay Caused by Authorities

Clause 8.5 Delay Caused by Authorities of Red Book, Yellow Book, and Saver Book read as follows:

8.5 Delay Caused by Authorities

*If the following conditions apply, namely: (a) the Contractor has diligently followed the procedures laid down by the relevant legally constituted public authorities in the Country; (b) these authorities delay or disrupt the Contractor's work; and *(c) the delay or disruption was Unforeseeable*, then this delay or disruption will be considered as a cause of delay under sub-paragraph (b) of Sub-Clause 8.4 [Extension of Time for Completion].*

Note: In the Siler Book, (c) the text marked as * ----- * to be replaced with the following text:

the delay or disruption was not reasonably foreseeable by an experienced contractor by the date for submission of the Tender,

This Sub-Clause, like Sub-Clause 8.4, makes no mention of the financial consequences, because they would depend upon the particular circumstances of the construction process.

16.2.3 Progress Reports

Regarding Progress reports, Clause 4.21 Progress Reports of FIDIC Red, Yellow Book, and Silver Book (subject to replacement of paragraph marked*) read as follows:

4.21 Progress Reports

Unless otherwise stated in the Particular Conditions, monthly progress reports shall be prepared by the Contractor and submitted to the Engineer in six copies. The first report shall cover the period up to the end of the first calendar month following the Commencement Date. Reports shall be submitted monthly thereafter, each within 7 days after the last day of the period to which it relates.

Reporting shall continue until the Contractor has completed all work which is known to be outstanding at the completion date stated in the Taking-Over Certificate for the Works.

*Each report shall include: *(a) charts and detailed descriptions of progress, including each stage of design (if any), Contractor's Documents, procurement, manufacture, delivery to Site, construction, erection and testing; and including these stages for work by each nominated Subcontractor (as defined in Clause 5 [Nominated Subcontractors]); (b) photographs showing the status of manufacture and of progress on the Site; (c) for the manufacture of each main item of Plant and Materials, the name of the manufacturer, manufacture location, percentage progress, and the actual or expected dates of: (i) commencement of manufacture, (ii) Contractor's inspections, (iii) tests, and (iv) shipment and arrival at the Site; (d) the* *details described in Sub-Clause 6.10 [Records of Contractor's Personnel and Equipment]; (e) copies of quality assurance documents, test results and certificates of Materials; (f) list of notices given under Sub-Clause 2.5 [Employer's Claims] and notices given under Sub-Clause 20.1 [Contractor's Claims]; (g) safety statistics, including details of any hazardous incidents and activities relating to environmental aspects and public relations; and (h) comparisons of actual and planned progress, with details of any events or circumstances which may jeopardise the completion in accordance with the Contract, and the measures being (or to be) adopted to overcome delays.*

Note: In Yellow Book and Silver Book replace the text id (a0 marked* with the following text:

(a) charts and detailed descriptions of progress, including each stage of design, Contractor's Documents, procurement, manufacture, delivery to Site, construction, erection, testing, commissioning and trial operation;

Unless this Sub-Clause is amended (or deleted) in the Particular Conditions, the Contractor is required to submit monthly reports. The Sub-Clause specifies them in some detail, but it is recognised that less detail may be appropriate for some projects. This detailed report on the progress during the month is considered to be an essential part of competent project management. Under Sub-Clause 14.3, the Contractor's Statement has to be submitted together with supporting documents which include the report in accordance with Yellow Book 4.15 Sub-Clause 4.21. The period for payment under paragraph (b) of Sub-Clause 14.7 does not commence until all these supporting documents have been received. The Contractor is to provide these reports regularly, until he has completed all work which is known to be outstanding at the completion date stated in the Taking-Over Certificate for the Works; namely, the work which is mentioned in Sub-Clause 11.1(a).

16.3 CONTRACTS VARIATIONS AND ADJUSTMENTS

16.3.1 General

Although Variations are a source of many disputes, Employers are, by and large, unwilling to enter into contracts which prevent them from requiring changes to be made, other than after the taking-over. Variations can be initiated by any of three ways: (i) The Variation may be instructed without prior agreement as to feasibility or price, which may be appropriate for urgent work, or in respect of Red Book's Works which are designed by (or on behalf of) the Employer. (ii)The Contractor may initiate his own proposals, which may be approved as a Variation, or he may be given other instructions which constitute a Variation. (iii) A proposal may be requested, in an endeavour to reach prior agreement on its effect and thereby minimise dispute. This "request" would typically not constitute a Variation. the proposal may, however, be approved as a Variation, or other instructions may be issued which constitute a Variation.

16.3.2 Right to Vary

Clause 13.1 Right to Vary of Red Book read as follows:

13.1 Right to Vary

Variations may be initiated by the Engineer at any time prior to issuing the Taking-Over Certificate for the Works, either by an instruction or by a request for the Contractor to submit a proposal.

The Contractor shall execute and be bound by each Variation, unless the Contractor promptly gives notice to the Engineer stating (with supporting particulars) that the Contractor cannot readily obtain the Goods required for the Variation.

Upon receiving this notice, the Engineer shall cancel, confirm or vary the instruction.

Each Variation may include: (a) changes to the quantities of any item of work included in the Contract (however, such changes do not necessarily constitute a Variation); (b) changes to the quality and other

characteristics of any item of work; (c) changes to the levels, positions and/or dimensions of any part of the Works; (d) omission of any work unless it is to be carried out by others; (e) any additional work, Plant, Materials or services necessary for the Permanent Works, including any associated Tests on Completion, boreholes and other testing and exploratory work; or (f) changes to the sequence or timing of the execution of the Works.

The Contractor shall not make any alteration and/or modification of the Permanent Works, unless and until the Engineer instructs or approves a Variation

Clause 13.1 Right to Vary of Yellow Book and Silver Book read as follows:

13.1 Right to Vary

Variations may be initiated by the Engineer (Employer in Silver Book) at any time prior to issuing the Taking-Over Certificate for the Works, either by an instruction or by a request for the Contractor to submit a proposal. A Variation shall not comprise the omission of any work which is to be carried out by others.

The Contractor shall execute and be bound by each Variation, unless the Contractor promptly gives notice to the Engineer (Employer in Silver Book) stating (with supporting particulars) that (i) the Contractor cannot readily obtain the Goods required for the Variation; (ii) it will reduce the safety or suitability of the Works; or (iii) it will have an adverse impact on the achievement of the Schedule of Guarantees. Upon receiving this notice, the Engineer (Employer in Silver Book) shall cancel, confirm or vary the instruction.

Variations may be initiated by the Engineer at any time prior to issuing the Taking-Over Certificate for the Works, either by an instruction or by a request for the Contractor to submit a proposal. The Contractor must execute and be bound by each Variation, unless the Contractor promptly gives notice to the Engineer stating (with supporting particulars) that (i) the Contractor cannot readily obtain the Goods required for the Variation, or (ii) such Variation triggers a substantial change in the sequence or progress of the Works. Upon receiving this notice, the Engineer must confirm, vary, or cancel, the instruction.

Each Variation may include, but not limited to: (a) changes to the quantities of any item of work included in the Contract (however, such changes do not necessarily constitute a Variation); (b) changes to the quality and other characteristics of any item of work; (c) changes to the levels, positions and/or dimensions of any part of the Works; (d) omission of any work unless it is to be carried out by others; (e) any additional work, Plant, Materials or services necessary for the Permanent Works, including any associated Tests on Completion, boreholes and other testing and exploratory work, or (f) changes to the sequence or timing of the execution of the Works. The Contractor, however, must not make any alteration and/or modification of the Permanent Works, unless and until the Engineer approves a Variation or issue instruction.

16.3.2 Value Engineering

Clause 13.2 Value Engineering of Red Book provides:

13.2 Value Engineering

The Contractor may, at any time, submit to the Engineer a written proposal which (in the Contractor's opinion) will, if adopted, (i) accelerate completion, (ii) reduce the cost to the Employer of executing, maintaining or operating the Works, (iii) improve the efficiency or value to the Employer of the completed Works, or (iv) otherwise be of benefit to the Employer.

The proposal shall be prepared at the cost of the Contractor and shall include the items listed in Sub- Clause 13.3 [Variation Procedure].

If a proposal, which is approved by the Engineer, includes a change in the design of part of the Permanent Works, then unless otherwise agreed by both Parties: (a) the Contractor shall design this part, (b) sub-paragraphs (a) to (d) of Sub-Clause 4.1 [Contractor's General Obligations] shall apply, and (c) if this change results in a reduction in th contract value of this part, the Engineer shall proceed in accordance with Sub-Clause 3.5 [Determinations] to agree or determine a fee, which shall be included in the Contract Price.

This fee shall be half (50%) of the difference between the following amounts: (i) such reduction in contract value, resulting from the change, excluding adjustments under Sub-Clause 13.7 [Adjustments for Changes in Legislation] and Sub-Clause 13.8 [Adjustments for Changes in Cost],and (ii) the reduction (if any) in the value to the Employer of the varied works, taking account of any reductions in quality, anticipated life or operational efficiencies.

However, if amount (i) is less than amount (ii), there shall not be a fee.

Clause 13.2 Value Engineering of Yellow Book and Silver Book provide:

13.2 Value Engineering

The Contractor may, at any time, submit to the Engineer (Employer in Silver Book) a written proposal which (in the Contractor's opinion) will, if adopted, (i) accelerate completion, (ii) reduce the cost to the Employer of executing, maintaining or operating the Works, (iii) improve the efficiency or value to the Employer of the completed Works, or (iv) otherwise be of benefit to the Employer.

The proposal shall be prepared at the cost of the Contractor and shall include the items listed in Sub Clause 13.3 [Variation Procedure].

The Contractor is not under any duty to submit value engineering proposals. He may be reluctant to do so, unless he seems likely to benefit from his endeavours, but may wish to propose changes, e.g. in the following situations: (i) The proposal may appear to be of benefit to the Contractor, in which case he may offer a reduction in the Contract Price in order to encourage the Employer's acceptance (especially if the proposal would not otherwise appear to be of benefit to the Employer). (ii) The proposal may appear to be of benefit to the Employer, by improving the quality of the Works (by reducing the cost of maintenance or operation, or improving productivity or efficiency). This might involve an increase in the Cost, and thus in the Contract Price.

Red Book 13.2 concludes with sub-paragraphs covering the possibility that the value engineering proposal may involve a change in the Employer's (or Engineer's) design of the Permanent Works. Problems sometimes arise in these situations, usually because the Parties failed to agree (or even consider) aspects such as design liability. They are entitled to agree what they wish, but the sub-paragraphs define the position if they fail to reach and record their agreement.

16.3.3 Variation Procedure

Clause 13.3 Variation Procedure on Red Book provides:

13.3 Variation Procedure

If the Engineer requests a proposal, prior to instructing a Variation, the Contractor shall respond in writing as soon as practicable, either by giving reasons why he cannot comply (if this is the case) or by submitting: (a) a description of the proposed work to be performed and a programme for its execution, (b) the Contractor's proposal for any necessary modifications to the programme according to Sub-Clause 8.3 [Programme] and to the Time for Completion, and (c) the Contractor's proposal for evaluation of the Variation.

The Engineer shall, as soon as practicable after receiving such proposal (under Sub-Clause 13.2 [Value Engineering] or otherwise), respond with approval, disapproval or comments. The Contractor shall not delay any work whilst awaiting a response. Each instruction to execute a Variation, with any requirements for the recording of Costs, shall be issued by the Engineer to the Contractor, who shall acknowledge receipt.

Each Variation shall be evaluated in accordance with Clause 12 [Measurement and Evaluation], unless the Engineer instructs or approves otherwise in accordance with this Clause.

Clause 13.3 Variation Procedure on Yellow Book and Silver Book provide:

13.3 Variation Procedure

If the Engineer requests a proposal, prior to instructing a Variation, the Contractor shall respond in writing as soon as practicable, either by giving reasons why he cannot comply (if this is the case) or by submitting: (a) a description of the proposed design and/or work to be performed and a programme for its execution, (b) the Contractor's proposal for any necessary modifications to the programme according to Sub-Clause 8.3 [Programme] and to the Time for Completion, and (c) the Contractor's proposal for adjustment to the Contract Price.

The Engineer shall, as soon as practicable after receiving such proposal (under Sub-Clause 13.2 [Value Engineering] or otherwise), respond with approval, disapproval or comments. The Contractor shall not delay any work whilst awaiting a response.

Each instruction to execute a Variation, with any requirements for the recording of Costs, shall be

issued by the Engineer to the Contractor, who shall acknowledge receipt.

Upon instructing or approving a Variation, the Engineer shall proceed in accordance with Sub- Clause 3.5 [Determinations] to agree or determine adjustments to the Contract Price and the Schedule of Payments. These adjustments shall include reasonable profit, and shall take account of the Contractor's submissions under Sub-Clause 13.2 [Value Engineering] if applicable.

As noted previously, Variations can be initiated by any of three ways: (i)The Variation may be instructed without prior agreement as to feasibility or price, which may be appropriate for urgent work, or in respect of Red Book' Works which are designed by (or on behalf of) the Employer. (ii) The Contractor may (at his option) initiate his own proposals, which may then be approved as a Variation, or he may be given other instructions which constitute a Variation. (iii) A proposal under Sub-Clause 13.3(a)-(c) may be requested, in an endeavour to reach prior agreement on its effect and thereby minimise dispute. This "request" would typically not constitute a Variation, unless it is an "instruction". Again, the proposal may be approved as a Variation, or other instructions may be issued which constitute a Variation.

Unlike "instructions" (see Red Book/Yellow Book 3.3 and Silver Book 3.4), the Contractor is not obliged to comply with a "request". He is required to respond, but his response may: (i) be in the form described in sub-paragraphs (a) to (c) inclusive of Sub-Clause 13.3, (ii) be in the form of a reasoned explanation of his inability to comply, or (iii) comprise some documents in the form described in sub-paragraphs (a) to (c), together with an explanation of his inability to provide the other requested submittals. For example, the Engineer or Employer might have requested detailed design drawings of a potential major Variation.

16.3.4 Adjustments for Changes in Legislation

Clause 13.7 adjustment for changes in legislation of all three FIDIC Books provides.

13.7 adjustment for changes in legislation

The Contract Price shall be adjusted to take account of any increase or decrease in Cost resulting from a change in the Laws of the Country (including the introduction of new Laws and the repeal or modification of existing Laws) or in the judicial or official governmental interpretation of such Laws, made after the Base Date, which affect the Contractor in the performance of obligations under the Contract.

If the Contractor suffers (or will suffer) delay and/or incurs (or will incur) additional Cost as a result of these changes in the Laws or in such interpretations, made after the Base Date, the Contractor shall give notice to the Engineer and shall be entitled subject to Sub-Clause 20.1 [Contractor's Claims] to: (a) an extension of time for any such delay, if completion is or will be delayed, under Sub- Clause 8.4 [Extension of Time for Completion], and (b) payment of any such Cost, which shall be included in the Contract Price. After receiving this notice, the Engineer shall proceed in accordance with Sub-Clause 3.5 [Determinations] to agree or determine these matters

The Contract Price needs to be adjusted to take account of any increase or decrease in Cost resulting from a change in the Laws of the Country (including the introduction of new Laws and the repeal or modification of existing Laws) or in the judicial or official governmental interpretation of such Laws, made after the Base Date, which affect the Contractor in the performance of obligations under the Contract. If the Contractor suffers (or will suffer) delay and/or incurs (or will incur) additional Cost as a result of these changes in the Laws or in such interpretations, made after the Base Date, the Contractor must give notice to the Engineer and will be entitled to: (a) an extension of time for any such delay, if completion is or will be delayed; and (b) payment of any such Cost, which shall be included in the Contract Price. After receiving this notice, the Engineer must proceed to agree or determine these matters in accordance with contract provisions.

Notwithstanding the foregoing, the Contractor must not be entitled to an extension of time if the relevant delay has already been taken into account in the determination of a previous extension of time and such Cost must not be separately paid if the same already have been taken into account in the indexing of any inputs to the table of adjustment data in accordance with the contract provisions.

16.3.5 Adjustments for Changes in Cost

Clause 13.8 of FIDIC Red Book and Yellow Book provide:

13.8 Adjustment for Changes in Cost

The Contract Price shall be adjusted to take account of any increase or decrease in Cost resulting from a change in the Laws of the Country (including the introduction of new Laws and the repeal or modification of existing Laws) or in the judicial or official governmental interpretation of such Laws, made after the Base Date, which affect the Contractor in the performance of obligations under the Contract.

If the Contractor suffers (or will suffer) delay and/or incurs (or will incur) additional Cost as a result of these changes in the Laws or in such interpretations, made after the Base Date, the Contractor shall give notice to the Engineer and shall be entitled subject to Sub-Clause 20.1 [Contractor's Claims] to: (a) an extension of time for any such delay, if completion is or will be delayed, under Sub-Clause 8.4 [Extension of Time for Completion], and (b) payment of any such Cost, which shall be included in the Contract Price.

After receiving this notice, the Engineer shall proceed in accordance with Sub-Clause 3.5 [Determinations] to agree or determine these matters. In this Sub-Clause, "table of adjustment data" means the completed table of adjustment data included in the Appendix to Tender. If there is no such table of adjustment data, this Sub-Clause shall not apply.

If this Sub-Clause applies, the amounts payable to the Contractor shall be adjusted for rises or falls in the cost of labour, Goods and other inputs to the Works, by the addition or deduction of the amounts determined by the formulae prescribed in this Sub-Clause. To the extent that full compensation for any rise or fall in Costs is not covered by the provisions of this or other Clauses, the Accepted Contract Amount shall be deemed to have included amounts to cover the contingency of other rises and falls in costs.

The adjustment to be applied to the amount otherwise payable to the Contractor, as valued in accordance with the appropriate Schedule and certified in Payment Certificates, shall be determined from formulae for each of the currencies in which the Contract Price is payable. No adjustment is to be applied to work valued on the basis of Cost or current prices. The formulae shall be of the following general type: ***P****n = **a** +* ***b L****n + **c E**n + **d M**n +...**L**o **E**o **M**o where: "**P**n" is the adjustment multiplier to be applied to the estimated contract value in the relevant currency of the work carried out in period "n", this period being a month unless otherwise stated in the Appendix to Tender; "**a**" is a fixed coefficient, stated in the relevant table of adjustment data, representing the nonadjustable portion in contractual payments; "**b**", "**c**", "**d**",*

*... are coefficients representing the estimated proportion of each cost element related to the execution of the Works, as stated in the relevant table of adjustment data; such tabulated cost elements may be indicative of resources such as labour, equipment and materials "**L**n", "**E**n", "**M**n", ... are the current cost indices or reference prices for period "n", expressed in the relevant currency of payment, each of which is applicable to the relevant tabulated cost element on the date 49 days prior to the last day of the period (to which the particular Payment Certificate relates); and "**L**o", "**E**o", "**M**o", ... are the base cost indices or reference prices, expressed in the relevant currency of payment, each of which is applicable to the relevant tabulated cost element on the Base Date.*

The cost indices or reference prices stated in the table of adjustment data shall be used. If their source is in doubt, it shall be determined by the Engineer. For this purpose, reference shall be made to the values of the indices at stated dates (quoted in the fourth and fifth columns respectively of the table) for the purposes of clarification of the source; although these dates (and thus these values) may

not correspond to the base cost indices.

In cases where the "currency of index" (stated in the table) is not the relevant currency of payment, each index shall be converted into the relevant currency of payment at the selling rate, established by the central bank of the Country, of this relevant currency on the above date for which the index is required to be applicable.

Until such time as each current cost index is available, the Engineer shall determine a provisional index for the issue of Interim Payment Certificates. When a current cost index is available, the adjustment shall be recalculated accordingly.

If the Contractor fails to complete the Works within the Time for Completion, adjustment of prices thereafter shall be made using either (i) each index or price applicable on the date 49 days prior to the expiry of the Time for Completion of the Works, or (ii) the current index or price: whichever is more favourable to the Employer.

The weightings (coefficients) for each of the factors of cost stated in the table(s) of adjustment data shall only be adjusted if they have been rendered unreasonable, unbalanced or inapplicable, as a result of Variations.

Clause 13.7 of FIDIC Red Book and Silver Book provide:

13.8 Adjustment for Changes in Cost

The Contract Price shall be adjusted to take account of any increase or decrease in Cost resulting from a change in the Laws of the Country (including the introduction of new Laws and the repeal or modification of existing Laws) or in the judicial or official governmental interpretation of such Laws, made after the Base Date, which affect the Contractor in the performance of obligations under the Contract.

If the Contractor suffers (or will suffer) delay and/or incurs (or will incur) additional Cost as a result of these changes in the Laws or in such interpretations, made after the Base Date, the Contractor shall give notice to the Employer and shall be entitled subject to Sub-Clause 20.1 [Contractor's Claims] to: (a) an extension of time for any such delay, if completion is or will be delayed, under Sub-Clause 8.4 [Extension of Time for Completion], and (b) payment of any such Cost, which shall be added to the Contract Price.

After receiving this notice, the Employer shall proceed in accordance with Sub-Clause 3.5 [Determinations] to agree or determine these matters.

If the Contract Price is to be adjusted for rises or falls in the cost of labour, Goods and other inputs to the Works, the adjustments shall be calculated in accordance with the provisions in the Particular Conditions.

The amounts payable to the Contractor, if applicable, must be adjusted for rises or falls in the cost of labour, Goods and other inputs to the Works, by the addition or deduction of the amounts determined by the prescribed formulae. To the extent that full compensation for any rise or fall in Costs is not covered, the Accepted Contract Amount must be deemed to have included amounts to cover the contingency of other rises and falls in costs. The adjustment to be applied to the amount otherwise payable to the Contractor, as valued in accordance with the appropriate Schedule and certified in Payment Certificates, shall be determined from formulae for each of the currencies in which the Contract Price is payable. No adjustment is to be applied to work valued on the basis of Cost or current prices.

The cost indices or reference prices stated in the table of adjustment data must be used. If their source is in doubt, it must be determined by the Engineer. For this purpose, reference must be made to the values of the indices at stated dates for the purposes of clarification of the source; although these dates (and thus these values) may not correspond to the base cost indices. In cases where the "currency of index" is not the relevant currency of payment, each index must be converted into the relevant currency of payment at the selling rate, established by the central bank of the Country, of this relevant currency on the above date for which the index is required to be applicable.

Until such time as each current cost index is available, the Engineer must determine a provisional index for the issue of Interim Payment Certificates. When a current cost index is available, the adjustment must be recalculated accordingly. If the Contractor fails to complete the Works within the Time for Completion, adjustment of prices thereafter shall be made using either (i) each index or price applicable on the date 49 days prior to the expiry of the Time for Completion of the Works, or (ii) the current index or price, whichever is more favourable to the Employer. The weightings (coefficients) for each of the factors of cost stated in the table(s) of adjustment data shall only be adjusted if they have been rendered unreasonable, unbalanced or inapplicable, as a result of Variations.

16.4 MEASUREMENT AND EVALUATION

16.4.1 General

This is only applicable for Red Book. Red Book Clause 12 is based upon the principle that the Works are to be valued by measuring the quantity of each item of work under Sub-Clause 12.2, and applying the appropriate rate per unit quantity or the appropriate lump-sum price under Sub-Clause 12.3. Alternatively, GPPC 14 refers to the possibility of replacing Clause 12 by appropriate Particular Conditions, for a lump-sum contract or a cost-plus contract.

16.4.2 Works to be Measured

Clause 12.1 Works to be Measured of the Red Book read as follows:

12.1 Works to be Measured

The Works shall be measured, and valued for payment, in accordance with this Clause. Whenever the Engineer requires any part of the Works to be measured, reasonable notice shall be given to the Contractor's Representative, who shall: (a) promptly either attend or send another qualified representative to assist the Engineer in making the measurement; and (b) supply any particulars requested by the

Engineer. If the Contractor fails to attend or send a representative, the measurement made by (or on behalf of) the Engineer shall be accepted as accurate.

Except as otherwise stated in the Contract, wherever any Permanent Works are to be measured from records, these shall be prepared by the Engineer.

The Contractor shall, as and when requested, attend to examine and agree the records with the Engineer, and shall sign the same when agreed. If the Contractor does not attend, the records shall be accepted as accurate.

If the Contractor examines and disagrees the records, and/or does not sign them as agreed, then the Contractor shall give notice to the Engineer of the respects in which the records are asserted to be inaccurate. After receiving this notice, the Engineer shall review the records and either confirm or vary them. If the Contractor does not so give notice to the Engineer within 14 days after being requested to examine the records, they shall be accepted as accurate.

Sub-Clause 12.1 describes the procedure for measuring the quantity of each item of work. Quantities should preferably be agreed between the representatives of the Engineer and the Contractor, as a continuing process, and as the execution of the Works proceeds. Although the second paragraph empowers the Engineer to take the initiative in requiring a measurement to be made, this activity should be regarded as a joint activity. The "Schedules" are defined as including a "Bill of Quantities". It should prescribe the basis for measuring each item of the Permanent Works, whether from the Drawings, on-Site measurement or from records.

The Contractor may be required (by the Specification, typically) to prepare detailed records, and the Contract may state that the quantities shall be based upon such records except to the extent of any errors therein. If the Bill of Quantities indicates that quantities are to be based upon records, but there is no indication as to who should prepare these records, they must be prepared by the Engineer in accordance with the penultimate paragraph of Sub-Clause 12.1.

14.4.3 Method of Measurement

Clause 12.2 Method of Measurement of the Red Book read as follows:

12.2 Method of Measurement

Except as otherwise stated in the Contract and notwithstanding local practice: (a) measurement shall be made of the net actual quantity of each item of the Permanent Works, and (b) the method of measurement shall be in accordance with the Bill of Quantities or other applicable Schedules.

This clause describe what is typically referred to as the "method of measurement" applicable to the Works. This method relates primarily to what quantities are to be applicable to the evaluation, rather than to the measuring techniques (although they may also be described), and plays an important part in the whole evaluation of the Contract Price. This method (or principles) of measurement may comprise: (i) principles for measurement which are specified in a preamble to the Bill of Quantities; (ii) a publication which specifies principles of measurement and which is incorporated (by reference) into the Bill of Quantities; or (iii) for a contract which does not contain many or complex items of work, principles included in each of the item descriptions in the Bill of Quantities.

Each item of the Works is to be measured in accordance with such principles/method of measurement, which take precedence over the general principle described in sub-paragraph (a) of this Sub-Clause. Sub-paragraph (a) specifies that, unless such specified principles (or other provisions in the Contract) state otherwise, measurement shall be made of the net actual quantity of each item of work, notwithstanding local practice. It may be unfair to assume that an international contractor is familiar with all aspects of local practice on these matters.

It is important to verify, before the Bill of Quantities is issued to tenderers, that it includes the correct quantities and item descriptions of the work defined in the Drawings and Specification. Clause 12 requires the work to be measured and valued, based upon the Bill of Quantities and/or other appropriate Schedules. Generally, tenderers will have limited opportunity to verify the correctness of the Bill of Quantities which they receive. However, during the measurement of the completed works, omissions in the original Bill of Quantities may be discovered, or be alleged by a Party. In such a case, a dispute may arise as to whether an additional Bill item will be required, or as to whether the work is covered by another item in the Bill of Quantities.

Although resolution of the matter may need to take account of various provisions in the Contract and of the applicable Laws, it is suggested that the effect of this Clause 12 would typically be as follows: (i) If the Bill of Quantities includes (either incorporated by reference or specified) principles of measurement which clearly require that an item of work be measured, and if the Bill of Quantities contains is no such item, then an additional Bill item will required in order to satisfy the requirement for measurement in accordance with such principles.(ii) If the Bill of Quantities includes (either incorporated by reference or specified) principles of measurement which do not clearly require that a particular item of work be measured, and the work was as described in the Contract and did not arise from a Variation, then measurement in accordance with such principles does not require the addition of a new Bill item. (iii) If the Bill of Quantities does not include principles of measurement for a particular item of work, and the work was as described in the Contract and did not arise from a Variation, then measurement in accordance with such principles does not require the addition of a new Bill item.

16.4.4 Evaluation

Clause 12.3 Evaluation of Red Book read as follows:

12.3 Evaluation

Except as otherwise stated in the Contract, the Engineer shall proceed in accordance with Sub-Clause 3.5 [Determinations] to agree or determine the Contract Price by evaluating each item of work, applying the measurement agreed or determined in accordance with the above Sub-Clauses 12.1 and 12.2 and the appropriate rate or price for the item.

For each item of work, the appropriate rate or price for the item shall be the rate or price specified for such item in the Contract or, if there is no such item, specified for similar work. However, a new rate or price shall be appropriate for an item of work if: (a) (i) the measured quantity of the item is changed by more than 10% from the quantity of this item in the Bill of Quantities or other Schedule, (ii) this change in quantity multiplied by such specified rate for this item exceeds 0.01% of the Accepted Contract Amount, (iii) this change in quantity directly changes the Cost per unit quantity of this item by more than 1%, and (iv) this item is not specified in the Contract as a "fixed rate item"; or (b) (i) the work is instructed under Clause 13 [Variations and Adjustments], (ii) no rate or price is specified in the Contract for this item, and (iii) no specified rate or price is appropriate because the item of work is not of similar character, or is not executed under similar conditions, as any item in the Contract.

Each new rate or price shall be derived from any relevant rates or prices in the Contract, with reasonable adjustments to take account of the matters described in sub-paragraph (a) and/or (b), as applicable. If no rates or prices are relevant for the derivation of a new rate or price, it shall be derived from the reasonable Cost of executing the work, together with reasonable profit, taking account of any other relevant matters. Until such time as an appropriate rate or price is agreed or determined, the Engineer shall determine a provisional rate or price for the purposes of Interim Payment Certificates.

The Engineer is required to agree or determine the value of each item of work, applying measured quantities to rates and prices in accordance with this Sub-Clause. Most measured quantities should be agreed without resorting to the determination referred to in the first sentence. The principles/method of measurement will, by defining what is to be measured, define what is appropriate for valuing each item in the Bill of Quantities: (i) a "rate" per unit quantity (such as $4/m3 for work measured by volume), which in some languages is referred to as a "unit price" or (ii) a lump sum "price" (such as $4000 for an item of work which is not to be measured).

The second paragraph confirms that, for each item, the appropriate rate or price shall be that stated in the Contract, either for such item or for "similar" work. The question as to the similarity of work may be resolved by referring to the description in sub-paragraph (b)(iii), which refers to similarity in terms of work being of similar character and executed under similar conditions. Sub-paragraph (a) specifies four criteria which are applicable without reference to Clause 13, and a new rate shall only be appropriate if all four criteria are satisfied. The first two criteria relate to the change in quantity; the third criterion relates to its effect on Costs; and the fourth criterion allows adjustment of some items to be precluded.

If the four criteria in sub-paragraph (a) are satisfied, the Bill rate would typically be changed in proportion to such change in Cost per unit quantity which was the direct result of the change in quantity. In other words, the rate per unit quantity would be adjusted pro rata to the proportion (Cqm/QM) / (Cqb/QB). Having passed the three criteria which specify percentages, the new rate should not take account of the criterion percentages in (a)(i), (ii) and (iii). Although these percentages preclude adjustment of some items, changes to the rates should not be based upon differences between actual and criterion percentages.

16.5 CONTRACT PRICE AND PAYMENTS

16.5.1 The Contract Price

Clause 14.1 The Contract Price of Red Book read as follows;

14.1 The Contract Price

Unless otherwise stated in the Particular Conditions: (a) the Contract Price shall be agreed or determined under Sub-Clause 12.3 [Evaluation] and be subject to adjustments in accordance with the Contract; (b) the Contractor shall pay all taxes, duties and fees required to be paid by him under the Contract, and the Contract Price shall not be adjusted for any of these costs except as stated in Sub-Clause 13.7 [Adjustments for Changes in Legislation]; (c) any quantities which may be set out in the Bill of Quantities or other Schedule are estimated quantities and are not to be taken as the actual and correct quantities: (i) of the Works which the Contractor is required to execute, or (ii) for the purposes of Clause 12 [Measurement and Evaluation]; and (d) the Contractor shall submit to the Engineer, within 28 days after the Commencement Date, a proposed breakdown of each lump sum price in the Schedules. The Engineer may take account of the breakdown when preparing Payment Certificates, but shall not be bound by it.

Clause 14.1 The Contract Price of Yellow Book read as follows;

14.1 The Contract Price

Unless otherwise stated in the Particular Conditions: (a) the Contract Price shall be the lump sum Accepted Contract Amount and be subject to adjustments in accordance with the Contract; (b) the Contractor shall pay all taxes, duties and fees required to be paid by him under the Contract, and the Contract Price shall not be adjusted for any of these costs, except as stated in Sub-Clause 13.7 [Adjustments for Changes in Legislation]; (c) any quantities which may be set out in a Schedule are estimated quantities and are not to be taken as the actual and correct quantities of the Works which the Contractor is required to execute; and (d) any quantities or price data which may be set out in a Schedule shall be used for the purposes stated in the Schedule and may be inapplicable for other purposes.

However, if any part of the Works is to be paid according to quantity supplied or work done, the provisions for measurement and evaluation shall be as stated in the Particular Conditions. The Contract Price shall be determined accordingly, subject to adjustments in accordance with the Contract.

Clause 14.1 The Contract Price of Silver Book read as follows;

14.1 The Contract Price

Unless otherwise stated in the Particular Conditions: (a) payment for the Works shall be made on the basis of the lump sum Contract Price, subject to adjustments in accordance with the Contract; and (b) the Contractor shall pay all taxes, duties and fees required to be paid by him under the Contract, and the Contract Price shall not be adjusted for any of these costs, except as stated in Sub-Clause 13.7 [Adjustments for Changes in Legislation].

This Sub-Clause sets out the fundamental principles of the Contract as regards money, which differ between the three Books. Under Red Book or Yellow Book, Sub-Clause 1.1.4.2 states that the Contract Price is defined in Sub-Clause 14.1. Red Book 14.1(a) defines the Contract Price by reference to Sub-Clause 12.3, to the effect that the Works are to be valued by measurement. Yellow Book 14.1(a) defines the Contract Price as being the same as the (lump sum) Accepted Contract Amount. In both Books, the definitions are subject to any contrary provisions contained in the Particular Conditions, and the Contract Price includes adjustments under other Sub-Clauses.

Under Red Book or Yellow Book, which define a fixed "Accepted Contract Amount", the General Conditions describe the Contractor's entitlements to additional Costs in terms of such adjustments being "included in the Contract Price". Under Silver Book, Sub-Clause 1.1.4.1 defines the Contract Price as the agreed amount stated in the Contract, subject to adjustments in accordance with the Contract, without any reference to Sub-Clause 14.1. Silver Book 14.1(a) does not therefore define the Contract Price, but simply refers to it being the lump sum upon which payments are based. Silver Book refers to the accepted contract amount as the "Contract Price stated in the Contract Agreement" and describes the Contractor's entitlements to additional Costs in terms of such adjustments being "added to the Contract Price".

Sub-paragraph (b) confirms that the Contractor pays duties and taxes under other provisions of the Contract: see Sub-Clause 1.13. The Contract Price is thus deemed to include these taxes and duties, together with associated administrative Costs, based on the rates applicable at the Base Date. If the rates of duty/tax increase after the Base Date, Sub-Clause 13.7 applies. Note that Sub-Clause 14.1 commences with the words "Unless otherwise stated in the Particular Conditions", which may include contrary provisions under which the Contractor may be entitled to exemption from, or to reimbursement of, taxes and/or duties.

Red Book 14.1(c) states that the quantities in the Bill of Quantities are only estimates. They do not define the extent of the Contractor's obligations to execute the Works, and they are not to be assumed to be correct for the purposes of final measurement. However, if the final measurement results in a quantity which is less than 90%, or more than 110%, of the quantity stated in the Bill of Quantities included in the Contract, the criterion in Sub-Clause 12.3(a)(i) is satisfied and either Party should consider whether the criteria in Sub-Clause 12.3(a)(ii) to (iv) have also been satisfied. Red Book 14.1(c) similarly states that quantities (if any) which may be stated in a Schedule are only estimates and do not define the extent of the Contractor's obligations. Under this lump sum form of Contract, the Contractor bears the risk of the quantities being different to his estimates. If any quantities are included in a Schedule, it should be clear as to who estimated the quantities and for what purpose they are included in the Contract. Sub-paragraph (d) prevents them being used for unintended purposes, such as when either Party seeks to adjust the Contract Price because of an increase or decrease in a quantity.

Under Yellow Book, the contract documents should therefore not include a Bill of Quantities unless its purpose is clearly stated. If a Bill of Quantities is included, so that part of the Works can be paid according to quantity supplied or work done, the provisions for measurement and evaluation must be stated in the Particular Conditions, in accordance with the final paragraph of P&DB 14.1.

Under Silver Book, the contract documents do not include "Schedules", so Saver Book does not contain provisions similar to Yellow Book 14.1(c)&(d). If part of the Works is to be paid according to quantity supplied or work done, appropriate provisions must be included in the Particular Conditions.

16.5.2 Advance Payment

All three FIDIC Books cover this topic under 14.2 Advance Payment.

The Employer must make an advance payment, as an interest-free loan for mobilisation and cash flow support, when the Contractor submits a guarantee in accordance as per contract provisions. The total advance payment, the number and timing of instalments (if more than one), and the applicable currencies and proportions, must be as stated in the Contract Data. The Engineer must deliver to the Employer and to the Contractor an Interim Payment Certificate for the advance payment or its first instalment after receiving a Statement and after the Employer receives (i) the Performance Security and (ii) a guarantee in amounts and currencies equal to the advance payment as per contract provisions. This guarantee must be issued by a reputable bank or financial institution selected by the Contractor, and must be in the form annexed to the Particular Conditions or in another form approved by the Employer.

The Contractor shall ensure that the guarantee is valid and enforceable until the advance payment has been repaid, but its amount must be progressively reduced by the amount repaid by the Contractor as indicated in the Payment Certificates. If the terms of the guarantee specify its expiry date, and the advance payment has not been repaid by the date 28 days prior to the expiry date, the Contractor must extend the validity of the guarantee until the advance payment has been repaid.

Unless stated otherwise in the Contract Data, the advance payment must be repaid through percentage deductions from the interim payments determined by the Engineer in accordance with the contract provisions. If the advance payment has not been repaid prior to the issue of the Taking-Over Certificate for the Works or prior to termination or Force Majeure (as the case may be), the whole of the balance then outstanding must immediately become due and, payable by the Contractor to the Employer.

16.5.3 Interim Payment

All three FIDIC Books cover this topic under 14.3 Application for Interim Payment Certificates.

The Contractor must submit a Statement in six copies (unless otherwise specified) to the Engineer after the end of each month, in a form approved by the Engineer, showing in detail the amounts to which the Contractor considers himself to be entitled, together with supporting documents which must include the report on the progress during this month in accordance with Progress Reports.

The Statement must include the following items, as applicable, which must be expressed in the various currencies in which the Contract Price is payable, in the sequence: (a) the estimated contract value of the Works executed and the Contractor's Documents produced up to the end of the month (including Variations but excluding items: any amounts to be added and deducted for changes in legislation and changes in cost and the deduction of amounts certified in all previous Payment Certificates; (c) any amount to be deducted for retention, calculated by applying the percentage of retention stated in the Contract Data to the total of the above amounts, until the amount so retained by the Employer reaches the limit of Retention Money (if any) stated in the Contract Data; (d) any amounts to be added for the advance payment (if more than one instalment) and to be deducted for its ; (e) any amounts to be added and deducted for Plant and Materials in accordance; (f) any other additions or deductions which may have become due under the Contract or otherwise, including those under *Claims, Disputes and Arbitration* clause; and (g) the deduction of amounts certified in all previous Payment Certificates. Schedule of Payments, Plant and Materials intended for the Works, and Issue of Interim Payment Certificates will be in accordance with contract provisions.

16.5.4 Schedule of Payments

All three FIDIC Books cover this topic in detail under 14.4 Schedule of Payments

A schedule of payments allows both Parties to plan their likely cash flow. Therefore, Red Book/Yellow Book 14.4(b) invalidates Sub-Clause 14.5, which would otherwise have introduced a variable aspect of cash flow. However, the schedule of payments may state that Sub-Clause 14.5 will apply. If there is no such schedule of payments, the last paragraph requires the Contractor to submit non-binding estimates every three months. They should tabulate his estimate of the payment to which he expects to become entitled during each quarterly period for the duration of the Contract. Unless instructed otherwise, the Contractor would be entitled to assume that "quarterly period" means January-March, April-June, July-September and October-December. Neither Party will be bound by the Contractor's estimates, so there is no reason for him to be required to amend them.

16.5.5 Payment

Clause 14.7 Payment of Red Book and Yellow Book read as follows;

14.7 Payment

The Employer shall pay to the Contractor: (a) the first instalment of the advance payment within 42 days after issuing the Letter of Acceptance or within 21 days after receiving the documents in accordance with Sub-Clause 4.2 [Performance Security] and Sub-Clause 14.2 [Advance Payment], whichever is later; (b) the amount certified in each Interim Payment Certificate within 56 days after the Engineer receives the Statement and supporting ; and (c) the amount certified in the Final Payment Certificate within 56 days after the Employer receives this Payment Certificate. Payment of the amount due in each currency shall be made into the bank account, nominated by the Contractor, in the payment country (for this currency) specified in the Contract.

Clause 14.7 Timing of Payments of Silver book read as follows:

14.7 Payment

Except as otherwise stated in Sub-Clause 2.5 [Employer's Claims], the Employer shall pay to the Contractor: (a) the first instalment of the advance payment within 42 days after the date on which the Contract came into full force and effect or within 21 days after the Employer receives the documents in accordance with Sub-Clause 4.2 [Performance Security] and Sub-Clause 14.2 [Advance Payment], whichever is later; (b) the amount which is due in respect of each Statement, other than the Final Statement, within 56 days after receiving the Statement and supporting documents; and (c) the final amount due, within 42 days after receiving the Final Statement and written discharge in accordance with Sub-Clause14.11 [Application for Final Payment] and Sub-Clause 14.12 [Discharge].

Payment of the amount due in each currency shall be made into the bank account, nominated by the Contractor, in the payment country (for this currency) specified in the Contract

The Employer is required to pay the first instalment of the advance payment (or the whole payment, if it is made in one instalment) within six weeks of entering into the Contract, or within three weeks of receiving the securities described in Sub-Clauses 4.2 and 14.2. When entering into the Contract, the Employer will typically be able to calculate the amount of this first payment, and should immediately initiate arrangements for making prompt payment. Under Silver Book, the Employer's obligation is stated in sub-paragraph (b) as being to pay the amount which "is due", subject to Sub-Clause 2.5 but irrespective of the Employer's notice under silver Book 14.6 and irrespective of any non-binding determinations under Silver Book 3.5. This amount due may incorporate reductions to which the Employer is entitled, having claimed compensation from the Contractor in accordance with Sub-Clause 2.5 and having received no notice of dissatisfaction.

If the Contractor notifies dissatisfaction with the Employer's determination under the last paragraph of Silver Book 3.5 (i) the determination is of no effect, and the Employer cannot rely upon it as entitling him to recover such compensation; (b) he must still pay the amount which "is due", irrespective of the Employer's own determination under Sub-Clause 3.5; and (iii) the answer to the question as to what amount "is due" may be determined by reference to the provisions on which the Employer based his claim, either by agreement or under the dispute resolution procedures described in Clause 20. For example, the DAB may decide the amount which was due, having been informed of the (lesser or greater) amount actually paid by the Employer. If the DAB decides that the Employer had paid less than the amount which was due under EPCT 14.7(b), the Contractor would be entitled to financing charges under Silver Book 14.8.

Under Red Book or Yellow Book, the Contractor's entitlement under sub-paragraph (b) is payment of the amount stated in the Engineer's Interim Payment Certificate. The Employer must make payment in full, irrespective of any entitlement to compensation arising from any claim which the Employer may have against the Contractor. If the Employer considers himself entitled to claim against the Contractor, notice and particulars must first be submitted under Sub-Clause 2.5. The Employer's entitlement is then to be agreed or determined, and incorporated as a deduction in a Payment Certificate. This procedure, as prescribed in Sub-Clause 2.5 (notice, particulars, and agreement or determination), may require less time than the 28 days mentioned in the first paragraph of Sub-Clause 14.6. By not timing payment to the date when the Engineer issues the Interim Payment Certificate, the Employer has more time to pay if the Certificate is issued promptly.

The Contractor has some degree of protection under Sub-Clauses 14.8 and 16.1 if certification is delayed. Note that his entitlement to financing charges under Sub-Clause 14.8 is calculated for a period which is "deemed to commence on the date for payment specified in Sub-Clause 14.7 [...], irrespective (in the case of its subparagraph (b)) of the date on which any Interim Payment Certificate is issued". For example, if the Certificate is a week late, the Contractor will be entitled to financing charges under Sub-Clause 14.8 unless the Employer manages to accelerate his procedures and comply with Sub-Clause 14.7.

The Employer is required to make payment into the Contractor's bank account(s), with provision being made for the Contract to have specified the country or countries of the Contractor's bank(s). For each of the currencies of payment, a "payment country" may have been specified, which might be the country of the currency of payment. Alternatively, all payments may have been specified as being made into the Contractor's bank in his country or the "Country". When pricing their tenders, tenderers will take account of the option to specify a payment country, and of the periods for payment. Longer periods for payment increase the Contractor's financing costs, so tenderers would wish to increase their prices accordingly.

16.5.6 Delayed payment

Clause 14.8 Delayed Payment of all three FIDIC Book deals with this aspect in detail.

The Contractor is entitled to financing charges (in some countries called "interest") if he does not receive payment in accordance with the appropriate sub-paragraph of Sub-Clause 14.7. Its sub-paragraph (b) entitles the Contractor to payment of: (i) under Red Book/Yellow Book, the amount certified by the Engineer, irrespective of any claim which the Employer may have against the Contractor, or (ii) under Silver Book, the amount which is actually due.

Under Red Book/Yellow Book, the date on which the Interim Payment Certificate is issued is not relevant when calculating these financing charges. Financing charges are calculated for a period which is "deemed to commence on the date for payment specified in Sub-Clause 14.7", even if the Engineer had not issued an Interim Payment Certificate by such "date for payment". This period applies even if no Interim Payment Certificate is issued, although it would then be difficult to establish the amount to which the "annual rate" is to be applied. If the Certificate is a week late and the Employer accelerate his procedures and complies with Sub-Clause 14.7, the Contractor will not be entitled to financing charges.

The Contractor is entitled to these financing charges without being required to give notice and, under Red Book/Yellow Book, without a Payment Certificate. However, it may be preferable for financing charges to be included in Payment Certificates under Red Book/Yellow Book, for accounting purposes. Financing charges are to be calculated at the annual rate of three percentage points above the discount rate of the central bank in the country of the currency of payment. If this rate is considered inappropriate when tender documents are being prepared, a new rate may be defined in the Particular Conditions.

16.5.7 Payment of Retention Money

Clause 14.9 Payment of Retention Money of all three FIDIC Book deal with this aspect in detail.

Retention Money is retained under Sub-Clause 14.3(c) and is released in instalments based upon the Taking-Over Certificates issued under Clause 10. Under

Red Book, the first releases are made when Taking-Over Certificates are issued for Sections and/or parts of the Works, under Sub-Clause 10.1 and/or Sub-Clause 10.2 respectively. The release is defined as two-fifths of the proportion calculated by dividing the estimated contract value of the Section or part, by the estimated final Contract Price. Only two-fifths (not half) of this proportion are stated as being released at this stage. If half had been released, there might be very little balance (of the half of Retention Money) to be released on completion of the Works, because of the arithmetical possibilities attributable to Variations.

Under Yellow Book or Silver Book, the first releases are made when Taking-Over Certificates are issued under Sub-Clause 10.1 for Sections which have passed all tests, including Tests after Completion (if any). The release is defined as the relevant percentage of the first half of Retention Money, such percentage being defined in the last paragraph as the percentage value of the Section as stated in the Appendix to Tender (under P&DB) or as stated in the Contract (under Silver Book).

Retention Money is not released when a Taking-Over Certificate is issued for a part of the Works, because it might be difficult to define an amount to be released. Also, the taking over of a part of the Works is inconsistent with Silver Book 10.2 and seems unlikely to be a frequent occurrence under Yellow Book 10.2.

The balance of the first half of the Retention Money is released when the Taking-Over Certificate is issued for the Works. Under Yellow Book or Silver Book, the Works must also have passed all tests, including Tests after Completion. If Tests after Completion are unduly delayed by the Employer, Yellow Book/Silver Book 12.2 would apply, entitling the Contractor to the financing cost attributable to the delayed release of Retention Money.

The date on which each Section is completed is to be stated in its Taking-Over Certificate. On this date, the Defect Notification Period commences, the duration of which is to be stated in the Appendix to Tender (under Red Book or Yellow Book) or in the Particular Conditions (under Silver Book).

16.5.8 Final Payment

Clause 14.11 Application for Final Payment Certificate of Red and yellow Book reads as follows:

14.11 Application for Final Payment Certificate

Within 56 days after receiving the Performance Certificate, the Contractor shall submit, to the Engineer, six copies of a draft final statement with supporting documents showing in detail in a form approved by the Engineer: (a) the value of all work done in accordance with the Contract; and (b) any further sums which the Contractor considers to be due to him under the Contract or otherwise.

If the Engineer disagrees with or cannot verify any part of the draft final statement, the Contractor shall submit such further information as the Engineer may reasonably require and shall make such changes in the draft as may be agreed between them. The Contractor shall then prepare and submit to the Engineer the final statement as agreed. This agreed statement is referred to in these Conditions as the

"Final Statement". However if, following discussions between the Engineer and the Contractor and any changes to the draft final statement which are agreed, it becomes evident that a dispute exists, the Engineer shall deliver to the Employer (with a copy to the Contractor) an Interim Payment Certificate for the agreed parts of the draft final statement. Thereafter, if the dispute is finally resolved under Sub-Clause

20.4 [Obtaining Dispute Adjudication Board's Decision] or Sub-Clause 20.5 [Amicable Settlement], the Contractor shall then prepare and submit to the Employer (with a copy to the Engineer) a Final Statement.

Clause 14.11 Application for Final Payment of Silver Book reads as follows:

14.11 Application for Final Payment

Within 56 days after receiving the Performance Certificate, the Contractor shall submit, to the Engineer, six copies of a draft final statement with supporting documents showing in detail in a form approved by the Employer: (a) the value of all work done in accordance with the Contract; and (b) any further sums which the Contractor considers to be due to him under the Contract or otherwise.

If the Employer disagrees with or cannot verify any part of the draft final statement, the Contractor shall submit such further information as the Employer may reasonably require and shall make such changes in the draft as may be agreed between them. The Contractor shall then prepare and submit to the Employer the final statement as agreed. This agreed statement is referred to in these Conditions as the "Final Statement".

However if, following discussions between the Parties and any changes to the draft final statement which are agreed, it becomes evident that a dispute exists, the Employer shall pay the agreed parts of the draft final statement in accordance with Sub- Clause 14.6 [Interim Payments] and Sub-Clause 14.7 [Timing of Payments]. Thereafter, if the dispute is finally resolved under Sub-Clause 20.4 [Obtaining Dispute Adjudication Board's Decision] or Sub-Clause 20.5 [Amicable Settlement], the Contractor shall then prepare and submit to the Employer a Final Statement.

This Sub-Clause sets out the procedure for settling the financial aspects of the Contract. The Contractor must initiate the procedure by the date eight weeks after the issue of the Performance Certificate under Sub-Clause 11.9. He may feel able to initiate it as soon as the Defect Notification Periods have all expired. If agreement is not achieved and a dispute exists, the Contractor is entitled to prompt payment in respect of the agreed parts of his draft final statement. If the dispute is then resolved under Sub-Clause 20.4 (by the DAB's decision) or under Sub-Clause 20.5 (by amicable settlement), a Final Statement is to be prepared in accordance with the outcome, so that the following Sub-Clauses can then be applicable. If the dispute is not resolved under Sub-Clause 20.4 or 20.5, it would probably need to be resolved under Sub-Clause 20.6: by arbitration.

After resolution by arbitration, which may be considerably later, there may be no need for a Final Statement, so Sub-Clause 14.11 does not require it to be prepared. For example, the only necessary documentation may have been prepared or defined by the arbitrator(s). If there is no Final Statement, Sub-Clause 14.12, Sub-Clause 14.13 and sub-paragraph (a) of Sub-Clause 14.14 cannot apply.

16.5.9 Payment in Applicable Currencies

Clause 14.15 Currencies of Payment of all three FIDIC Book read as follows:

14.15 Currencies of Payment

The Contract Price shall be paid in the currency or currencies named in the Appendix to Tender. Unless otherwise stated in the Particular Conditions, if more than one currency is so named, payments shall be made as follows: (a) if the Accepted Contract Amount was expressed in Local Currency only: (i) the proportions or amounts of the Local and Foreign Currencies, and the fixed rates of exchange to be used for calculating the payments, shall be as stated in the Appendix to Tender, except as otherwise agreed by both Parties; (ii) payments and deductions under Sub-Clause 13.5 [Provisional Sums] and Sub-Clause 13.7 [Adjustments for Changes in Legislation] shall be made in the applicable currencies and proportions; and (iii) other payments and deductions under sub-paragraphs (a) to (d) of Sub-Clause 14.3 [Application for Interim Payment Certificates] shall be made in the currencies and proportions specified in sub-paragraph (a)(i) above; (b) payment of the damages specified in the Appendix to Tender shall be made in the currencies and proportions specified in the Appendix to Tender; (c) other payments to the Employer by the Contractor shall be made in the currency in which the sum was expended by the Employer, or in such currency as may be agreed by both Parties; (d) if any amount payable by the Contractor to the Employer in a particular currency exceeds the sum payable by the Employer to the Contractor in that currency, the Employer may recover the balance of this amount from the sums otherwise payable to the Contractor in other currencies; and (e) if no rates of exchange are stated in the Appendix to Tender, they shall be those prevailing on the Base Date and determined by the central bank of the Country.

This Sub-Clause prescribes the currencies in which payments are to be made, subject to the provisions which may be contained in the Contract Agreement or (under Red Book or Yellow Book) in the Appendix to Tender. If these provisions state that all payments are to be made in one named currency, this Sub-Clause becomes inapplicable, subject to any Particular Conditions.

Sub-paragraph (a) only applies if payments are expressed in Local Currency but are to be made (partly or wholly) in other currencies, applying agreed proportions and rates of exchange. This method of payment is often considered appropriate for a Red Book contract, where the alternative of a multi-currency Bill of Quantities may be unduly complicating, and may also give an unrealistic indication of the proportions of Cost in the various currencies. For a lump sum contract under Yellow Book or Silver Book, it may be considered preferable to define each of the amounts due in each of the currencies in which payment is to be made. In this event, payments will be due in such currencies, and subparagraph (a) will not apply. When tender documents are being prepared, the effect of this Sub-Clause should be reviewed in the light of the intended method of defining payments in applicable currencies.

If the Contract provides for payment of the Contract Price in more than one currency, then the amount payable in each of the applicable currencies must be specified. For this purpose, reference must be made to the actual or expected currency proportions of the Cost of the varied work, and to the proportions of various currencies specified for payment of the Contract Price.

16.5.10 Provisional Sums

Each Provisional Sum must only be used, in whole or in part, in accordance with the Engineer's instructions and the Contract Price must be adjusted accordingly. The total sum paid to the Contractor to include only such amounts, for the work, supplies or services to which the Provisional Sum relates, as the Engineer shall have instructed. For each Provisional Sum, the Engineer may issue instruction for: (a) work to be executed (including Plant, Materials or services to be supplied) by the Contractor and valued; and/or ; (b) Plant, Materials or services to be purchased by the Contractor, from a nominated Subcontractor or otherwise, and for which there shall be included in the Contract Price: (i) the actual amounts paid (or due to be paid) by the Contractor as per contract provisions, and (ii) a sum for overhead charges and profit, calculated as a percentage of these actual amounts by applying the relevant percentage rate (if any) stated in the appropriate Schedule. If there is no such rate, the percentage rate stated in the Contract Data shall be applied. The Contractor, however, is required to substantiate producing quotations, invoices, vouchers and accounts or receipts, upon demand from the Engineer.

16.5.11 Daywork

For work of a minor or incidental nature, the Engineer may instruct that work outside contract (i.e. variations or extra work to be executed on a daywork basis. The work must then be valued in accordance with the Daywork Schedule included in the Contract in accordance with prescribed procedure. One copy of each statement will, if correct, or when agreed, be signed by the Engineer and returned to the Contractor. The Contractor must then submit priced statements of these resources to the Engineer, prior to their inclusion in the next Statement of Application for Interim Payment Certificates.

16.5.12 Release From Performance

Clause 19.7 Release from Performance under the Law of FIDIC Red Book, Yellow Book, and Silver Book read as follows:

19.7 Release from Performance under the Law

Notwithstanding any other provision of this Clause, if any event or circumstance outside the control of the Parties (including, but not limited to, Force Majeure) arises which makes it impossible or unlawful for either or both Parties to fulfil its or their contractual obligations or which, under the law governing the Contract, entitles the Parties to be released from further performance of the Contract, then upon notice by either Party to the other Party of such event or circumstance: (a) the Parties shall be discharged from further performance, without prejudice to the rights of either Party in respect of any previous breach of the Contract; and (b) the sum payable by the Employer to the Contractor shall be the same as would have been payable under Sub-Clause 19.6 [Optional Termination, Payment and Release] if the Contract had been terminated under Sub-Clause 19.6.

If any event or circumstance outside the control of the Parties (including, but not limited to, Force Majeure) arises which makes it impossible or unlawful for either or both Parties to fulfil its or their contractual obligations or which, under the law governing the Contract, entitles the Parties to be released from further performance of the Contract, then upon notice by either Party to the other Party of such event or circumstance: (a) the Parties shall be discharged from further performance, without prejudice to the rights of either Party in respect of any previous breach of the Contract; and (b) the sum payable by the Employer to the Contractor shall be the same as would have been payable under Optional Termination, Payment and Release.

Chapter 17

ISO 9000 – QUALITY MANAGEMENT IN CONSTRUCTION

17.1 INTRODUCTION

The ISO 9000 family addresses various aspects of quality management and contains some of ISO's best known standards. The standards provide guidance and tools for companies and organizations who want to ensure that their products and services consistently meet customer's requirements, and that quality is consistently improved. Standards in the ISO 9000 family include:

- ISO 9001:2008 - sets out the requirements of a quality management system
- ISO 9000:2005 - covers the basic concepts and language
- ISO 9004:2009 - focuses on how to make a quality management system more efficient and effective
- ISO 19011:2011 - sets out guidance on internal and external audits of quality management systems.

17.2 TRANSITION OF ISO 9001: 2008 TO ISO 9001:2015

The main changes in the new version of ISO 9001:2015 are:

- the adoption of the HLS as set out in Annex SL of ISO Directives Part One;
- an explicit requirement for risk-based thinking to support and improve the understanding and application of the process approach;
- fewer prescribed requirements;
- less emphasis on documents;
- improved applicability for services;
- a requirement to define the boundaries of the QMS;
- increased emphasis on organizational context;
- increased leadership requirements; and
- greater emphasis on achieving desired outcomes to improve customer satisfaction.

The International Accreditation Forum (IAF) which monitors certifications/accreditations and the ISO Committee on Conformity Assessment (CASCO) have agreed a three year transition period from the publication date of ISO 9001:2015. The transition period will begin in dd September 2015 and end in dd September 2018.

Validity of certifications to ISO 9001:2008: ISO 9001:2008 certifications will not be valid after the end of September 2018. From March 2017 all initial certifications under accreditation shall be to ISO 9001:2015.

Guidance for transition: For any organisation the degree of change necessary will be dependent upon the maturity and effectiveness of the current management system, organisational structure and practices, therefore an impact assessment is strongly recommended in order to identify realistic resource and time implications.

Organizations using ISO 9001:2008: Organizations using ISO 9001:2008 are recommended to take the following actions:

- identify organizational gaps which need to be addressed to meet new requirements;
- develop an implementation plan;
- provide appropriate training and awareness for all parties that have an impact on the effectiveness of the organisation;
- update existing quality management system (QMS) to meet the revised requirements and provide verification of effectiveness;
- where applicable, liaise with your certification body for transition arrangements.

17.3 THE COST OF QUALITY

The cost-effectiveness of quality management depends upon reducing quality related costs. These are of three kinds. namely: (a) Prevention Costs; (b) Appraisal Costs; and (c) Failure Costs.

(a) Prevention costs: The costs of any action taken to investigate prevent or reduce defects and failures. Some examples of such costs include: (i) Establishing and maintaining a quality management system. (ii) Preparation of quality plans. (iii) Analysis of performance data for quality improvement purposes. (iv) Calibration and maintenance of equipment or instrumentation used to set quality standards or evaluate quality. (v) Quality training. (vi) Pre-qualification of outside suppliers, sub-contractors/ consultants, etc.

(b) Appraisal costs: The costs of assessing whether work has been carried out to the required standard or not. Some examples of such costs include: (i) the verification, checking or testing of the organization's final output immediately before delivery to the client/customer. (ii) The verification, checking or testing of goods or services supplied by others. (iii) The verification, checking or testing of the organization's own work whilst it is in progress. (iv) Reviewing the results of such verification, checking or test data.

(c) Failure costs: The costs incurred through failure to achieve the specified quality first time. These are often sub-divided into: internal failure costs and external failure costs. Internal failure costs are costs incurred before transfer of ownership to the client/customer and External failure costs are those incurred after that transfer. Some examples of such costs include: (i) Repeated or modified work of one's own or of an outside supplier. (ii) Rejected work of one's own or of an outside supplier. (iii) Trouble-shooting. (iv) Downgrading of any form. (v) Dealing with client/customer complaints claims and litigation. (vi) Analysis of defects or failures re-verification, checking or testing.

In conclusion, we can say that every £ (or $) by which quality-related costs can be reduced contributes straight to profit or can be used to reduce overall costs, thereby improving competitiveness. It should be noted that, it is very much easier to enhance the profit margin through reducing quality-related costs than to do so by increasing turnover. However, it is important that quality management should be very cost-effective and though quality does not come free but such costs not only increase efficiency but also contribute to profits or to greater competitiveness.

17.4 QC AND QA UNDER FIDIC CONTRACTS

17.4.1 Quality in Construction Process

Construction site is a changing, contractually oriented and uncertain environment and differs with production factory where environment is relatively controlled. The quality in the construction project is obtained by conscientious application of a formal Quality Assurance Program implemented through a Quality Control Plan in the form of Practical Procedures and communicated among all parties involved in the project.

QA being part of the total management system, its effectiveness is directly related to the overall performance of the company and therefore, should be applied throughout the company. Since time is money in a project environment, therefore a formal QA System must be able to improve the time efficiency of a project to justify the cost of QA System. QA assistance is not only meeting the budget constraints of the project but also building up confidence that the work will be completed within the original program period and consequently contributing to the long-term prosperity of the company.

A formal QA system also benefits management in so far as delegating the routine function thus concentrating more on the technical development and problem solving of the business. Because of this delegation of function a formal QA System acts as an excellent vehicle to train junior members of the team for engineering and management function and ultimately serve to promote confidence throughout the company's organization.

Experience has shown that majority of errors that occur in the project environment are associated with lack of training, inadequate supervision and poor communication with the management team. A well applied QA System would lead to the satisfaction of the client and as a consequence increases substantially the ability of the company to maintain business and expands its client base.

Furthermore, QA is here to stay and shall be used more and more in the future as it will become impossible within a relatively short period of time to complete the major project without an adequate Quality Management System. The critics of QA System may argue that the associated cost of a formal QA System will eat into profit margins, without appreciating the fact that cost of QA System is relatively insignificant in comparison with the overall benefit accrued by the client which is more than matched by the effects of increased efficiency resulted thereof.

QA awareness and its inherent benefits must be communicated to all those associated with its development and implementation so that they should be convinced that it will ultimately benefit the business. The Top Management of all associated organizations with construction projects must accept that QA is not only desirable but also essential. The ethos of QA is clear: quality cannot be inspected in; it must be planned for built in.

The QA is, as much as anything, an issue of attitude. When the responsibility for checking quality is with the inspector, the responsibility is then quite wrongly perceived to be removed from the producer. This is bad attitude as it leads to failures by the producers and place unlimited burdens on the inspector. Thus if clients add QA clauses to their contracts, medium size contractors will respond positively without excessive difficulties because QA is the current buzz word for good management which in practice is the most economic form of management practice. Quality in the construction is obtained by conscientious application of a formal QA Program implemented through a Quality Control Plan in form of practical procedures and communicated among all parties involved in the project.

Since quality and costs are twins and quality has to be paid for, therefore appropriate allowance must be made in the project budgets. All concerned with the pursuit of quality should identify their respective system boundary; determine their own philosophy and quality goals and related responsibilities and ensure the successful implementation of the quality system in their respective fields.

Quality is both a discipline and a tribute to attitude and standards and investing in it can only result in significant benefits for the owner, design consultants, the construction contractors, the end-users and ultimately the public at large. Quality Philosophy and approach to quality achievement should go hand in hand to bring quality consciousness which may hasten the pace of change in the years to come.

17.4.2 Contractor's Specific Obligations to Control Quality of Works

Clause 4.9 Quality Assurance of Red Book, Yellow Book, and Silver Book read as follows:

4.9 Quality Assurance

The Contractor shall institute a quality assurance system to demonstrate compliance with the requirements of the

Contract. The system shall be in accordance with the details stated in the Contract. The Engineer (in Silver Book Employer) shall be entitled to audit any aspect of the system.

Details of all procedures and compliance documents shall be submitted to the Engineer (in Silver Book Employer) for information before each design and execution stage is commenced. When any document of a technical nature is issued to the Engineer (in Silver Book Employer), evidence of the prior approval by the Contractor himself shall be apparent on the document itself.

Compliance with the quality assurance system shall not relieve the Contractor of any of his duties, obligations or responsibilities under the Contract.

The Contractor is required to institute a quality assurance system in accordance with the details stated in the Contract, unless no such details are so stated. The international standard ISO 9001 introduced the concept of quality assurance, but it may be inappropriate for some Works or for work in some countries. If this Sub-Clause is to apply, details of the quality assurance system should be included in the Contract, and could have been proposed by tenderers

Under the current competitive business environment, business enterprises, particularly major companies are becoming more and more quality conscience having objectives to produce high level products and services to meet their customers'/clients' requirements.

In this context, it must be remembered that quality is not something that occur automatically and it is not enough to establish whether the result of work performed meets the requirements. But it demands avoidance of faults during the various work stages through corporate efforts in directing and controlling various processes, e.g., planning, design & development, purchasing, production, inspection, testing, etc. Therefore, the aim should be directed towards achieving a high degree of quality in all of the operational areas of the respective company. The company top management should issue a quality policy. Based on the quality policy, a comprehensive quality system needs to be developed and introduced in all organizational units in the form of a QA Program.

The purpose of QA Program, particularly on any major construction project should be to make optimum use of both QA documents and organization as management tools and take all those planned and systematic actions necessary to provide adequate confidence that all the elements of work will satisfy given requirements for quality. It is important to remember in this context that for effectiveness, Quality Assurance usually requires a continuing evaluation of factors that affect the adequacy of the design or specification or both for intended application as well as verification and audits of construction, installation and inspection operations.

It is the responsibility of Quality Assurance Organizational Unit Managers to ensure that all briefing, planning, design, specification, construction and final inspections are carried out in accordance with the QA Procedures and Policies set out in the Quality Manual and where indicated abide by the associated documents. In producing the Quality Manual, it is important to recognize all the salient features and factors that determine the quality of the output. The most significant feature of Quality Assurance is that it is self-correcting as by keeping a record of what is done, it is possible through feedback to see where procedure are weak or not being followed, and corrective action taken.

Chapter 18

RISK MANAGEMENT & RESPONSIBILITY IN CONSTRUCTIONAL PROJECTS

18.1 RISK MANAGEMENT

The primary objectives of Risk Analysis and Management are to: (i) keep the cost of projects to a minimum; (ii) achieve greater certainty of total costs; (iii) identify the likely cost range for a project; (iv) ensure the project can be delivered. These objectives are achieved through the identification of potential risks, assessment of their impact on the project should they materialize, and the development of appropriate actions for their management. Accordingly, Risk Management is a core element of project management and as such should be implemented by all professionals managing contracts or projects.

The techniques are applicable to all scales of project, independent of size or nature; and should be properly understood by all key personnel from the planner and project manager through to the engineer and designer. It should be noted that as project budgets tighten so do the risks associated with the planning, development, design and implementation of projects. Therefore, through understanding the risks involved in projects and implementing cost effective techniques to reduce these risks, budget spending can be more accurately estimated and monitored, thereby ensuring that optimum efficiencies are achieved on all projects.

Projects contain a number of uncertainties that result in time and cost uncertainties, affecting the project deliverability. To manage these uncertainties, they need to be quantified. Risk is an uncertainty that can be quantified either from historical information or from an educated estimate. Risk Management is a process designed to allow for, remove or reduce the uncertainties or risks, which could threaten the achievement of project objectives. Risk Management should be regarded as an integral part of project management and not just as a set of tools or techniques.

All major projects have many inherent risks that might include varying ground conditions, resource availability, and requirements of third parties, each have an impact on the ability to deliver a particular project. Risks that remain unresolved at production or construction usually result in cost increases. Any resulting delay and consequential effects on a contract can be attributed to individual changes resulting from uncertainties built into the contract. Given that the changes are the result of the uncertainties (risks), the cost impacts can be directly related to residual risks transferred into the construction phase.

It is wise to use, a wealth of knowledge on risk management and the process for dealing with project risks from previous projects, in the form of risk analysis and management procedures to minimize the number of unplanned events during project development.

As the management of risks commences at the initial feasibility stage and is a continuous dynamic process, requiring reaction to new information and investigations during the development of a project, therefore, the assessment of risks aims to determine the likely financial impact that each risk will have on the project. In this context the financial effect of time related risks should be included to provide the overall financial impact.

At the early stages of project development, the analysis of risks provides an assessment of the ability to deliver a project. These strategic risks should be considered as part of the risk analysis to assess the programming and financial impact on the project. Where projects have high risk to achieve specific objectives, the risks and their potential costs can be highlighted so that project development can take full account of these risks.

To ensure that each project provides the best overall value for money, all of the important risks need to be identified and assessed at the earliest possible stage of a project. Risk analysis and risk management aims to predict, from the inception of a project through to production/construction, the allowance that needs to be included to estimate the project outturn cost and also risk analysis and risk management provides critical information relating to the choice of a preferred project. Risks at the early stages of a project are of a more strategic nature but during project development, strategic risks begin to recede and engineering risks become more dominant. However, due to the changing nature of a project's risk environment, a formal risk analysis should be undertaken at important stages of the procurement process corresponding with updates of the project cost estimate.

Where there are several risk response or mitigation measures available, the object is to identify those which reduce the total cost of risk and give the best value for money solution. It is important to understand that responsibility for managing each identified risk should be allocated to the party best placed to exercise the most effective control over it, and during the design phase, individual specialists may be identified to manage risks on behalf of their clients. The Risk Allowance, which is an estimate of the financial allowance for dealing with the remaining risks at that stage, should be reported along with the other costs to provide the project outturn cost estimate. The nature of the residual risks and the cost of dealing with these will provide information to help to make an informed choice of the form of contract to be used for procurement. Risk Analysis and Management process can be subdivided into the following three distinct phases, namely: Identification; (ii) Assessment; and (iii) Management:

Identification: Determine what could go wrong. This is best achieved by brainstorming in a Workshop forum.

Assessment: Understand how the Risks occur, quantify their possible effects on the project and identify options for their reduction.

Management: The process of evaluating options for reducing the Risks and quantifying their possible effects on the project and identify options for their reduction. The management of all risks should be a continuous process, built into these procedures and risk management is shown below:

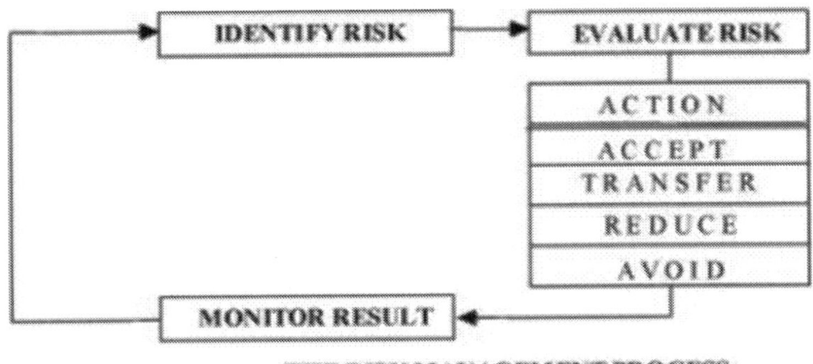

THE RISK MANAGEMENT PROCESS

To identify risk is the most important element of the risk management process. This is a technique which requires comprehensive knowledge of organizational tools such as organization chart, site plans and geographic data and material flow diagrams, etc., of the activities of the organization, etc. Once identified that a risk exists, then to evaluate it, the next step in the process is to determine whether it falls within acceptable limits. Many methods have been used for risk evaluation ranging from: a very simple statistical review to a highly complex hazard analysis. It is of utmost importance that evaluation obtained is realistic and to achieve that the risk manager needs to be able to call on all the skill within the organization as well as external specialists. Once risk is adequately evaluated the risk manager should be able to prescribe the correct action for each individual risk. If risks are unacceptable to the organization then these need further treatment, e.g., reduce, transfer or avoid, etc.

Most common risks could be transferred (by exchanging uncertain large losses for certain small losses, i.e., insurance, etc.), or risk reduction by loss prevention which can take the form of training, process modification, etc. Since processes, conditions and people are all subject to change, it is important that there is a regular monitoring process which can ensure that any new risks are not neglected or previous accepted risks have become unacceptable and to determine that action taken is still effective and relevant.

18.2 TRANSFER OF RISK

Construction companies enter into contracts on a regular basis, therefore it is critical to understand what risk such companies can attempt to transfer and what risk they are being asked to assume. While In this respect before making decision about transferring of risk some major issues need to be addressed, such as the following:

Indemnification: It is defined as "compensation for actual loss or damage." Under common law, one party is responsible for indemnifying another party for the consequences of one's negligent acts. Contractually speaking, however, indemnification can have broader connotation. There are three basic types of indemnities: (i). Limited Form Indemnity - a limited form indemnity merely stating that the inseminator will hold harmless and indemnify the indemnitee for the consequences of the indemnitor's negligence; (ii) Intermediate Form Indemnity – this form indemnity requires the indemnitor to hold harmless and indemnify the indemnitee for anything and everything except the indemnitee's sole negligence; and (iii) Broad Form Indemnity – this form indemnity requires the indemnitor to hold harmless and indemnify the indemnitee for anything and everything, including the indemnitee's sole negligence.

Accordingly, before agreeing to an indemnification agreement, one need to understand exactly what risk is being transferred and whether or not one is in a position to assume the risk. Furthermore, one need to take into consideration laws of the country where project is executed that might affect the risk transfer. In this context FIDIC Contracts' Clause 17 refers of which sub-clause for the transfer of risk of the Contractor as well as Employer are discussed herein above.

The factors affecting risk transfer: These include, but not limited to: (i) Control of the risk - which is in the best position to control the risk? Example –a construction contractor, as opposed to an owner might better control jobsite accidents due to contractual management requirements. (Ii) Knowledge of the risk - Does one party's knowledge of risk make them more logical to assume risk? Example –a demolition contractor using explosives to demo a building might be the logical choice to assume risk of injuries and damages due to their unique expertise. (iii) Statutory or common law limitations on risk transfer - may limit risk that can be transferred via contract example - when a statute or common law prohibits one party from assuming another party's sole negligence. (iv) Custom and practice- generally accepted modes (e.g. Employer to Contractor; Contractor to subcontractor). (v) Bargaining position: the bigger the entity the more likely to transfer risk to smaller entity; the more competitive the marketplace, the more risk a company is likely to accept in negotiations; and those entities with a reputation for a firm bargaining position may obtain a preferred risk position because of their reputation.

Transference of Risk *Versus* Optimum Project Cost: decisions made by the Owner and his design professional as to which risks will be transferred to the Contractor will have a significant effect on the ultimate cost of the project as the Contractor will, in most cases, endeavour to level the playing field based upon his perception of the project risks he has undertaken by ensuring that he is appropriately compensated for accepting those risks. Of course, in each tendering situation, the Contractor will have to decide if the additional money which he may attempt to charge through to the Owner is worth the risks that have been allocated to him in the contract documents.

An excellent initiative of transference of risk can be seen in public private partnerships (PPP) projects. These projects typically involve a number of separate contractual relationships, and it is incumbent on the parties to foresee the most likely project risks to be encountered by each of the project participants and deal with these appropriately in the individual PPP contracts. An example of typical PPP contracts which are affected by distribution of risk include the Concession Agreement – the agreement between the public sector Owner and the private sector project company by which the project concession is granted.

There is also usually a Design/Build construction contract between the private sector project company and the Design/Build Contractor to design and build the project. In addition, there is an Operation and Maintenance contract between the project company and the Operator/Manager to operate and maintain the project during part or all of the PPP concession period. PPP contracts illustrate the transference of risk as well as the necessity for project participants to tailor their contracts to the project under consideration, and not vice-versa. There is no one standard contract form that can fit every type of contract contingencies. Each contract must be drafted to meet the requirements for each individual project, and this includes the allocation of risks between the contracting parties.

These risks should be allocated to the parties who have the best ability to bear them: This is important to optimize project results for the owner from a cost and time point of view. In the PPP example, the assessment of which parties will be affected by a particular element of risk, and in what way, will be complicated and difficult to clarify since the project participants typically assume several different roles, e.g., the Design/Build Contractor may also be one of the shareholders of the project company and/or the Operator. In most PPP projects, risk allocation factors such as the following will operate: (i) Market risk will be assumed by the project company. (ii) Design, construction and commissioning risk will be assumed by the Design/Build Contractor. (iii) Operation and maintenance-related risks will be assumed by the Operator. (iv)The majority of any political risk and delays by authorities will generally be allocated to the public sector Owner through the Concession Agreement between the Owner and the project company. (v) Any residual risk will be borne, in the first instance, by the project company, who will frequently attempt to transfer this risk to the Owner.

In this context, an excellent example in this regard is the philosophy used in the FIDIC major Forms of Contracts (Red Book, Yellow Book, and Silver Book). FIDIC Books share the Project Risks between the Employer and the Contractor as shown in the diagram below.

Provisions that deal with risk allocation between the project Owner and the Design/Build Contractor and the Operation and Maintenance Contractor may be drafted so as to mirror the language of the Concession Agreement between the project Owner and the project company. A practical solution to potential ambiguities between the various contracts often includes the use of "if and when" language in the Design/Build construction contract, for example, stating that the Design/Build Contractor is entitled to extensions of time under certain circumstances if and when such extensions are granted to the project company under the Concession Agreement with the Owner. The project company may also wish to see an overriding provision in the Design/Build.

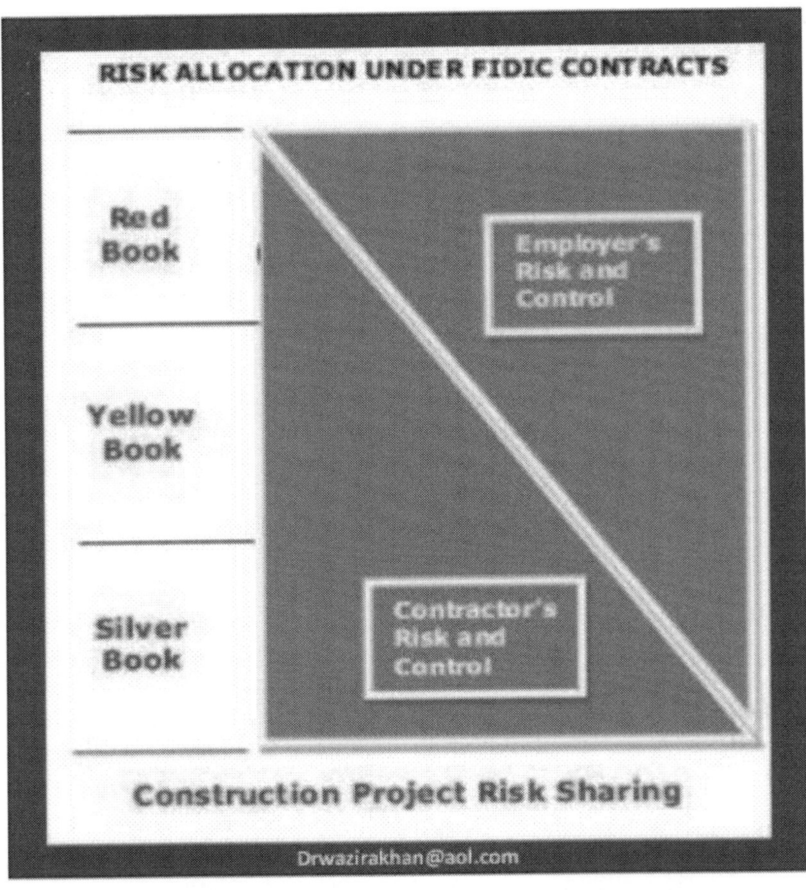

Contract such that the Design/Build (FIDIC Yellow Book and Silver Book and for that matter Gold Book) Contractor is under an obligation to perform so that the project company is not in breach of its obligations in the Concession Agreement. Completion risks, containing elements of design, construction and commissioning risk, as well as other residual risks, will be a factor for all of the principal project participants. Certain parties will typically bear the greatest level of such risk, in particular, the Design/Build Contractor. Ultimately, however, decisions made by the project Owner and his advisors, be they architects, engineers or project managers, in the initial stages of contract tender preparation, will have a major effect in setting the tone for the future construction relationship between the parties.

In this reference whilst it is important to appreciate that principles of equity and fairness should apply in allocating risk in contracts, simply allocating risk to the weaker party who is less likely to bear it. It must be remembered always that unequal or overwhelmingly one-sided contracts, throwing all of the major risks on to the Contractor, rather than making for a smooth cooperative process throughout the term of construction, can result in a breakdown of relationships during the course of a project, thereby giving way to claims and disputes and difficulty in achieving an overall successful project, as one party or the other perceives that it is being taken advantage of and that it has signed a less than fortuitous contract. FIDIC Contracts set out under Clause 17 in detail the risk and responsibilities of the parties involved in the international construction project.

For the management of risk transfer mechanism, FIDIC Contracts set out under clause 18 Insurance, which is generally advisable to protect both Parties from the financial consequences of unexpected loss, damage or liability. At any given time, it is difficult for any published form of contract to define the precise extent of insurance cover which will be reasonably available for all Works for which the respective Book may be used. Clause 18 specifies insurance requirements in terms of the cover which is typically available, but the Contract may have to take account of the cover which is actually available. The primary purpose of insurance is to ensure that the Contractor has the financial capability to execute the Works irrespective of fortuitous loss or damage. Where a risk is allocated to the Employer, the insurance should (wherever possible) enable the Employer to pay for the rectification of damage caused by an Employer's risk.

Furthermore, if the Contractor fails to complete the Works, the insurance should enable the Employer to pay another contractor to rectify loss or damage to incomplete work. The liabilities of the Parties, other than in relation to effecting insurance, are not to be interpreted from this Clause 18. It is these liabilities, in accordance with the other terms of the Contract, which will be relevant whenever an element of loss or damage is not covered by insurance, e.g., an insurer may bear the amount of a claim except for the deductible. Although the listing of Employer's risks takes account of the extent to which insurance cover is available in many countries, the listing is not intended to reflect insurance practice. In some cases, those risks which may be uninsurable are included as Employer's risks, although they are to be insured wherever possible. However, the availability or otherwise of insurance does not determine a Party's risks.

Chapter 19

SUMMARY AND CONCLUSION

Construction industry is essentially a service industry as what is sold to the client is not a product but a capacity to produce (Winch, 2002). Unlike manufacturing industry and retail sectors, construction industry is an agglomeration of projects than a discrete or a fixed constellation of firms (Groak, 1994).

Construction industry is an important contributor to the national economy and without adequate construction capacity aspirations for economic growth cannot be accomplished, thereby implying that economic activity and self-identity are two primary drivers for construction activity, which are inextricably linked together. Researchers have found that the capital assets of any country predominantly consist of its built environment assets and in the UK built environment assets, such as: housing, infrastructure and other buildings represents 76% (£3800 billion) of a total assets base worth around £5000 billion at 2005 prices (Morledge, Smith, and Kashiwagi, 2006).

However, since there is, by and large, an extended time period between the initiation of project procurement process and its eventual completion and handover to the client, this time period may encompass significant changes in economic activity, which in turn may provoke changes to the initial rationale of the construction process. Also unlike the manufacturing industry and retail sectors the supply process of construction industry is more of an inconsistent network than a well coordinated and carefully managed supply chain.

These inherent problems of construction industry bring conceptual difficulties for clients coming to the industry with value propositions associated with delivery of projects, thereby needing considerable assistance from the professionals in formulating a suitable framework of the project implementation process i.e. project strategy for the client who is in fact is purchasing undefined, unspecified project where both price and delivery are vague at the outset.

Such a framework include: carrying out a detailed assessment of the: client's characteristics, client's overall needs and goals by identifying specific primary and secondary objectives of the project, and the risks inherent in the proposal, and then determining the environment in which the project will be delivered and finally selecting the most appropriate method of project procurement (Masterman, 2002).

Selecting a suitable method of project procurement is fundamental to the success of a project. In the past, by and large, traditional method of project procurement based on price-led traditional practices were used, the main method consisted of procuring designer to design the job and then selecting a constructor on the basis of low bid and the construction management function was carried out by client's in-house project team or through a project manager separately procured by the client.

However, traditional methods are being replaced over the past three decades by less conventional approaches based on the principles of building trust between all parties by incorporating more co-operative means of project implementation. However, increased trust and collaboration tend to be resisted where a cultural rooted in conformance with the contract and price exists and gained only limited increased support from experienced construction clients where they can see that progressive measurable value-based improvement has been accomplished by adopted such practices.

Construction contract management is the process that enables parties to a contract to meet their obligations in order to deliver the objectives required from the contract with the central aim to achieve the scope as agreed in the contract and achieve value for money. The foundations for contract management are laid in the stages before contract award, including the procurement process. Contract management may involve aiming for continuous improvement in performance over the life of the facility and building a good working relationship between the parties and other having interest in the project.

The factors essential for good contract management include: (a) good preparation; (b) an accurate assessment of needs translated into a clear output-based specification; (c) effective evaluation procedures and selection; (d) allocation of risk; (e) the quality control of works; and (f) procedures for communication and dispute resolution.

Contract administration is an integral and important element of contract management and overlaps with monitoring and performance assessment. It encompasses various activities that need to be completed on a day-to-day basis, including: (a) developing and maintaining contact details of key people involved in the contract; (b) understanding the notice provisions; (c) scheduling meetings and other actions required by the contract delivery and acceptance of the goods or services; (d) making payments; (e) maintaining complete records for the contract itself; and

(f) establishing and maintaining contract documentation.

In this context, it is important that the most up-to-date version of the contract incorporating any variations is formally evidenced in writing and appropriately stored. This provides the basis for making payments and the ongoing management of the contract. It is likely by the contract management phase that a system for maintaining documents for the particular contract will already have been established. If this is not the case, a recordkeeping system containing all appropriate documentation should be established in accordance with the employer's recordkeeping policy and practices. If a system already exists it should be reviewed to ensure that it is appropriate to the contractual arrangement. Any additional recordkeeping requirements should be identified and any gaps in documentation addressed.

Contruction contract administration handles the formal administration of the contract and changes to the contract documentation. Contract administration is concerned; with the mechanics of the relationship between the parties; the implementation of procedures defining the interface between the parties; and the smooth operation of routine administrative functions. Contract administration, however requires appropriate resourcing. In the Contract administration functions, clear administrative procedures ensure that all parties to the contract understand who does what, when, and how.

The procedures that combine to make up contract administration include, but not limited to: (i) contract maintenance and change control; (ii) charges and cost monitoring; (iii) ordering procedures; (iv) payment procedures; (v) budget procedures; (vi) resource management and planning; (vii) management reporting; (viii) asset management.

Procedures should also be established to keep the contract documentation up to date and to ensure that all documents relating to the contract are consistent, and that all parties have a common understanding. For a large or complex contract, a formal document management procedure is critically important, thereby requiring some form of change control procedure.

The contract administrator is the individual responsible for administering the construction contract(s). The contract administrator may be the architect, and indeed the JCT (Joint Contracts Tribunal) standard form of contract describes the role as 'architect / contract administrator' but the contract administrator could be the lead consultant, the cost consultant, or a client representative. GC Works (NB GC Works contracts are no longer being updated by the government) and NEC (New Engineering Contract) contracts describe the contract administrator as the 'project manager', ICE 7th (Institution of Civil Engineers, now also dropped in favour of NEC) refers to the 'engineer' and design and build contract such as JCT DB 05 (design and build) refer to the 'employer's agent'. Under FIDIC Contracts, the contract administrator is Engineer under Red and Yellow Book contracts and Employer’s representative under Silver Book contracts

After a contract has been signed there are a number of matters that should be addressed to provide the foundation for successful contract management. An early step is to ensure that sufficient resources and senior management support are available to manage the contract. It is equally important to understand both the contract provisions and contractual relationships at the outset by the contract management team. In the case where the contract administrator has been involved in earlier procurement phases, it is expected that the contact administrator will already have knowledge of issues relevant to implementation.

Contract administrators are appointed by the client and usually act as the client's agent. When certifying or giving an assessment or decision, the administrator has to act honestly and reasonably and their decisions are open to challenge via the dispute resolution procedure unless the contract makes their decisions final and conclusive. For example on NEC contracts the assessments, notifications and certificates of the project manager can be reviewed under the dispute resolution procedure as a result of 'any action or

Construction contract administrator's role will generally include: (1) Inviting and processing tenders. (2) Preparing contract documents for execution. (3) Administrating change control procedures. (4) Seeking instructions from the employer in relation to the contract. (5) Issuing instructions such as variations, or relating to prime cost sums or making good defects. (6) Evaluating claims. (7) Chairing construction progress meetings. (8) Preparing and issuing construction progress reports. (9) Co-ordinating and instructing site inspectors. (10) Agreeing defects reporting procedures. (11) Ensuring that project documentation is issued to the client. (12) Issuing certificates of practical completion and interim certificates. (13) Collating and issuing schedules of defects. (14) Issuing the certificate of making good defects. (15) Issuing the final certificate. And (16) Agreeing commissioning and testing procedures.

I must be remembered that on a construction management contract, the role of contract administrator might be attributed to the construction manager. On management contracts (where the works contracts a replaced by the management contractor) the management contractor will perform the role of contract administrator.

BIBLIOGRAPHY

1. Berends, T. C. 2000. Cost plus incentive fee contracting: Experience and structuring. International Journal of Project Management 18:165–171.
2. Broome, J. C., and R. W. Hayes. 1997. A comparison of the clarity of traditional construction contracts and the new engineering contract. International Journal of Project Management 15(4):255–261.
3. Bubshait, A. A. 2003. Incentive/disincentive contracts and its effects on industrial projects. International Journal of Project Management 21:63–70.
4. Bubshait, A., and S. A. Almohawis. 1994. Evaluating the general conditions of a construction contract. International Journal of Project Management 12(3):133–136.
5. Bubshait, K., and I. Manzanera. 1990. Claim management. International Journal of Project Management 8(4):222–228.
6. Carty, G. J. 1995. Construction. Journal of Construction Engineering and Management 121(3):319–328. Central Unit on Purchasing (CUP). 198–194.
7. Corbett, E. 2000. FIDIC's new rainbow 1st Edition: An advance. The International Construction Law Review 17(2):253–275.
8. Fenn, P., D. Lowe, and C. Speck. 1997. Conflict and dispute in construction. Construction Management and Economics 15:513–518. The Fe´de´ration Internationale des Inge´nieurs-Conseils (FIDIC). 1999.
9. Griffiths, F. 1989. Project contract strategy for 1992 and beyond. International Journal of Project Management 7(2):69–83.
10. Herten, H. J., and W. A. R. Peeters. 1986. Incentive contracting as a project management tool. International Journal of Project Management 4(1):34–39.
11. Hughes, W., and Y. Maeda, Y. 2003. Construction contract policy: Do we mean what we say? FiBRE—Findings in Built and Rural Environments, RICS

Foundation, The Royal Institution of Chartered Surveyors, London.

12. Rugby, UK: IChemE. www.icheme.org The Institution of Civil Engineers (ICE), 1995. The engineering and construction contract: Guidance notes. London: Thomas Telford. ———. 1995. The new engineering and construction contract (NEC). 1995. The Institution of Civil Engineers. London: Thomas Telford.
13. Jergeas, G. F., and V. G. Cooke. 2000. Law of tender applied to request for proposal process. Project Management Journal 28(4):21–34. Joint Contracts Tribunal (JCT), 2002. JCT contracts. London. The Joint Contracts Tribunal Ltd.
14. Kangari, R. 1995. Risk management perceptions and trends of U.S. construction. Journal of Construction Engineering and Management 121(4):422–429.
15. Khan, Wazir A. Applied Management for Engineers and technologists ISBN 0-9526436-2-6, avialablr from Amazon
16. Khan, Wazir A. Professional Manual on Total Quality Management - ISBN 0-9526436-1-8
17. Professional Manual on Total Project Management (Volume 1: CM General Perspective)- ISBN 0-9526436-3-4
18. Khan, Wazir A. Professional Manual on Total Project Management (Volume 2: CM Commercial Perspective)- ISBN 0-9526436-4-2
19. Khan, Wazir A. Professional Manual on Claims Management and Dispute Resolution in Construction Process 0-9526436-7-7
20. Kumaraswamy, M. M., and K. Yogeswaran. 2003. Substantiation and assessment of claims for extensions of time. International Journal of Project Management 21:27–38.
21. Latham, M. 1994. Constructing the team: Final report of the government/industry review of procurement and contractual arrangements in the UK construction industry. London: The Stationery Office.
22. Lowe, D. J., P. Fenn, and S. Roberts. 1997. Commercial management: An investigation into the role of the commercial manager within the UK construction industry. CIOB Construction Papers, No. 81, 1–8.

23. Morris, N. and Ndekugri, I. (2013). The Timetable Challenges of Adjudicators under the Housing Grants, Construction and Regeneration Act 1996, *Construction Law Journal*, 29(5), 343-366.
24. Ndekugri, I., Daeche, H. and Zhou, D. (2013). The Project Insurance Option in Infrastructure Procurement, *Journal of Engineering, Construction and Architectural Management*, 20(3), 267-289.
25. Ndekugri, I., Braimah, N. and Gameson, R. (2008). Delay Analysis within Construction Contracting Organisations, *Journal of Construction Engineering and Management*, American Society of Civil Engineers, 134(9), 692-700. http://fidic.org/node/6159.
26. Paterson, F. A., and P. Britton, eds. 2000. The Construction Act: Time for review. London: Centre of Construction Law & Management. King's College.
27. Sadeh, A., D. Dvir, and A. Shenhar. 2000. The role of contract type in the success of R&D defense projects under increasing uncertainty. Project Management Journal 31(3):14–22.
28. Seppala, C. R. 2000. FIDIC's new standard forms of contract: Force majeure, claims, disputes and other clauses. The International Construction Law Review 17(2):125–252.
29. Shadbolt, R. A. 1999. Resolution of construction disputes by dispute review boards. The International Construction Law Review 16(1):101–111. Specific Interest Group on Contracts and Procurement (SIGCP). 1998.
30. Smith, C., D. Topping, and C. Benjamin. 1995. Joint ventures. In The Commercial Project Manager. J. R. Turner, Maidenhead, UK: McGraw-Hill.
31. Smith, N. J., and S. H. Wearne. 1993. Construction contract arrangements in EU countries. Loughborough, UK: European Construction Institute.
32. Thomas, H. R., G. R. Smith, and D. J. Cummings. 1995. Have I reached substantial completion? Journal of Construction Engineering and Management 121(1):121–129.
33. Turner, J. R., and R. A. Cochrane. 1993. The goals and

methods matrix: coping with projects with ill-defined goals and/or methods of achieving them. International Journal of Project Management 11(2): 93–102.

34. Turner, J. R., and S. J. Simister. 2001. Project contract management and a theory of organisation. International Journal of Project Management 19(8):457–464.
35. Van Dunne, J. 2002. The changing of the guard: Force majeure and frustration in construction contracts: The foreseeability requirement replaced by normative risk allocation. The International Construction Law Review 19(2):162–186.
36. Van Houtte, V. 1999. The role and responsibility of the owner. The International Construction Law Review 16(1):59–79. Veld, J. in't, and W. A. Peeters. 1989.
37. Wang, W., K. I. M. Hawwash, and J. G. Perry. 1996. Contract type selector (CTS): A KBS for training young engineers. International Journal of Project Management 14(2):95–102.
38. Ward, S., and C. Chapman. 1994. Choosing contractor payment terms. International Journal of Project Management 12(4):216–221.
39. Wearne, S. H. 1992. Contract administration and project risks. International Journal of Project Management 10(1):39–41.
40. Wearne, S. H. 1999. Contracts for goods and services. In Project management for the process industries. G. Lawson, S. Wearne, and P. Iles-Smith. Rugby, UK: Institution of Chemical Engineers. Wright, D. 1994. A "fair" set of model conditions of contract: Tautology or impossibility? International Construction Law Review 11(4):549–555.

Printed in Poland
by Amazon Fulfillment
Poland Sp. z o.o., Wrocław